William Carlos Williams and Autobiography

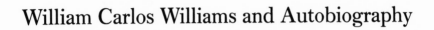

William Carlos Williams and Autobiography

The Woods of His Own Nature

Ann W. Fisher-Wirth

The Pennsylvania State University Press
University Park and London

Library of Congress Cataloging-in-Publication Data

Fisher-Wirth, Ann W.
William Carlos Williams and autobiography : the woods of his own
nature / Ann W. Fisher-Wirth.

p. cm.
Includes index.
ISBN 0-271-00653-6
1. Williams, William Carlos, 1883–1963. 2. Poets, American—20th
century—Biography. 3. Autobiography in literature. I. Title.
PS3545.I544Z98 1989
811'.52—dc19

[B]

88–19620
CIP

Contents

Preface   vii

Acknowledgments   xi

Abbreviations   xiii

Introduction   1

1   Fit to Be Imitated: *The Autobiography of William Carlos Williams*   17

2   An Innocent Sort of Child: *The Autobiography of William Carlos Williams*   31

3   In Every Way True to Nature: *A Dream of Love*   45

4   A World Lost: "Philip and Oradie"   63

5   Making Something of Oneself: "Pastoral," "Love Song," "Queen-Ann's Lace," "The Crimson Cyclamen"   87

6   A Song of a Man and a Woman: "Asphodel, That Greeny Flower"   115

Epilogue   181

Notes   185

Index   211

*For my children
and for Peter*

Preface

I have taken the subtitle for this book from William Carlos Williams's late poem "The Dance," which seems to me best to express—though through a series of metaphors—Williams's sense of the self. The poem describes the way snow spins upon its axis as it falls, always heading earthward, but spinning, whirling, gliding, entering into a dance with other snowflakes. "Only the dance is sure!" Williams writes,

> make it your own.
> Who can tell
> what is to come of it?
>
> in the woods of your
> own nature whatever
> twig interposes, and bare twigs
> have an actuality of their own
>
> this flurry of the storm
> that holds us,

> plays with us and discards us
> dancing, dancing as may be credible.
>
> (*PB*, 32–33)

We are the falling snow, the dance of our lives incessantly changing and fluid, caught and discarded in the flurry of the storm. Then, in a switch of metaphor, we become the woods on which the snow alights. There is a self, this seems to say; there are twigs that catch the snow and give it shape, form, pattern, imposing a structure upon the otherwise blank swirl of phenomena. And as we fall toward death, there is the chance of expressing the truth of ourselves, of acting authentically, or "dancing as may be credible."

In this book, I consider some of Williams's writings as autobiography. The number of works I discuss at length is relatively small, for I have wanted to spend time with each, to learn what it reveals of Williams's conception of the self, its relation to the world and to the act of writing. I have chosen works which represent different problems confronting an autobiographer, and different resolutions to these problems. I begin with two chapters on *The Autobiography of William Carlos Williams,* a conventional autobiography in which Williams constructs a public persona based on the idea of innocence and the consequent suppression of the knowledge of both sexuality and death. I contrast, then, Williams's play *A Dream of Love,* a confession of guilt in which Williams explores one of his central conflicts: the conflict between marriage and adultery. The next two chapters form a kind of diptych, too. "Philip and Oradie," Williams's long, early, unpublished "*Endymion* poem," is his first attempt to arrive at a sense of his identity through writing, the veiled autobiography of an aspiring artist. It is Williams's foray into what Keats calls the egotistical sublime; in it, language and experience are held in thrall to the overweening ego of Williams's persona, the persecuted and alienated prince. The failure of "Philip and Oradie" and the death of prince Philip give rise, then, to "The Wanderer," the poem of initiation which marks the poet's baptism in the "filthy Passaic River." With this poem, the poet becomes what we know as William Carlos Williams: a writer of negative capability, whose sense of himself is found in contact with the "weeds, bearing seeds," the flotsam of experience. Some of the poems which enact this process of surrender to experience are the subject of chapter 5. Finally, chapter 6 is a reading of "Asphodel, That Greeny Flower," the long, late love poem to Flossie which is Williams's deepest and fullest autobiography.

This book does not pretend to be a comprehensive survey of Williams's writings. In particular, it does not contain full treatments of *Kora in Hell* and *Paterson,* though I refer to both in passing. About *Paterson,* a great deal has already been written; it has been the subject of countless articles and chapters, and several books. With the recent publication of Roy Miki's *Prepoetics of William Carlos Williams,* the same is becoming true of *Kora in Hell.* As well as Miki's book, fine essays have been written about it, notably Gerald Bruns's "De Improvisatione," but much of *Kora* still remains unmined. It presents a tantalizing instance of autobiography as improvisation and the self as a collage of charged or radiant fragments; in this sense, it is an important precursor of *Paterson.* But as even a quick look at *Kora in Hell* will show, it either seems to mean very little or to lead off in all directions at once, establishing a complex and nearly endless web of correspondences and possibilities. Some of these remain murky, no matter how familiar one is with the work; most of those who have written best on *Kora* offer only sporadic interpretations of the improvisations themselves. A brief treatment of either *Paterson* or *Kora in Hell* as autobiography would be inadequate; a full treatment of either is not possible within the limits of the book I have chosen to write.

Acknowledgments

Over the years, many people have helped me with this book. I am grateful to James Laughlin, of the New Directions Publishing Corporation, and to Donald Gallup, formerly Curator of the Collection of American Literature at the Beinecke Library, Yale University, for permission to quote from William Carlos Williams's unpublished poem "Philip and Oradie" and Williams's other papers and manuscripts at Yale. I am also grateful to the librarian at Yale who spent hours searching through Williams's uncatalogued papers for the manuscript of "Philip and Oradie," and finally found it in a shoebox.

This book would not have been possible without financial assistance of various kinds. From Claremont Graduate School, the National Endowment for the Humanities, and the University of Virginia, I received research fellowships and summer grants. From the Danforth Foundation, I received a Graduate Fellowship which freed me from teaching for more than a year at a time when the obstacles to completing this book seemed overwhelming.

Ida Garrison, Elizabeth Nelke, Debbie Shea, and Barbara Smith, all of the English department at the University of Virginia, helped me prepare my manuscript. Darcy O'Brien, the late Charles Holmes, Robert Mezey, and Ray Nelson shared their knowledge of Williams's poetry with me and gave me excellent editorial suggestions. Peter Wirth's criticisms helped me clarify my argument in its final stages. James Cox, David Levin, Paul Mariani, and A. K. Weatherhead read the manuscript and encouraged me when I needed it toward the end. My editor, Philip Winsor, has been a pleasure to work with, for his expertise and courtesy. William Spengemann has helped me without stint from my first year of graduate school to the present.

I owe my friends and family a great debt, and I hope that my thanks here will in part repay them. From my mother, Irma Randall Mitchell, I learned to love literature; to her and to John Fisher, I am very grateful for assistance and encouragement over the years. My thanks to Rebecca for rooting for me. My husband, Peter Wirth, and my children, Pascale, Jessica, Lucas, and Caleb, are more deeply a part of this book than I can say.

Abbreviations

I use the following abbreviations for the works by William Carlos Williams which I cite in this study. Since the editions of Williams's works which are widely available are those by New Directions Publishing Corporation, it is to these editions that I refer:

A   *The Autobiography of William Carlos Williams* (New York: New Directions, 1967).

B   *The Build-up* (New York: New Directions, 1968).

CEP   *The Collected Earlier Poems of Williams Carlos Williams* (Norfolk, Connecticut: New Directions, 1951).

CLP   *The Collected Later Poems of William Carlos Williams,* revised edition (New York: New Directions, 1967).

CP   *The Collected Poems of William Carlos Williams: Volume I: 1909–1939,* ed. A. Walton Litz and Christopher Mac-Gowan (New York: New Directions, 1986).

DL   *A Dream of Love,* in *Many Loves and Other Plays* (New York: New Directions, 1965).

DW   *The Descent of Winter,* in *Imaginations,* ed. Webster Schott (New York: New Directions, 1970).

FD   *The Farmers' Daughters: The Collected Stories of William Carlos Williams* (New York: New Directions, 1961).

GAN   *The Great American Novel,* in *Imaginations.*

IAG   *In the American Grain* (New York: New Directions, 1956).

IWW   *I Wanted to Write a Poem: The Autobiography of the Works of a Poet,* ed. Edith Heal (New York: New Directions, 1978).

K   *Kora in Hell,* in *Imaginations.*

N   *A Novelette and Other Prose,* in *Imaginations.*

P   *Paterson I–V* (New York: New Directions, 1963), 8th paperbook printing.

PB   *Pictures from Brueghel and Other Poems* (New York: New Directions, 1962).

"Rome"   "Rome," ed. Steven Ross Loevy, in *The Iowa Review,* 9, no. 3 (1978), 1–65.

SA   *Spring and All,* in *Imaginations.*

SE   *Selected Essays of William Carlos Williams* (New York: New Directions, 1969).

SL   *The Selected Letters of William Carlos Williams,* ed. John C. Thirlwall (New York: McDowell, Obolensky, 1957).

VP   *A Voyage to Pagany* (New York: New Directions, 1970).

YALC   Dr. Williams's manuscripts, typescripts, and papers in the Collection of American Literature, Yale University Library.

Y, MW   *Yes, Mrs. Williams: A Personal Record of My Mother* (New York: McDowell, Obolensky, 1959).

The artist is always and forever painting only one thing: a self portrait.

—William Carlos Williams

Introduction

Though in recent years a great deal has been written about the poetry and prose of William Carlos Williams, and though he has been the subject of several biographical studies, critics have paid remarkably little attention to his autobiography. One exception is Sherman Paul, whose brief discussion of this work in *The Music of Survival* perceptively characterizes it and places it in the context of Williams's other writings, of which the late poem "The Desert Music" is Paul's primary theme.[1] Another is Herbert Leibowitz, whose *American Poetry Review* essay entitled "You Can't Beat Innocence" offers a full and detailed description of Williams's book, aptly discussing its limitations, but failing sufficiently to consider the reasons for these limitations.[2] By and large, however, critics have mentioned *The Autobiography of William Carlos Williams* only in passing, and have considered it merely as a storehouse of accurate or inaccurate information about the author's life, friends, and other publications, rather than as a literary document in its own right, or as yet another stage in Williams's lifelong voyage of exploration and discovery.

This neglect extends as well to critics of autobiography, who have attempted to define and explore the artistic and psychological aspects, and to set the limits, of the genre. But they can hardly be faulted for their neglect, for perhaps the most surprising thing about Williams's autobiography, given his experimental approach to both poetry and prose, is that in its form and central conception it is so unexperimental and therefore so unsurprising. It is true that Williams's artistry raises this autobiography above many others in matters of technique: in the organic metaphor of "Root, Branch, & Flower"[3] which governs the work's structure and reveals Williams's conception of the pattern of his life; in the contrapuntal arrangement of chapters which illuminate the life's various facets and play off against one another to develop certain themes; and in the deftness, versatility, and occasionally great beauty of the writing. But these matters, although important, are peripheral to the central assumption which underlies this work and defines its kinship with the countless other examples of conventional autobiography.

This assumption is that autobiography, as it has commonly been defined, can still be written. Though plenty of writers never question this assumption, implicit within it are a number of beliefs. One must believe, primarily, that there is a self which can be known, perhaps not in all the details of its history, but in the truth which emerges when the pattern of the life is seen. This self corresponds to the Christian soul; it can be intuited or revealed, but neither created nor destroyed, by its temporal experience. Its metaphor could be said to be the hazelnut, rather than Hesse's walnut or pomegranate,[4] Woolf's aureole, or Barthes' onion: it is conceived to be a round, firm, and single center within the shell of the temporal body, rather than a center which is double, multiple, hazy, or simply nonexistent. Then, given such a self, one must believe that one can attain to a fixed point of view, arrive by means of time at a timeless understanding, and rest at this narrative standpoint while one recounts the story of one's life. Just as the first belief derives from the Christian idea of the soul, this second belief derives from the Christian (specifically Augustinian) notion of redemption through faith, which redemption issues in a timeless clarity of vision and, consequently, in a final, complete, and perfect narrative point of view. And third, one must believe that what Elizabeth Bruss has called "autobiographical acts"[5] can be performed in prose, by confining oneself to fact, and by writing retrospectively. This belief follows from the first two: once one conceives the self to be single, final, perfect, and complete, it suffices for language to report, to represent, the pattern of events which led from root to flower, from nascence to realization. Language need not invent, create, project, or in any way call attention to its formative powers, its poetic or fictive reality as language.

It is possible to write an autobiography by confining oneself to retrospective and factual prose, just as it is possible to write blank-verse tragedy or compose sonatas. But the drift of both art and psychology since the advent of Romanticism has made the process highly problematic: current ways of thinking about the nature of the self, time, memory, and the process of artistic creation practically guarantee that to adhere to conventional form is to write only one of two possible kinds of autobiography. The first of these possible kinds, the one most often recognized as autobiography both by ordinary readers and by many theorists of the genre, and generally written by those who wish to "tell the story" of their lives, is what may be called public autobiography. The archetypal *Autobiography* in this mode is Benjamin Franklin's. It is true that, to some extent at least, the public autobiographer is motivated by what Roy Pascal has defined as the deepest impulse of those who work in the genre: the desire to enact "'Selbstbesinnung.'" The German word *Selbstbesinnung,* derived from *Sinn* ("sense" or "meaning"), literally means "self-reflection" or "self-recollection"; Pascal translates it as "a search for one's inner standing."[6] Overridingly, however, the public autobiographer's desire is that exemplified by Franklin: to offer a life history the pattern and discoveries of which are fit to be learned from or imitated.[7] Fidelity to the truth of the life's experience as it actually unfolded, whether that be in tension, chaos, ecstasy is simplified, even at times deliberately distorted, in order that it be made to conform to a prevenient pattern. This pattern, in its most general form, corresponds to Williams's metaphor of "Root, Branch, & Flower": Events of the past are selected and depicted in such a way that they seem to lead inevitably to the flowering which is the narrative present. As Pascal writes, autobiography involves "the reconstruction of the movement of a life, or part of a life, in the actual circumstances in which it was lived. . . . Autobiography is the shaping of a past. It imposes a pattern on a life, constructs out of it a coherent story."[8] In order to construct a coherent story, the autobiographer must have decided first upon a particular point of view from which to interpret his past, a particular "self" to "be" so that he can depict that self's becoming. The problem, however, is that the process of composition soon becomes circular and circumscribed: The point of view validates the process of selection, and the process of selection validates the point of view. No wonder that, as Pascal remarks, the effect of an authorial "emergence from shadows into daylight"[9] is an absolute condition of conventional autobiography.

The pattern of conventional autobiography derives its energy, in part, from past works written in the genre: Accounts of spiritual conversion, for instance, are still modeled on Saint Augustine's, while Franklin's secularized reworking of Augustine has become the dominant model for subsequent accounts of temporal success. But, of course, one need not read Augustine, Franklin, or anyone else in order to write an autobiography. In its broad outlines, the conventional form has become an unstated cultural assumption, and the public autobiographer plays off against the archetypal roles implicit in the formative myths of his society.[10] Therefore, even when he would appear to reject the social order—as in a hypothetical *Autobiography of an Anarchist* or *Confessions of a Killer*—in reality he upholds it, by conceiving of the self primarily in its social function, and by claiming the right to reside in one of society's many rooms.

Public autobiography, then, is socially oriented and socially defined. This mode, examples of which are legion, is generally taken for the whole of autobiography. But it is not. There is another mode as well, although works of this latter sort often fall outside the generic limits of autobiography as conventionally defined: They are not retrospective prose narratives which tell the story of their authors' lives. They are poems, fictions, meditations, improvisations—works in which form is determined by content, and content is determined by the writer's overwhelming desire to enact the search for inner standing so often sacrificed by writers of public autobiographies. This other mode may be called private autobiography. Much of the serious imaginative writing since the Romantic movement falls within this category, the archetype of which is a work contemporaneous with Franklin's but seminal to Romanticism, *The Confessions of Jean-Jacques Rousseau.*[11]

Rousseau's initial premises in writing his autobiography are the premises of Romantic epistemology: that one's experience is the only ground of knowledge; and that each self, both as it is given and as it is formed by experience, is unique. "I am made unlike anyone I have ever met," Rousseau writes, to explain his belief that the enterprise upon which he has embarked in beginning his *Confessions* is one "which has no precedent"; "I will even venture to say that I am like no one in the whole world." Consequently, adherence to conventional form gives way to narrative fidelity to the truth of one's experience as the private autobiographer's overriding compulsion, for without this fidelity each step of the way there can be no final discovery of the meaning of one's life or the nature of one's inner standing. As Rousseau defines his topic, it is nothing less comprehensive than a portrait of the self "in every way true to nature"[12]—for to depict less than "all that has happened to me, all that I have done, all that I have felt" would be to prejudge and therefore to falsify the picture, rather than to clarify the self's position for its own understanding, or to "make my soul transparent to the reader's eye."[13]

To "make my soul transparent to the reader's eye": As this phrase indicates, Rousseau's *Confessions* by no means serves an entirely private function. "Transparent," Rousseau hoped, would mean understood, and understood would mean loved, forgiven. His belief in his own uniqueness makes it impossible for him to create an autobiography fit for imitation, but he writes nonetheless with his public firmly in mind. The locus of atonement is difficult to fix: at times it seems atonement would take place in the mutual acknowledgment of "depravities"; at others, in the innocence of a remembered or imagined life in nature. But wherever or however atonement might happen, the wish for atonement runs as a current of pain throughout the pages. When we first meet Rousseau, he defiantly asserts his kinship with all mankind, not in God but in human nature: "So let the numberless legion of my fellow men gather round me, and hear my confessions. Let them grown at my depravities, and blush for my misdeeds. But let each one of them reveal his heart at the foot of Thy throne with equal sincerity, and may any man who dares, say 'I was a better man than he.'"[14] When we last see him, he is reading from the *Confessions* to a group of friends, still trying to convince them that no one "who will examine my nature, my character, my morals, my liking, my pleasures, and my habits with his own eyes" could "believe me a dishonourable man." Even as he reads, he watches their reactions; in a profoundly ambiguous passage he tells us: "Madame d'Egmont was the only person who seemed moved. She trembled visibly, but quickly controlled herself, and remained quiet, as did the rest of the company. Such was the advantage I derived from my reading and my declaration."[15]

In one sense, of course, all autobiography seeks to fulfill both a public and a private function. As Georges Gusdorf writes, with regard to what I have been calling public autobiography,

> Such is without doubt the most secret intention of all attempts at Souvenirs, Memoirs, or Confessions. The man who tells the story of himself seeks himself across his story. . . . The confession, the effort of remembrance, is at the same time a quest for a hidden treasure, a final liberating word, redeeming at the last moment a destiny which doubted its own value.[16]

Beneath the avowed project of the public autobiographer are profound and private intentions. The same is true in reverse for the private autobiographer: Beneath his avowed project are profound and public intentions. One sees this in Rousseau, whose insistence upon his uniqueness and upon narrative fidelity to the truth of his own experience finally cuts two ways. On the one hand, his uniqueness isolates him; on the other, it enables him to become a spokesman for all people in their own uniqueness—if, that is, they are brave enough and perceptive enough to meet him on the common ground of their terrible isolation. This doubleness of desire—both to create a self "in every way true to nature" and to create a self which will serve as a model for others—leads in the *Confessions* to an enormously complex and painful set of problems. The farther Rousseau goes into the heart of his own experience, the greater becomes his sense of separateness. The greater this sense of separateness, the more urgent the pleas for forgiveness and reconciliation; and the more urgent the pleas, the more desperate the suspicion that to plead his case only loses him further ground, only lends fire to the conspiracies against him—conspiracies which need not be political, need only be those of an audience's or readers' indifference and impatience, in order to be damning. Because there can be no resting place, no enduring unity between private and public desire, the *Confessions* become nearly endless, and endless the labyrinthine passages of self-investigation and self-exoneration, and the undercurrent, which rises again and again to a cry, of abandonment and pain. Insofar as the reader is moved, his or her reactions tend to resemble those of Madame d'Egmont, who "trembled visibly" when at last the *Confessions* fell into silence—trembled both, I daresay, from empathy and horror, both from knowing herself to be like, and knowing herself to be different from, Rousseau.

For the fact is that, though autobiographies may seek to fulfill both a public and a private function, they cannot entirely realize this aim. The wish to offer a life history fit for imitation runs counter to the wish to enact a search for one's inner standing, and has done so ever since the loss of absolute certainty in a God that was both the deepest truth of the self and the principle of social communion. No autobiographer has completely resolved this dilemma since Saint Augustine, whose *Confessions* bequeathed what Augustine did not perceive to be a problem to all later writers in that genre. Of all autobiographers, Augustine alone had what Pascal calls a fully "meaningful standpoint";[17] lifted beyond sin, beyond erroneous vision and a sense of isolation by his miraculous conversion, he could stand still, and in so standing, sempiternal, interpret his life as replete with meaning. Public and private desires—the desire to serve as a model for others and the desire to seek out his inner standing—were one and the same, for God, the Truth, was within the self, and the self was within God. Every word of the *Confessions* was an act of prayer, a perfect circle, coming from God and addressed to God, encompassing both the deepest reaches of Augustine's own soul and the universe of his brothers. However, once God gives way as the center "which is everywhere,"[18] or once the experience of conversion becomes even a fraction less than final and absolute, public and private desires in autobiography begin to conflict and divide. What come to signify, therefore, are the choices made in the process of creation. An autobiographer may arrange his experience in order to elucidate a conventional pattern, and so follow Franklin's example, or he may allow the pattern to emerge through a faithful investigation into the heart of his experience, and so follow Rousseau's.

Or he may do both, at different times in his life; he may come to see that the self inheres not in any one work but in the pattern which evolves over a lifetime of creation. This is the course followed by William Carlos Williams, all of whose work can be seen as the creation of a self by discovering that self in the act of writing.[19] And this is one lesson brought home to him by the book he entitled *The Autobiography of William Carlos Williams,* which was supposed to close a life but which in fact opened on to the unsuspected world of the late poems: that it is no longer possible—and no longer necessary—to write a single, final, and comprehensive autobiography.

The Autobiography of William Carlos Williams is an important public statement. It is Williams's primary attempt to present the pattern of his experience "in the American grain," and his fullest account of the major figures, events, and stages in his life. But it is not the autobiography of William Carlos Williams. There is no such thing, in fact, as the autobiography of William Carlos Williams. Rather, there are autobiographies, of which the *Autobiography* is simply one among many. As Louis Simpson remarks, "With other writers we must be on guard against thinking that they are writing about themselves—with Williams the reverse is true: almost everything he wrote is autobiography."[20]

Simpson's remark is accurate on the level at which he intends it. Williams nearly always wrote from his own experience, about himself, his family, his friends and patients, Rutherford or Paterson, the filthy Passaic River, the trees and flowers that grew in Kipp's woods or his garden; he nearly always wrote, that is, autobiographically. The remark is revealing, however, in a deeper sense as well. Williams's poems, stories, novels, plays, and improvisations are not just depictions of the "local." They are themselves the locale, the place in which Williams explores the ground of his experience, and on this ground discovers his inner standing. They are examples of what I have called private autobiography.

That "Philip and Oradie," "Queen-Ann's Lace," and "The Crimson Cyclamen" (to take three examples from subsequent chapters of this study) are private autobiographies may seem mere playing with words. Surely "Philip and Oradie" is a jejune imitation of Keats's *Endymion,* "Queen-Ann's Lace" is a poem describing a woman's desire through the metaphor of a wildflower, and "The Crimson Cyclamen" is an elegy for William's friend Charles Demuth. Surely. But these descriptions, though true, are not binding; for to say that autobiography must be "about" oneself, must confine itself to the "facts," must be written in prose from a retrospective point of view, as conventional definitions say it must be, is to come upon twentieth-century literature with an outmoded guide to autobiography.

Like the *Guide Bleu,* the outmoded guide to Europe that Roland Barthes demolishes in *Mythologies,* conventional definitions of autobiography succumb to the "disease of thinking in essences," which, Barthes argues, "is at the bottom of every bourgeois mythology of man." Like the *Guide Bleu,* conventional definitions of autobiography answer "none of the questions which a modern traveler can ask himself while crossing a countryside which is real *and which exists in time.*" And the danger of thinking in essences—of expecting Europe to conform to its monuments and cathedrals, or expecting modern autobiography to conform to great autobiographies written in the past—is that it blinds the traveler to the abundance of the terrain. As Barthes remarks of the *Guide,* "To select only monuments suppresses at one stroke the reality of the land and that of its people, it accounts for nothing of the present, that is, nothing historical, and as a consequence, the monuments themselves become undecipherable, therefore senseless. What is to be seen is thus constantly in the process of vanishing."[21]

The process Barthes describes can be seen in certain critical works on autobiography. Judging recent autobiographies in terms of Rousseau's *Confessions,* for instance, Pascal reluctantly concludes that, "in face of the great richness of modern autobiography in so far as it tells of the development of a specific gift and task, its success in representing the whole man is relatively meager."[22] To Pascal, in other words, modern autobiography fulfills the public but not the private dimension of its task. It seems to me, however, that Pascal is seeking "the whole man" where "the whole man" no longer fits, and overlooking the many places where one can find him. That "the whole man" no longer is found in conventional autobiographies is by no means cause for lamentation; it does not bespeak a diminished present overshadowed by the monuments of the past. For Rousseau emerges whole in his *Confessions* solely by virtue of his determination to allow the form of his work to arise from its necessary contents, which are nothing less than all of himself, "in every way true to nature." Just so with private autobiographers of the twentieth century: They emerge whole in their work solely by virtue of their own determination to allow the form of that work to arise from its necessary contents, not from the form or contents of Rousseau. And whatever that form becomes—whether poetry, fiction, drama, or fugitive improvisations—the wholeness, "the whole man," is there insofar as, within the work, the writer discovers the place of his inner standing.

In fact, self-recollection or the search for inner standing need not involve the narrative recapitulation of one's own biography at all. As Barrett J. Mandel argues, "the truth is not in [the] pictures" which constitute one's recollections, "but *behind* them."[23] Mandel writes,

> Consciousness, and not the true self, flashes pictures before the eye, pictures we take to be the real me—my true story. It is customary to believe that we see the truth about ourselves in the mirror of our thoughts. . . . [However], *myself* and its story are products of the mind. Since the mind is the only part of us that is conscious and conscious of itself, we mistakenly assume that this consciousness is conterminous with who we are. Actually the conscious mind is rooted in the unseen (but not unseeing) being—the *source* of consciousness. Autobiographies, like all works of art, emanate ultimately from the deeper reality of being.[24]

Searching for one's inner standing has, in the deepest sense, to do with recollecting or centering oneself, finding oneself in the presence of oneself, rather than with rehearsing one's memories. As Proust shows so brilliantly in *Remembrance of Things Past,* at least what he calls involuntary memory can be the means of access to the realm of inner standing, but it is also possible to recollect the self, to center the self, and to write the self without reference to the memories and events which constitute one's biography.

It may even be more possible. "'Je' est un autre," Rimbaud remarks. Williams is often most present when he does not say "I," but rather surrenders to the phenomenon he focuses on, so that he becomes inseparable from and for the moment entirely contained in, implicit in, the process of transformation his language both enacts and describes. His poem "Young Sycamore," for instance, begins with the reflection or injunction, "I must tell you / this young tree," but then quickly closes the gap between self, tree, poem, and reader by dropping the "I," dropping the stance of observation, and entering bodily, as it were, by means of a thrusting, penetrant, unfinished language into the living, unfinished process of the tree (*CP,* 266; *CEP,* 332). Poet and reader join "in present passion" (*SA,* 149), in attentiveness to the poem; "so long as you read," Williams remarks in *Spring and All,* "we are from henceforth . . . locked in a fraternal embrace, the classic caress of author and reader. We are one" (*SA,* 89). And tree and reader join, by means of language. Williams's language is homely, prosaic, American; his tree has a

> round and firm trunk
> between the wet
> pavement and the gutter
> (where water
> is trickling)

—but the tree's creation *ex nihilo* participates in the ancient mystery Rainer Maria Rilke describes in *The Sonnets to Orpheus:*

> A tree sprang up. O sheer transcendence!
> O Orpheus sings! O tall tree in the ear![25]

Mandel affirms the presence of a deep self which is inaccessible to both consciousness and language.[26] Though this deep self cannot be approached or expressed directly, its presence is felt at the moment of creativity. Any version of one's past is just a version, but, as Mandel remarks, "in ratifying [the version of] the past, the autobiographer discloses the truth of his or her being in the present. Thus, personal history is put forth in a certain light. The past may be an illusion, but the light of now is never an illusion. What it illuminates, it makes real. *Now* is the only source of light."[27] This *now* is what Williams focuses on, in what I am calling his private autobiographies. "The reader knows himself as he was twenty years ago," he writes in *Spring and All*, "and he has also in mind a version of what he would be, some day. Oh, some day! But the thing he never knows and never dares to know is what he is at the exact moment that he is. And this moment is the only thing in which I am at all interested" (*SA*, 89). The space of the poem or other work is the plenteous space; whether or not the work refers to biographical data from Williams's past, it can be described as a private autobiography insofar as it serves as locus for the poet's act of self-centering and self-recollecting, his search for a sense of inner standing.

There is, of course, a trend in contemporary literary and psychoanalytic theory away from this conception of the deep self. Jacques Lacan, Jacques Derrida, Michel Foucault, Roland Barthes, and others have argued both against the concept of an unmediated and sovereign "I" and against the concept of "an author as a subjective presence who originates and is thus responsible for a discourse or a piece of writing."[28] Instead, as James Olney writes, summarizing their position with regard to autobiography,

> the text itself takes on a life of its own, and the self that was not really in existence in the beginning is in the end merely a matter of text and has nothing whatever to do with an authorizing author. The self, then, is a fiction and so is the life, and behind the text of an autobiography lies the text of an 'autobiography': all that is left are characters on a page, and they too can be 'deconstructed' to demonstrate the shadowiness of even their existence.[29]

All we can write, then, are fictions about a fiction, versions of a self which "takes shape by and in its language rather than using language as a vehicle to express its own transcendental being."[30]

The mistake postmodern theory makes, however, is to privilege language above that which presumably it seeks to signify. The self may be an illusion, but it is no more an illusion than language, thought, the cycles of birth and death, the manifold creation—all the phenomena symbolized in Hindu mythology by the dance of Shiva. All may be equally illusory, but if this is so, then all is equally real. Though on the one hand such a belief makes autobiography meaningless, on the other hand it frees the autobiographer illimitably, for the self, which is nothing and nowhere, is at the same time present at every moment and in every gesture of its dance; all of its manifestations are both illusory and revealing.

My definition of private autobiography as the place in which a writer discovers his or her inner standing tends to turn all modern literature worth reading into autobiography: who could say, for instance, that *Finnegans Wake, One Hundred Years of Solitude,* "The Love Song of J. Alfred Prufrock," and *My Ántonia* were not the place of their authors' inner standing? This only seems, however, to be a disadvantage, for in fact, as countless writers and critics have averred, much of the serious imaginative writing at least since the Romantic movement *is* autobiography.[31] "I have gradually come to understand what every great philosophy until now has been," Nietzsche writes: "the confession of its author and a kind of involuntary, unconscious memoir. . . . Nothing at all about the philosopher is impersonal."[32] If this is true of philosophy, which has always claimed to teach impersonal truths, how can it not be true of other forms of imaginative writing? As Jorge Luis Borges eloquently observes, "A man sets himself the task of portraying the world. Through the years he peoples a space with images of provinces, kingdoms, mountains, bays, ships, islands, fishes, rooms, instruments, stars, horses, and people. Shortly before his death, he discovers that that patient labyrinth of lines traces the image of his face."[33]

Louis Simpson's remark, that nearly everything Williams wrote is autobiography, serves well as my point of departure. In the remainder of this book, I apply the remark to certain of Williams's works, in order to see not *whether* but *how* they are autobiographies: what each reveals of Williams's conception of the self, its relation to the world, and its relation to writing. My principle of order in the following chapters is neither chronological nor generic, though chronological patterns and generic shifts and developments do occur. Rather, I move from most obvious to least obvious, from most conventional to least conventional, of Williams's experiments with autobiography. His most conventional is, of course, *The Autobiography of William Carlos Williams;* as will become clear later on, "The Crimson Cyclamen"—in which neither its author, Williams, nor its subject, the painter Charles Demuth, is mentioned—seems to me to be a good example of Williams's least conventional autobiographies. Along this fictive line, Williams's play *A Dream of Love;* his unpublished "*Endymion* poem," "Philip and Oradie"; and various of the poems written during his middle years mark points of exploration between the two extremes.

In the first two chapters of this book, my subject is *The Autobiography of William Carlos Williams*. Chapter 1 discusses the affinities of Williams's *Autobiography* with Franklin's *Autobiography,* and the ways in which Williams's *Autobiography* is a deliberately public statement, presenting a self made fit for imitation. Chapter 2 discusses "innocence," for "innocence" is the key to Williams's public persona. As the chapter points out, "innocence" conceals as much as it reveals; in certain important ways, it represents Williams truly and releases self-expression, while in other ways more important, it constricts him and proves a lie.

If the *Autobiography* is Williams's "songs of innocence," *A Dream of Love* is his "songs of experience." Chapter 3 examines the play as a private autobiography, the archetypal work behind which is not Franklin's *Autobiography,* but *The Confessions of Jean-Jacques Rousseau*. Like Rousseau in *The Confessions,* Williams struggles in *A Dream of Love* to reveal himself "in every way true to nature," in the hope of creating a ground on which the self can commune with others. The anguish of the play is that, like Rousseau in *The Confessions,* Williams cannot know whether the world will embrace him, recognizing itself in him, or whether it will revile him in his pain.

The Autobiography, the subject of chapters 1 and 2, is the self-portrait of a man who has written poetry, but not of a man who could write poetry. *A Dream of Love,* the subject of chapter 3, is the self-portrait of a man who could write poetry—who was, in fact, writing poetry. With chapter 4, which discusses "Philip and Oradie," the distance between autobiography and poetry vanishes; the autobiography is the poem itself. However, one way to describe the problem with "Philip and Oradie" is to say that the distance between the self and the poem does not vanish: that the poem, its language, its experience, remain in thrall to an overweening ego, rather than becoming the space in which the poet can enact, discover, and forget about himself, by surrendering to the processes of creation.

As an autobiography, "Philip and Oradie" describes a world dying and just hints, in its final lines, at a new world powerless to be born. The continuous birth which we have come to know as the poetry of William Carlos Williams and which begins in "The Wanderer," with Williams's symbolic death and rebirth in the "filthy Passaic River," his waters of creation, is the subject of chapter 5. And finally, chapter 6 discusses Williams's long poem to Flossie, "Asphodel, That Greeny Flower." Written in sickness and age, "Asphodel" may be Williams's single finest poem. With its candor and nakedness, its wisdom and authority, Williams comes about as close as any post-Augustinian autobiographer can, in it, to fusing private and public autobiography. Each of my first five chapters stands on its own, and isolates for discussion one set of choices or problems confronting Williams as autobiographer; each may be seen as well as a step on the way to "Asphodel," Williams's richest, deepest, and perennially flowering autobiography.

1

Fit to Be Imitated:
The Autobiography of William Carlos Williams

Benjamin Franklin is one of the exemplars of "denial" in William Carlos Williams's book of historical essays, *In the American Grain*. Essentially, what Williams dislikes about Franklin are the qualities he also finds both in the Puritans and in his own contemporaries, men (though seldom women) of twentieth-century America: a concern with Calvinist purity, or the appearance thereof; a nervous and tormented obsession with power over nature or over others; a betrayal of the actual, the present, what Williams calls "the wilderness," for the sake of some imagined future secular or religious salvation. As Williams writes in "Jacataqua," his essay condemning the conditions of modern American life, "Ben Franklin, who started black, with an illegitimate son, was forced to turn white, poor Richard, to save himself later. He saw the hell and warned us, warned us to save our pennies" (*IAG,* 179). This kind of safety, this conventional wisdom, Williams thoroughly despises. In his view, Franklin lacked both the courage and the abandon which would enable him to descend "to the ground of his desire" and thereby enter into the cyclical processes of creation (*IAG,* 136). Franklin's prudence and practicality cut him off from the fecund, untamed sources of life and true invention; according to Williams, though Franklin possessed genius he could not surrender to it, but made himself into a "dike keeper, keeping out the wilderness with his wits. Fear drove his curiosity" (*IAG,* 155). Consequently, "his energy never attained to a penetrant gist; rather it was stopped by and splashed upon the barrier, like a melon. His 'good' was scattered about him" (*IAG,* 153).

Williams does not scorn Franklin's discoveries—the most famous of which, after all, was as brilliant, and has proven to be as useful, as the discovery of radium by Madame Curie, whom Williams enshrines in *Paterson*—but the spirit which lies behind them. Like Daniel Boone or Père Sebastian Rasles of *In the American Grain,* Madame Curie exemplifies those qualities most truly "in the grain" as Williams sees it, qualities which he seeks to enact in his own art and life. Conversely, Franklin exemplifies the qualities against which Williams strives, but which have always held sway in our society (so that, in fact, to go against the prevalent grain is to be truly in the grain). In discovering electricity, for instance, Franklin deflects the power he fears, harnessing it to the service of industrial civilization; in this he resembles Alexander Hamilton, whom Williams castigates in *Paterson* for seeing only, and capitalizing upon, the industrial possibilities of the Passaic Falls. In contrast to these men's desire to harness power is Madame Curie's desire to release it; her patient, intense devotion to experimenting with seemingly inert materials at last breaks the atom, penetrating to the "radiant gist" which may "cure the cancer" (*P,* 109, 179). Franklin makes himself barren (hence, metaphorically, Williams's remark about the illegitimate son); his experiments are a form of manipulation and consequently of denial. He desires to avoid the "wilderness" altogether, or, failing that, to impose an order upon it. Madame Curie is "pregnant," "with ponderous belly, full / of thought" (*P,* 176–77). She intuits the order that lies within things as they are, the luminous "nothing" that would account for a gap in the Mendelief tables (*P,* 178–79). Dreaming, laboring, desiring, she becomes a type of the true poet, an alter ego for Paterson and Williams, whose goals are like hers, and who fear, as she must have, that

Saintlike you will never
separate that stain of sense,

. . .

—never separate that stain
of sense from the inert mass. Never.
Never that radiance.

(*P*, 108)

And when at last their desires are affirmed, when they discover the "luminosity of elements, the / current leaping," theirs is the true "invention," without which, as Williams writes, "nothing is well spaced . . ." (*P*, 176, 50).

Nearly all Williams's writing possesses exactly the qualities and enacts exactly the processes he so praises in the passages on Madame Curie. Her uranium is his anything: a tree, a woman, a marriage, Paterson, America,

. . . a city in itself, that complex
atom, always breaking down.
to lead.
　　　　　But giving off that, to an
exposed plate, will reveal   .

(*P*, 178)

His approach is almost always the same: He enters into the life of a thing or a complex experience, surrenders himself to it entirely, and thereby discovers the language and form which will reveal, and enact, its luminescence, its power and beauty. As a writer and as a man, Williams seems deliberately unfinished, delicately probing. His devotion is not primarily to results—in medicine, the cured patient; in life, the achieved serenity or fame; in art, the set-piece—but to the process of discovery itself.

Oddly enough, however, given Williams's antipathy toward Benjamin Franklin, his own *Autobiography* is remarkably Franklinesque. Franklin himself was highly unusual, but he shaped his life in his *Autobiography* to make it seem a suitable model for imitation, in the hope that all men might eventually be led to realize their common ground and brotherhood in Reason.[1] Therefore, all the peculiarities and peccadilloes, the things which a modern reader tends to find not only more interesting than the accounts of inventions or plans for self-improvement but also more essentially indicative of Franklin's genius, are either suppressed entirely or revealed only to be dismissed as "errata," passional aberrations on the high road to success. Williams, too, was highly unusual; one has only to try to explain who he was to the many people who still have never heard of him in order to realize afresh how complex a person he was and how much he accomplished. Poet, novelist, playwright, historian, essayist, correspondent, writer of short stories and improvisations; pediatrician, obstetrician, gynecologist, general practitioner; son, father, husband, and apparently incorrigible lover—and all these things with aplomb—in the variety of his accomplishments and the vigor of his life, Williams seems to resemble the actual Benjamin Franklin more than anyone else. But in writing his *Autobiography* he succumbed to what he deplored in Franklin: He harnessed the "wilderness" of his experience with the yoke of civilization.

Such a harnessing, of course, is common to public autobiography. The reasons for attempting it are legion. What I believe to have been Williams's reasons will emerge throughout this chapter and the next. There are two, however, which pertain to both Williams and Franklin. Though Williams did have his moments of disgust with ordinary people, both he and Franklin were ardently democratic. In writing their autobiographies, they seem to have felt that if they could provide others with a program for greatness, however simplified (even falsified) such a program must be, then others could attain it too. Furthermore, both men were passionately convinced of the necessity and correctness of their ideas. Therefore, both sought in their autobiographies to win others over to their convictions. Williams is quite explicit on this point: "What becomes of me," he writes, "has never seemed to me important, but the fates of ideas living against the grain in a nondescript world have always held me breathless" (*A,* Foreword).

Both these things—the belief in the essential equality and perfectibility of mankind, and the belief in one's own clarity of vision—help to account for the didacticism that pervades the two autobiographies. Franklin's instructions are explicit; they have inspired (or amused) generations of students. Williams's are more subtle and less systematic, but nonetheless evident. Franklin moralizes, turning directly to the reader, as when he writes, "I mention this industry [his own, for which he was commended while working as a printer] the more particularly and the more freely, tho' it seems to be talking in my own praise, that those of my posterity who shall read it may know the use of that virtue, when they see its effects in my favour throughout this relation."[2] Williams shows rather than tells. The chapter of the *Autobiography* entitled "Projective Verse" begins with a direct statement, a theme for consideration: "Until we have reorganized the basis of our thinking in any category we cannot understand our errors" (*A,* 329). The next few pages are given to quotation from Charles Olson's essay, "Projective Verse," which seemed to Williams to summarize many of his own ideas concerning the bases of poetry. Then, the subject switches to Charles and Musya Sheeler, an American painter and exiled Russian dancer, both close friends of Williams, in whose marriage he sees the same union of disparate elements, the same solicitude, the same ability to work from the ground, respecting and utilizing local phenomena, that would enable the "reconstruction of the poem" (*A,* 332). The chapter ends with an observation that encompasses Olson, the Sheelers, and Williams, and instructs future poets: "Nothing can grow unless it taps into the soil" (*A,* 334).

Now, an autobiographer who aims to instruct will seek to persuade not so much by philosophizing or exhorting as by manipulating the story of his life. Every event must be made to seem part of a larger pattern, so that the conclusions, the legacies, the meaning, may appear to spring necessarily from the happenstance of daily existence. And this pattern must not remain private; it must pertain, implicitly, to every reader. This is why, when one reads Saint Augustine's *Confessions,* or Franklin's *Autobiography,* or Williams's, one is not really free to disagree. Each author argues his essential typicality—Augustine as a redeemed sinner, Franklin as a man of Reason, Williams as an American "in the grain." Each author implies, therefore, that to disagree is to fail to see correctly. And such a failure is serious indeed; one would no more want to be a sinner in Saint Augustine's eyes than to be T. S. Eliot in Williams's.

We return, however, to the paradox: Williams wrote a Franklinesque autobiography, though he scorned Benjamin Franklin. He wrote a story of his life fit for imitation, though again and again throughout his career he spoke out against the destructive effects, for both art and life, of just such imitation. He who, as Sherman Paul observes, showed "in the story of his success as a poet, how others might live (must live) the literary life in America,"[3] was at pains elsewhere to discredit such ambitions, as in *In the American Grain,* where he said of Daniel Boone, "because of a descent to the ground of his desire was Boone's life important. . . . Not for himself surely to be an Indian, though [the Indians among whom he ventured] eagerly sought to adopt him into their tribes, but the reverse: to be *himself* in a new world, Indianlike" (*IAG,* 136–37). Part of Williams's greatness and much of his originality stem from his realization that no thing and no person exists in order to be copied, either in art or in life. In fact, what he most admires about both things and people are not their generic qualities, not their participation in some larger, abstract category ("the literary life in America," for instance), but their quiddities, their freedom from definition or translation, their "perfections" (*A,* 288). Perhaps one can become a man of Reason through a systematic process of imitation, but as Williams would be the first to insist, one cannot become a poet, or an interesting person, or an American "in the grain," by imitating anything—even by imitating Williams.[4]

Nevertheless, Williams did not practice these convictions in his *Autobiography.* Instead, he decided this time to forgo the experimental probings, the search for his inner standing, and write the public story of his life. One consequence of this decision is that, in the *Autobiography,* he ignores one of the primary tenets of his theory of artistic composition, that (as he quotes from Olson), "FORM IS NEVER MORE THAN AN EXTENSION OF CONTENT" (*A,* 330). The *Autobiography* does possess a certain freedom; Williams shakes the conventional form up just about as much as he can, juxtaposing memories, anecdotes, bits of information, without bothering much to fill in the gaps with interpretation. As a result, the writing itself is delightful. Fresh, lively, and highly informal, it is the prose of a man who has been writing for nearly fifty years and who has learned to write well spontaneously. The arrangement of anecdotes and chapters is delightful, too. Though the order of events is on the whole chronological,

Williams works at times within this form in a prose equivalent of Olson's "open field composition": seemingly disparate stories, like that of "A Maternity Case," in which the harried doctor delivers unexpected twins to an enormous sow of a mother, and the one about his meeting in Paris with Gertrude Stein (who asks him what she should do with her unpublished manuscripts and, when he advises her to save the best and burn the rest, replies, "But then writing is not, of course, your *métier*") are set side by side without commentary to reveal important linkages and underlying themes. Gertrude Stein does not suffer, quite, for being tucked alongside the fecund mother—the breakthrough she achieves with her "objective use of words" is as important as (and something like) the breakthrough of the objective second baby—but clearly the beds whence new life emerges are not elegant places to be. This the doctor knows, despite Stein's collections of paintings and breakable antique chairs. Though he admires her greatly, and though at the time of the trip to Paris he had felt like a country cousin among the expatriate artists, he has the last laugh after all, by writing so well about Stein and others in his *Autobiography* (*A*, 241–56, passim).

But no matter how delightful the writing, or the arrangement of anecdotes and chapters, the fact remains that the form precedes the contents. It does not grow specifically out of the workings of Williams's imagination, as an extension of content, but out of the generic conventions of public autobiography. Williams's *Autobiography* is a largely chronological, retrospective narrative, written from a fixed and disembodied point of view, which confines itself to the relation of those aspects of private experience which will serve to create the impression he desires, of the nature and the meaning of his life. And this, I think, is the book's central problem. If one is to write a public autobiography, too many things must be excluded. The process of selection is predetermined; therefore, the act of writing is not so much one of discovery as it is one of exposition. One is not an explorer, like Daniel Boone, descending again and again to the ground of one's desire; one is a tour guide, taking others over ground already charted. This kind of autobiography has its uses, of course, or it would not be written. It serves excellently for what Williams consciously wanted: It disseminates his ideas and shows us the man behind the ideas, a fascinating man, whose long-awaited fame was well deserved. It does other things as well: It provides a valuable context in which to place, and thus to understand, Williams's other writings. It creates an epoch, the epoch of Modernism, and chronicles fundamental changes in both life and art in America. It challenges us still in our assumptions about this country and adds to our knowledge of the search for true invention. But because its form is not open, not an extension of content, it is not free to do what Williams also needed: to help him arrive at a sense of his inner standing and, in a time of private hardship, thus to redeem his life.

Nor does the *Autobiography* give a particularly full impression of what Williams was actually like. The man it describes is a man of many parts, a brilliant man—but not, as Williams was, a man of genius. This is due in part to the fact that genius is indescribable; as Yeats said of truth, it can be embodied but not known; and even the most extraordinary people do a lot of mundane things over the course of a life. But it is also due to the choices made in the process of composition. In the *Autobiography,* everything is up front; though Williams refers to such things as the terror that "dominated my youth," a "terror that flared from hidden places and all 'heaven'," he does not really body them forth (*A,* 3). They remain named but not shown, elements in a poem which never gets written—not in the *Autobiography,* at any rate. Then too, many things are simply omitted. Here, there is no high loneliness, no fundamental sense of dislocation, no awareness of the dangers lurking within the self—things which it is by no means falsely romantic to say were present in Williams's experience.

The impression one receives from the body of Williams's writing, though not from the *Autobiography,* is that he was a complex man whose genius blossomed, like Yeats's, in a ground of irreconcilable oppositions. Tension, frustration, and a sense of loss (which he calls "damnation") were the necessary conditions of his creativity. At a fairly early age, he learned this fact about himself, and therefore deliberately did not make decisions which would give him a false sense of possession or force him into one camp or another, though the pressures upon him and within him to do so were great. He remained, for instance, the loyal son of both his father and his mother—both the practical English businessman and the passionate Latin *artiste manquée.* He remained both a doctor and a writer, though he complained loudly for years about the demands the practice of medicine made on his time and concentration; both a devoted family man and an independent wanderer, though the effects on both his sense of freedom and his marriage were severe; both a respectable citizen and a member of the avant-garde, though his friends in Greenwich Village accused him of selling out and the townsfolk of Rutherford thought he was crazy. Though at times he longed for expatriation, he chose to spend his life in Rutherford, New Jersey—halfway between New York City and the desolate back hills whence come girls like Elsie—Rutherford, New Jersey, a quintessential American place. He was tempted in ways only hinted at in the *Autobiography,* ways explored more fully in the other writings: perfection, suicide, bohemian abandon. Like Yeats, he greatly admired misfits, people "heroically lost, heroically found," who moved through the wilderness of their lives "improvising [their] music."[5] Yet for himself, the extremities he praised in others seemed too easy a resolution; as he sardonically remarks in *The Descent of Winter,* the suicide is "the perfect type of the man of action . . ." (*DW,* 255). Anything less than to hold all possibilities alive within himself would indicate a failure of the imagination. Therefore he vowed, while still in his twenties, to "be normal, undrunk, balanced in everything" (*A,* 51).

As part of the legacy of Romanticism, perhaps, society generally expects artists to be tormented and flamboyant. Often enough they are, sometimes in excess of their convictions. Given such a climate of expectation, Williams's program of being "normal, undrunk, balanced" was neither easy nor naive. It required, instead, a degree of courage and self-knowledge equal to Adrian Leverkuhn's when, in Mann's *Doctor Faustus,* he comes to the opposite decision and contacts syphilis for the sake of his art. The comparison is not entirely gratuitous; such a possibility was suggested to Williams by the Baroness Else von Freytag Loringhoven, an exile who lived in Greenwich Village around 1920, and who offered her diseased body for Williams's transformation. And *Kora in Hell* indicates that Williams understood the Romantic compulsion; in one of the improvisations, he writes,

> A man whose brain is slowly curdling due to a syphilitic infection acquired in early life calls on a friend to go with him on a journey to the city. The friend out of compassion goes, and,

thinking of the condition of his unhappy companion, falls to pondering on the sights he sees as he is driven up one street and down another. It being evening he witnesses a dawn of great beauty striking backward upon the world in a reverse direction to the sun's course and not knowing of what else to think discovers it to be the same power which has led his companion to destruction. At this he is inclined to scoff derisively at the city's prone stupidity and to make light indeed of his friend's misfortune. (*K,* 40)

But, as Williams realized, it is easier to go down in a blaze of glory than it is to survive. To survive is precisely what he decided to do—and decided again and again, at various points in his life.

During his twenties, then, Williams formulated the general design, and made many of the most important decisions, of his life. He decided to settle in Rutherford and to marry Florence Herman. He decided to write, rather than to paint, which had been a possibility. He decided not to try to support himself and his family by writing, but to practice medicine as well, and thereby make enough money to free him from the necessity of writing for popular acceptance. Though the poems he wrote in his twenties were frankly derivative, stemming much more from poetic tradition than from the conditions of his life, the decisions he made at the time prepared him for his thirties, when he freed himself from convention and began his long voyage of exploration and discovery. As he writes in the *Autobiography,* regarding his youthful intentions,

> I would live: that first, and write, by God, as I wanted to if it took me all eternity to accomplish my design. . . . I would marry (but not yet!) have children and still write, in fact, therefore to write. I would not court disease, live in the slums for the sake of art, give lice a holiday. I would not "die for art," but live for it, grimly! and work, work, work (like Pop), beat the game and be free (like mom, poor soul!) to write, write as I alone should write, for the sheer drunkenness of it, I might have added. (*A,* 51)

This passage, written in Williams's sixties, describes decisions taken forty years before, but as its fervor indicates, there remains a deep accord between the older man and his youthful self as to the wisdom of the life's design.

The *Autobiography,* however, charts too straight a course between youthful sproutings and mature exfoliation. In retrospect, a life may appear to have rooted, branched, and flowered, as a working title for Williams's *Autobiography* indicates that he felt his life had done. In retrospect, Williams may seem to himself to have been a budding poet with an instinctive sense of measure the first time he beat upon his tiny drum (*A,* 3). When he sees what has become of others—of his friend and rival Ezra Pound, for instance, confined to St. Elizabeth's and accused of treason—his own decision to stay in Rutherford may seem infinitely wiser than others' decisions to live abroad, basking in fame and reaping the benefits of a great poetic tradition (*A,* 335–44). When he sees how sturdy and rewarding his marriage has been, how it has warmed him time and again and even made room for his divagations, he may know his wife to be "the rock on which I have built" (*A,* 55). When he sees how writing and medicine have merged, the practice of each enriching the other, the frustrations of each are forgotten (*A,* 286–89, 356–62). And when he sees that he has come through at last, a sense of triumph colors the writing. Having succeeded, he finds the marks of success implicit all along.

Here is a passage from the *Autobiography* describing events which followed the Williamses' return from Europe in June 1924:

> My first job was to resume my practice of medicine. We were broke, of course, or near it, and that was important: I wasn't sure what would happen, but enough of my former patients came back to me to form the nucleus of a new practice. I was definitely committed to the practice of pediatrics and, being young, everything seemed rosy.
>
> The boys went back to camp, we spent a couple of weeks with them at the end of August, and that fall I had my tonsils out. Happy Days! (*A,* 235)

And here, in contrast, is a passage of autobiography written in 1929 during the influenza epidemic, describing equally inconsequential things:

RING, RING, RING, RING! There's no end to the ringing of
the damned—The bell rings to announce the illness of someone
else. It rings intimately in the warm house. That's your bread
and butter.

Is the doctor in? (It used to ring.) What is it? (Out of the
bedroom window.) My child has swallowed a mouse.—Tell
him to swallow a cat then. Bam! This is the second paragraph
of the second chapter of some writing on the influenza epidemic
in the region of New York City, January 11, 1929. In the
distance the buildings fail. The blue-white searchlight-flare
wheels over to the west every three minutes. Count. One.

The things—one thing I dislike about your book was that
you said that sex is beautiful. Did I? I thought I had said the
opposite. No, you said it somewhere.

She looked at me so queerly, so intently. (*N*, 275–76)

The first passage seems innocuous enough. It covers ground; it is unified and coherent, though written with spontaneity. It describes a bit
of the life, just as life seems to have happened. The second passage, in
contrast, would be considered by readers of traditional taste to be
barely publishable writing. But in fact, as Williams argues, the kind of
writing the first passage exemplifies is full of prevarication: "The com-
positions that are smoothed, consecutive are disjoined. Dis-jointed.
They bear no relation to anything in the world or in the mind" (*N*,
275). He despairs, at times, of breaking through the tidy sentences to
a true relation; as he knows, when the experiments fail, "the banality
wins, is rather increased by the attempt to reduce it" (*N*, 274). Nevertheless, throughout his career he strives toward another kind of unity,
the only kind he treasures, and which the second passage exemplifies,
for all its apparent incoherence. It is a unity of the present, in which
"all things enter into the singleness of the moment and the moment
partakes of the diversity of all things" (*N*, 282).

Such a unity will not constrain life, but release it, for, as Williams
believes, we live only now. The purpose of writing, therefore, must be
neither to rearrange the past nor to prepare for the future, but "to
refine, to clarify, to intensify that eternal moment in which we alone
live . . ." (*SA*, 89). If the present is redeemed, the rest will follow; all

of life, surrendered to the creative flow of the imagination, may become as rich, as complete within itself, as the moment Williams describes in *Kora in Hell,* in which,

> *Seeing the leaves dropping from the high and low branches the thought arises: this day of all others is the one chosen, all other days fall away from it on either side and only itself remains in perfect fullness. It is its own summer, of its leaves as they scrape on the smooth ground it must build its perfection.* (K, 82)

But, as Williams discovered, such a redemption of the present was the one thing beyond the power of his *Autobiography.*

2

An Innocent Sort of Child:
The Autobiography of William Carlos Williams

A Franklinesque version of innocence lies at the heart of *The Auto-biography of William Carlos Williams*. More than any other quality, Williams's innocence makes him appear as he wants to appear—quintessentially American, and therefore fit to serve as a model for other American writers in their own struggles to fulfill his legacy, making contact with their country, living and writing "in the American grain."

Williams wastes no time declaring his theme. "I was an innocent sort of child," he begins his *Autobiography*, "and have remained so to this day. Only yesterday, reading Chapman's *The Iliad of Homer*, did I realize for the first time that the derivation of the adjective venereal is from Venus! And I a physician practicing medicine for the past forty years!" (*A*, 3). The word "innocent" occurs from time to time throughout the book, taking on as it does so a peculiar set of connotations. For instance, Williams writes, "[A]s far as my wish is concerned, I could not be satisfied by five hundred women. As I said at the beginning, I was always an innocent child" (*A*, 55). And later, juxtaposing things which have passed away, with himself, who has endured, he comments, "innocence is hard to beat" (*A,* 76). Innocence seems, from these remarks, to be Williams's word for the source of his power. It makes him morally pure, unaware, as he says, of the venereal in Venus. Yet it gives him, too, a vigorous and virile imagination—which, combined with the purity, issues rather mysteriously in durability.

This last, I think, is no exaggeration. For more important than the recurrence of the word is the recurrence of the conception: Williams's sense of his own innocence, both as an American man and as an American artist, pervades the *Autobiography*.[1] The pattern of growth he presents is much like Franklin's. As a young man, he is wide-eyed, enthusiastic, eager for new experiences, whether these be fumigating the cockroaches in the lab at old French Hospital, smuggling a dead baby on the subway in a suitcase, dancing in his pajamas with the nurses on the roof, playing "hares and hounds" as a boy, or hiking across the fields discussing poetry with H.D. As a middle-aged man, he is plunged into life—into his family, his writing, his hectic medical practice, his connections with the avant-garde, and his whirlwind tour through Europe in 1924, a lengthy but skewed account of which falls just at the center of the *Autobiography*. Even in his sixties, after all that work, he seems as fresh for life as ever. The readings on college campuses, the trips to St. Elizabeth's to visit Ezra Pound, the journeys west with Floss in 1948 and 1950 to teach and read as a famous poet, the flurry of work at Yaddo to finish *Paterson, Book IV*—and his openness to fame, his obvious delight at having completed the *magnum opus*—the accounts of these make him seem forever young, at heart "the young doctor" still,

> . . . dancing with happiness
> in the sparkling wind, alone
> at the prow of the ferry!
> ("January Morning," *CP,* 100; *CEP,* 162)

As he presents himself in the *Autobiography,* Williams is not only fresh for life but also a little naive. He is naive, however, only with regard to the things about which Americans are supposed to be naive: corruption, sex, and Europe. This is part of Williams's charm, and part of Williams's strategy; it is also his primary reason for consternation. It makes him be, as he wants to be, "in the American grain"; it makes him likeable, good, and pure, but also sometimes vulnerable and foolish. Goodness and stubborn integrity are ascendant in Williams's story of his refusal, while an intern, to sign his name to unverified financial forms at Nursery and Child's Hospital, forms which were covering up graft and sexual corruption. The refusal cost him his job and put an end to his future as a wealthy pediatrician in New York City, but Williams's innocence in the affair is a virtue of which, in telling the story, he is justifiably proud (*A,* 102–5). Innocence seems, however, less a matter for pride in Williams's accounts of his attempts to gain experience with women, attempts that came to nothing when he looked too young to be taken seriously, didn't dare to follow a prostitute, dared to follow a prostitute but couldn't afford champagne. (His chagrin, though undoubtedly real, is once again part of the strategy, healthy American youths having until recently been expected to be both burning with lust and virgin.) But innocence ends happily with Williams's marriage to Floss; little is said about sex after that, except for a clever reminder that, even in his sixties, after a long and active life, this seeker after Venus is still charmingly obtuse at sniffing out the venereal:

> As Bob McAlmon said after the well-dressed Spanish woman passed us in Juarez (I had said, Wow! there's perfume for you!):
> "You mean that?" he said. "That's not perfume, I just call that whores." (*A,* 289)

Both pride and chagrin figure strongly in Williams's accounts of his sojourn in Europe. Though Williams and Floss spent several months in Italy and Vienna, the *Autobiography* recounts in detail only the time they spent in France, particularly in Paris. It circumvents, that is to say, the Dionysian longing for abandon, the themes of desire, chaos, and darkness that so fascinate and trouble Williams in the obscene, long-unpublished improvisations entitled "Rome" and in the Italian and Viennese sections of his first novel, an account of "Evans Dionysus Evans's" trip to Europe modeled closely on Williams's own, entitled *A Voyage to Pagany.*[2] The *Autobiography* focuses on Williams's reception among the European avant-garde and the American expatriate society in Paris; it emphasizes, therefore, the confrontation between innocence and experience that has been so central a theme in American writing, particularly in James and Twain.

As the *Autobiography* shows, and as other sources corroborate, Williams enjoyed a rising reputation both among the expatriates and among such European artists as Joyce, Brancusi, and Valéry Larbaud. His excitement at being fêted, however, was marred by his persistent feelings of unsophistication—feelings both symbolized and intensified by his one-sided feud with T. S. Eliot, whose poetry and expatriation Williams vehemently despised. "T. S. Eliot had come to Paris about then," Williams writes in the *Autobiography*, "appearing at the Dôme and other bars in top hat, cutaway, and striped trousers. It was intended as a gesture of contempt and received just that" (*A*, 217). Notice Williams's wording: One cannot tell whether Eliot felt contempt for Paris, or for Williams. For Paris, no doubt, but the statement hints at both pride and paranoia. For worst of all, Eliot did not enter the feud with Williams; he thought him too small to feud with, merely "of some local interest perhaps." Whatever Eliot's intentions, it was Williams who felt the contempt—in part because he truly disagreed with the expatriates' reasons for leaving America; in part because he saw beneath the glamor of expatriate society to the "cupidity, the bitchery, the half-screaming hysteria" that went on at the personal level; and in part because he felt like the boy with his face pressed against the sweetshop window (*A*, 215). Especially when Floss was sick and Williams had to go out alone—to a ballet where he identified with the little dancer who looked as if she'd break her arms and legs, contorting herself in her efforts to reach an indifferent audience—his sense of his own wrongness was painfully acute: "My old tux looked like two cents in all that extremity of mode" (*A*, 215).

Once, at Walter Arensberg's studio in New York, in the years before the war, Williams had tried to praise Marcel Duchamp for a painting, "The Sisters," that hung on Arensberg's wall:

> I finally came face to face with him as we walked about the room and I said, "I like your picture," pointing to the one I have mentioned.

> He looked at me and said, "Do you?"
> That was all. (*A*, 137)

Then, in Paris, Williams's close friend and host Robert McAlmon gave Williams an honorary dinner, which twenty or thirty people attended. Duchamp was there, as were the Joyces, Ford Madox Ford, Sylvia Beach, and others for whose attentions Williams had been grateful; and after a lively evening it came time for Williams to rise to the occasion:

> I said thank you, naturally, to Bob, thanked them for all their kindness and then told them that in Paris I had observed that when a corpse, in its hearse, plain or ornate, was passing in the streets, the women stopped, bowed their heads and that men generally stood at attention with their hats in their hands. (*A*, 195)

This is not a bad perception for a poem by William Carlos Williams. Once again, he was insisting on the emptiness of rhetoric and the universality of the local—and he was carrying fire to the enemy, proving that he needn't bow to Europe, showing that perhaps the eyes of a Rutherford yokel were clearer than the Parisians'. He was, subtly, getting revenge for Duchamp's snub, which had made him realize "then and there that there wasn't a possibility of my ever saying anything to anyone in that gang from that moment to eternity—but that one of them, by God, would come to me and give me the same chance one day and that I should not fail then to lay him cold—if I could" (*A*, 137). His speech did lay a few people cold, but not in the way he had intended. Like Mark Twain's speech at the Whittier Birthday Dinner, it stripped bare not the audience but the speaker, revealing in him both the scorn and the longing of the innocent from the West, the perpetual outsider. And the result was humiliation. "To relieve the bad moment, someone asked Bob to sing 'Bollicky Bill'" (*A*, 195). Bollicky Bill, indeed.

But as Williams said, innocence is hard to beat. For in public autobiography, one's end determines the nature of one's journey; and despite the setbacks, the humiliations, the long and difficult struggle for recognition, Williams's *Autobiography* is a paean of success. Splendidly, he fulfills the plan conceived in the radical innocence of his young adulthood: the plan to do it all; to marry, have children, practice medicine, and "write, write as I alone should write"; to become large enough to encompass both bourgeois responsibility and bohemian abandon (*A*, 51). Splendidly, he vindicates the choices he made in his process of self-creation. In a list resembling that of Proust's Baron de Charlus,[3] he itemizes the fates of his friends; compared with them he seems inordinately blessed. Many of them have died: Joyce, Stein, Stieglitz, the Baroness, Charles Demuth, Hart Crane, Marsden Hartley. Others, like Bob McAlmon, have faded into obscurity—McAlmon is "working for his brothers in El Paso." Most poignantly, "here is Pound confined to a hospital for the insane in Washington"; and with regard to Pound, at least, Williams seems not only inordinately blessed but also inordinately savvy (*A*, 318). For Pound, above all others, had tried for many years to talk Williams into expatriation; but if he had followed Williams's example (one imagines Williams thinking), if he had stayed at home, he would not have created the tragedy which culminated his life.

Williams wrote his *Autobiography* almost entirely between December 1950 and May 1951, only months after he completed *Paterson, Book IV,* and thus brought to fruition (as he thought then) the labor of his life.[4] This fact of its timing is the most important thing about the *Autobiography.* For more than anything else, the *Autobiography* is the story, not quite of the poet who could write *Paterson,* but of the poet who has written *Paterson,* who has thought of his poethood as embodied in and coterminous with *Paterson,* and who wants therefore now to enter into the poem, defending it, explaining it, passing it on to others, making it seem his life. Though critical opinions differed widely as to the merit of *Paterson* during the years of its publication,[5] and though Williams alternately suffered and rejoiced over his critics' reactions, the *Autobiography* leaves no doubt as to what *he* thought of the poem. As the *Autobiography* moves toward its close, his thoughts all turn to *Paterson,* the "reply to Greek and Latin with the bare hands" (and to Eliot and *The Waste Land*) that vindicated staying home and showed learning to know one place to be the most profound and difficult form of exploration (*P*, 2). His thoughts all turn to *Paterson,* the "image large enough to embody the whole knowable world about me," and he finds himself embodied there too, inexpressibly (*A*, 391).

The *Autobiography* ends with the description of a tour Williams made only "yesterday" around the terrain that became the poem, with his guest from New Orleans, John Husband, and his little grandson Paul. Williams's strategy here is brilliant and very moving. Showing Paterson to his companions, he draws them into his vision; and we— out-of-towners like John Husband, but also inheritors like Paul—we learn to see what Williams sees, for he draws us too. Up on Garrett Mountain, looking over the city, we learn through John Husband's words what it has come to be for Williams: both Paterson and *Paterson;* intimate, possessable, unified, complete; something, John Husband says, "you could visualize so distinctly, practically hold . . . in the hollow of your hand" (*A,* 393). Then we are told of the little house built just at the peak of the rocks by an artist, or a writer perhaps, a kindred spirit of Williams. Then we are taken down the back way, where the road is covered with melting ice, and come at last to the Falls.

Williams's language remains anecdotal, but at this point the chatty remarks take on a nostalgic beauty. "This," he tells John Husband,

> "This must have been about the spot where Mrs. Cummins stood before she fell or jumped into the stream below."
>
> "Yes, that was a story," said John.
>
> "And over there is where Sam Patch must have stood—that's the point."
>
> "Where?" said Paul.
>
> "There."
>
> "Did he jump from there?"
>
> "Yes, to retrieve the roller when they were running the bridge across."
>
> "Quite a story, quite a story." (*A,* 394)

It has indeed been quite a story, and now we are at its end, in the place where texts converge. As a young man Williams vowed to write "As I alone should write"; innocent, he thought he could do so. He has done so, for a lifetime, and finds himself now in the moment when his writing pays homage to his writing, when he passes on his legacy, looking out over the landscape of his life.

The words themselves, however, tell the reader one thing more— one thing that Williams may not have intended. The end of a story, the end of an autobiography, is not a termination. For even as Williams speaks and ceases speaking, he is standing next to the source of his language, the thunder of whose waters fills Paterson's eternal dreams—the endless Passaic Falls (*P,* 6).

When he wrote the *Autobiography,* Williams may have thought he was finished with poems.[6] But he wasn't, of course, and one of the poems in *Pictures from Brueghel* is for the grandson, older now, who was with him that day at the Falls. On the surface, it's a poem about catching fish:

> when you shall arrive
> as deep
> as you will need go
>
> to catch the blackfish
> the hook
> has been featly baited
>
> by the art you have
> and
> you do catch them . . .
> ("Paul," *PB,* 22)

Like so many of the poems in *Pictures from Brueghel,* "Paul" has its genesis in the *Autobiography,* which was supposed to close a life but which opened instead to an even deeper beginning.[7] For "Paul" arises from a question the child asks at the end of the book, but which his grandfather does not answer: "How deep is the water? . . . I mean at the deepest place?" (*A,* 394). Then like a fish the poem comes, to be one answer; it answers, however, by speaking with love and by speaking of art, not by measuring depth of water. For, as Williams came to see, in terms of autobiography, the question Paul asks in his innocence is the question that has no answer, the very best question of all.

One thing is certain, though: the water flows much more deeply than Williams permits us to see in his *Autobiography.* The *Autobiography* is not a deliberate falsification; Williams's other writings show that innocence, as he portrays it here, was a quality he did possess. But the

Autobiography is a one-sided self-portrait, in which certain facets of Williams's experience are cleverly highlighted and others firmly suppressed. Both the highlightings and the suppressions serve to strengthen the theme of innocence, as becomes clear once one perceives that the things suppressed are *eros* and *thanatos*—those great desires that drive the psyche and consternate Americans—while the things highlighted are the public virtues derived from sublimation. This is why, as I said, the *Autobiography* shows us the man who has written *Paterson,* but not quite the man who could write *Paterson.* Nor does it show us the man who would soon begin again, open up the "finished" product and find it truly never-ending: who would write *Paterson, Book V,* and the poems in *Pictures from Brueghel,* and leave behind notes for *Paterson, Book VI,* when, twelve years later, he died.

When Williams writes, "I was an innocent sort of child and have remained so to this day," he is both telling the truth and beginning to construct his public persona. With the very next sentence, however, the truth and the public persona begin fatally to diverge. For, though Williams may indeed have failed to see the connection between the words "venereal" and "Venus" until his good gray middle sixties,[8] he had perceived the connection between the things these words represent at least as early as *Kora in Hell,* in which (in the passage I quote in chapter 1) he meditates upon the "dawn of great beauty striking backward upon the world," which is both the setting sun and the terrible, godlike power that drives his friend the syphilitic (*K,* 40). He had, in fact, been obsessed by the connection, which was absolutely central to his calling as a poet. For the venereal is desire, the desire to make contact, to fuse, and to create, which impels indiscriminately the lover, the syphilitic, and the poet. And Venus is "Beautiful Thing," the "radiant gist," the goddess of love, without whom poems cannot be born. As Williams remarks in *Kora in Hell,* "It's all of the gods, there's nothing else worth writing of. They are the same men [and women] they always were—but fallen" (*K,* 61). And as he insists throughout his life, fallen, the gods fall farther still when mortal men and women turn away from love, denying the venereal.[9]

In the *Autobiography,* however, Williams's guise as a Franklinesque innocent forces him to play coy with his awareness of this connection. Convinced of its great importance, he is not willing to leave it alone;

he offers hints to the reader: "I am extremely sexual in my desires: I carry them everywhere and at all times. I think that from that arises the drive which empowers us all." Yet neither is he willing to state the connection fully. Given the social climate of the 1950s, one need not expect him to be candid about sex in so public a self-expression as his *Autobiography*. Half-said, however, is better left unsaid; to a woman, at least, he becomes offensive when he announces, "I do not intend to tell the particulars of the women I have been to bed with, or anything about them. Don't look for it. That has nothing to do with me" (*A*, Foreword).[10]

Whereas Williams is evasive with regard to *eros*, with regard to his own mortality he is mute. Perhaps, writing the *Autobiography*, he felt he had purged *thanatos* in *Paterson, Book IV*, in which he allows his desire for death its voice—

<blockquote>

Listen!

Thalassa!   Thalassa!

Drink of it, be drunk!

Thalassa

immaculata: our home, our nostalgic

mother in whom the dead, enwombed again

cry out to us to return

the blood dark sea!

nicked by the light alone, diamonded

by the light   from which the sun

alone lifts undamped his wings

of fire!

</blockquote>

—but turns away with the cry that the sea is "not our home! It is NOT / our home" (*P*, 202). Perhaps he felt he could remain identical with his persona, who, on the poem's last page, heads resolutely "inland, followed by the dog" (*P*, 203). But such resolution seems premature, given the conditions under which Williams wrote the *Autobiography*. Not only was he plagued by illness—he suffered a heart attack in February 1948, just after which he began the preliminary "Some Notes Towards an Autobiography"; he had a stroke in 1949; and on March 25, 1951, while racing to finish the *Autobiography*, he had an apoplectic stroke which could have killed him[11]—not only was he ill, but he had at least once nearly chosen his illness. A typescript passage at Yale describes his anginal attack and hints at a bitterness toward life and a carelessness toward death thoroughly suppressed in the final draft of the *Autobiography:*

> It was in this [icy] weather that I was at the hospital one day until one in the morning—a night cold and clear. I came out, backed my car out from where it stood, nosed into the curb, straightened the front wheels out and headed slightly down hill for home. The snow plough had banked the drifts here at least three feet on either side and I, trying to find some amusement for myself, kept skimming this high wall to my left until it caught my front wheel and I went into it a few feet and stopped. It was entirely my own fault. Unable to back out I went ahead turning the wheel hard to the right, it was down hill, thinking to pull out of it that way. I merely got myself in deeper and knew I had to shovel it. It was near one-thirty by that time.
>
> The only shovel I could find in the Hospital basement was a small half broken one, the others were locked up for the night—and the engineer couldn't find the key. So I shovelled. I shovelled until I began to feel some anginal pains which I recognized through my anger, and like the farmer who lost a finger in the hay chopper and kept going until he lost two more, I kept going.
>
> I did stop once, for breath, and looking at the snow, clean and white before me, thought to myself it wouldn't be a bad spot to drop dead in. In fact it looked positively attractive. The bitterness that overcomes us at times often takes that color.[12]

To suppress *eros* and *thanatos,* the psyche's desires for love (or life) and death, is to suppress the poem; and for Williams, to suppress the poem was to die:

> If a man die
> 　　　　it is because death

has first
possessed his imagination . . .
("Asphodel, That Greeny Flower," *PB,* 179)

Despite all its riches and all its information, the *Autobiography* suppresses the poem—not the poem already finished, not *Paterson, I–IV,* and all the other published books, but the poem unfinished, which Williams's own life was being lived to realize. This accounts for Williams's depression upon completing the *Autobiography,* a depression from which, as Sherman Paul beautifully argues, Williams's return to the poem with "The Desert Music" began painfully to release him (*PB,* 108–20). For if, Paul writes, Williams "needed *The Autobiography* to give his life permanence, he needed poetry to redintegrate the self—to restore, in contact with the world, the very chaos from which the ordering movement of imagination saved him." [13] And reintegration became possible precisely because, in "The Desert Music," Williams was able to surrender his Franklinesque innocence, surrender his public persona, and, descending once again into *thanatos* and *eros,* find himself in "the music" which was the ground of his desire.

From the beggars with "obscene fingers" who clutch at the poet's arm, "Give me penny please, mister," pulling him into their need; from the "old whore in / a cheap Mexican joint in Juárez, her bare / can waggling crazily," whose cold perfunctory eyes mock both her pathetic dance and the world's interpretations; and most of all from the shape on the bridge between Juárez and El Paso, the shape

> shapeless or rather returned
> to its original shape, armless, legless,
> headless, packed like the pit of a fruit
> into that obscure corner . . .

—from these figures of what the world calls desolation, the life-giving desert music is released. It begins in snatches that counter the other music, the "lying music" of "souls" and "loves" that the Indians sing at the restaurant, the music of social realities and secular expectations; and it swells as the poet listens, to encompass him in its singleness,

                          the music! the
              music! as when Casals struck
              and held a deep cello tone. . . .

The sound this music makes does not derive from human life, though
it sustains and embraces the human. Beyond life and death but "protecting" both, encompassing both, its nearest verbal equivalent would
seem to be the Buddhist "Om!", the sound and silence of being itself,
in which everything in the universe is grounded.[14]

Confronted by the music and the shape which is himself, the shape
of life-and-death united on the "interjurisdictional" bridge, Williams,
"speechless" at first, cries out in sudden enlightenment with a sense of
his vocation:

                        I *am* a poet! I
              am. I am. I am a poet, I reaffirmed, ashamed. . . .

This is the only possible form of recognition: just to speak one's name
in the music, to be what one must be. But the word seems odd,
"ashamed." Why should Williams be ashamed?

The reason connects, I think, with the question his grandson asked
at the end of the *Autobiography*, "How deep is the water? . . . I mean
at the deepest place?" In part Williams's shame arises because he has
doubted he was a poet, has thought his days for poetry gone. In part it
arises because, as "The Desert Music" makes clear, it can be shameful
to be a poet, to see otherwise than the world. "So this is William /
Carlos Williams, the poet," someone says at dinner in Juárez. "You
seem quite normal. Can you tell me? Why / does one want to write a
poem?" But in part it arises from something else entirely. "Innocent,"
Williams was clothed. Naked, he is ashamed. Not out of guilt, however—for the desert music obliterates both innocence and guilt—not
out of guilt, but out of privilege. For he has arrived, himself, as deep as
he will need go; facing the shape of the human, sensing the music
which sustained it in its life-and-death enfolded, he surrenders the innocence of pride for the humility of knowledge. In the space of the
desert music, it is nothing to be "William / Carlos Williams, the poet."
It is life itself, however, to be given a poem to write:

Now the music volleys through as in
a lonely moment I hear it. Now it is all
about me. The dance! The verb detaches itself
seeking to become articulate

> And I could not help thinking
> of the wonders of the brain that
> hears that music and of our
> skill sometimes to record it.

3

In Every Way True to Nature:
A Dream of Love

In the *Autobiography,* Williams succumbs to what he deplored in
Benjamin Franklin and harnesses the "wilderness" of his experience with the yoke of civilization. In his play *A Dream of Love,*
however, he casts aside the yoke and enters into the wilderness in order
to discover his inner standing. For this reason, just as the tutelary work
behind Williams's *Autobiography* can be said to be Franklin's *Autobiography,* the tutelary work behind *A Dream of Love* can be said to be
The Confessions of Jean-Jacques Rousseau. Candid, troubled, *A Dream
of Love* comes close to revealing Williams in all the truth of nature.
Like Rousseau's *Confessions,* it is a painfully naked work, which must
appeal for communion and atonement neither to God nor to society,
but to the individual and equally naked human: "May any man who
dares, say 'I was a better man than he.'"[1] This necessity stems from
guilt: Like the *Confessions,* it is a statement of transgression. Once
again like the *Confessions,* it is also a statement of pride and faith.[2] And
the sense that faith, pride, and guilt are inextricably intermingled—
that guilt enables faith and pride, and pride and faith necessitate

guilt—makes *A Dream of Love* one of Williams's most moving accounts of the daily business and burden of being human.

Or I should say, perhaps, the daily business and burden of being a poet. The extent to which the poet speaks for others has been a question often addressed but never fully resolved since the advent of Romanticism, with its rejection of dogma and its consequent insistence that one's own experience is the only ground of knowledge. This, of course, is also one of the main questions underlying Rousseau's *Confessions*. Williams shares Emerson's belief that the poet does indeed speak universal truth, that he is "representative"—"He stands among partial men for the complete man, and apprises us not of his wealth, but of the common wealth"—and that, though "the people fancy they hate poetry . . . they are all poets."[3] But Williams's sense of the implications of this belief is somewhat different from Emerson's, for Williams's conception of our human nature is not that it is contemplative, but that it is erotic. Nothing could be more troublesome, given the fact that our culture has firmly repressed the erotic. The pain that suffuses *A Dream of Love* derives from Williams's well-founded suspicion that, while poets are certainly human, others may not be human—may not be imaginative enough to perceive their erotic humanity, that is, or courageous enough to endure it. They may, therefore, reject poetry entirely. Or they may treasure the poem as something lovely, yet reject what the poet reveals of himself and the process of its creation. They may even love the poet, protect and adore him for his calling, yet find themselves unable to follow him all the way into the self, to discover that, in his self-revelation, he reveals them too. They may find themselves unable to acknowledge themselves as "poets." And when this denial happens, the poet is painfully isolated, painfully exposed. He discovers that he is not in the Eden he dreamed of, where he and others are naked, but in the recurrent nightmare where he is naked while others are clothed. He must take the chance, however, in order to fight against the hypocrisy that persists in seeing the poem as divorced from the poet, the human. For unless he can reveal himself in all the truth of nature, poems will seem to the world to be bloodless adornments merely, rather than speech in our common tongue, rooted in and flowering from our passion—acts of love for a dream of love, stemming from the seediness of our lives.

A Dream of Love is Williams's fullest investigation into the connection between "Venus" and "the venereal"—a connection of which he would later pretend not to have been aware. It is the autobiography not of the poet who has written *Paterson* but of the poet who could write *Paterson*—who was, in fact, writing *Paterson.*[4] It shares many themes with *Paterson,* particularly the themes of the pursuit of "Beautiful Thing" and of "love, that stares death / in the eye, love, begetting marriage . . ." (*P,* 106). It shares, as well, a source with *Paterson,* to which I would like to turn briefly: a poem published in 1936, in which Williams's dominant metaphors are "the city" and "the dream of love."

"Perpetuum Mobile: The City" contains a clear expression of Williams's understanding of the importance and the psychology of desire (*CEP,* 384–90; *CP,* 430–35). The poem moves as its title indicates, fluctuating rapidly between images of the city of man and of man's dream of the City (which Williams refers to elsewhere as "the radiant gist," "Beautiful Thing," or "love").[5] The two cities seem mutually opposed: the one whose beauty Williams expresses in an image which recalls the traditional Christian linking of the East, the rising sun, with the City of God, the risen Son—

> All at once
> > in the east
> rising!
>
> All white![6]

—and the other, the necessary language for which is contemporary images of violence, hypocrisy, greed, deceit, decay. The one is a flower,

> a locust cluster
> a shad bush
> > blossoming
>
> Over the swamps
> > a wild
> magnolia bud—,

which contains within itself the promise of harmony and fulfillment. In contrast, the other is "Milling about," with neither purpose nor termination; both meanings are implicit in "No end—." And the one is the realm of imagination, the place beyond words, the perfect poem; it is the City with

> ... stars
> of matchless
>   splendor
>
>   and
> in bright-edged
>   clouds
> the moon—.[7]

The other is the "Tearful city," where rain and grief hide the light, and life is bound and crushed by "iron reason."

But city and City are offspring of a single union—that of the self's embrace with the other which enacts the dream of desire. As in Williams's short lyric "Queen-Ann's-Lace," desire is the force behind all flowering; it mediates between cities and, in fact, causes them both to be. On the one hand, Williams deplores the acts committed by the inhabitants of the city; still, as the poem keeps insisting, men do what they do—rob banks, wage war—"For love." What seems simply random movement is in reality the hunger of the self for its perfection, its extension, its release. Consequently, even an act as inherently perverse, to Williams's mind, as that of the Black who has "wisps of long / dark hair" tied "wisp / by wisp" to his own hair, in an effort to transform his sexual identity, participates in the poem which "lives are being lived to realize" (*A*, 362).

Throughout his writing, Williams's metaphor for the most fruitful type of human action is marriage, because in marriage man's attempts to transcend the bonds of the self and make contact with the other can be most clearly seen. Like Shakespeare, Spenser, and Donne, Williams speaks of marriage as fruitful both in its moments of ecstatic union and in its promise, through children, of continuity; but Williams also finds great value in the tension brought about by marital frustration which, if earlier poets mentioned it, they were wont to deplore. "Perpetuum Mobile," then, is in part a poem in praise of marriage. In grand and quotidian ways it exemplifies the potency and the failure of desire.

In contrast to the violent, deceitful, or decadent desires of others who inhabit the city, the desire of the poet and his wife is pure—relatively speaking—because it impels them to work together to build a life:

> We have bred
> we have dug
> we have figured up
> our costs
> we have bought
> an old rug—.

And it causes them, "each / separately," to release the self in the sexual enactment of the dream

> of love
>   and of
> desire—
>
> that fused
> in the night—.

But though actively to dream calls forth the City, it "disappeared / when / we arrived." Unity falls back to multiplicity and the ideal to the real, for human desire has no power to abrogate time. Through repetition a note of despair begins to enter the poem: Having failed once, the dream begins to seem "a little false." Still, it is

> a dream
>   toward which
> we love—
> at night
>   more
> than a little
>   false—.

Possibly, then, the actors and not the dream are false; or possibly both; the punctuation of this passage stresses its ambiguity. Perhaps to dream is itself just another form of "delectable / amusement," no better and no worse than all the things people do when they live in the city.

The poem's strength is not that it offers a resolution to the question of desire—for there can be none, no absolute knowledge in a world governed by time and apprehended only through individual experience—but that it states the problem fruitfully. The poet has stood at the prow of the ferry and sought words for his experience in its fluidity. "Farewell!" is the poem's last word. As in marriage, however, the problem is not so easily solved, and the word is qualified by its subsuming title, "Perpetuum Mobile." Life is perpetual motion and death the only termination. Furthermore, not life but death opposes itself to the City, for in life "There is no end to desire." Nor is there any end to failure. Desire can never attain to a lasting state of fulfillment, for time and imperfect love are the only means by which man glimpses the eternal, which immediately gives way to the desiring self in time.

Given this dilemma, Williams finds himself in ambiguity. What F. C. Gardiner says of the medieval Christian pilgrim applies to him as well: He endures a dialectical, even paradoxical relationship with the object of his desire—one of "presence and absence, possession and non-possession, sight and faith." Though the paradox causes him anguish, he is not free to choose the cessation of desire, for, as Gardiner points out in his remarks on Gregory the Great, "The pilgrim who desires also possesses the object of his desire, even while not possessing it."[8] Perhaps the real miracle in Luke's account of the journey to Emmaus, which serves Gregory as text for his meditation on desire, is that of the power of human longing to call into being its version of "Beautiful Thing": "The two disciples love, and the object of their love walks with them; loving, they speak, and the person whom they discuss is there."[9]

But Williams's situation is a good deal more acute than the medieval Christian pilgrims'. For Williams there is no God, and consequently no City of God, to exist independently of man's actions and provide him with both a final home and an absolute scheme of values. True, there is "Beautiful Thing," "the radiant gist," "the City," which responds to man's deepest self and endures beyond all changes as the object of his desire; this, for Williams, is an absolute tenet of faith. As he writes in the *Autobiography,* "It is an identifiable thing, and its characteristic, its chief character is that it is pure, all of a piece and, as I have said, instant and perfect: it comes, it is there, and it vanishes. But I have seen it, clearly. I have seen it. I know it because it is there" (*A*, 289). But this sacred presence—which can be summoned but not named, embraced but not possessed, experienced but never fully described—is immanent, not transcendent; Williams's other absolute tenet is "no idea but in things." Consequently, the burden is on the poet; he must enter into the world, enter into experience, sensuously, physically. As *A Dream of Love* reveals, his virtue is at one with his capacity for transgression; sexually at least, true selfhood inheres not in chastity but in sin.

Adultery, the dramatic situation of *A Dream of Love,* has lost much of its power in recent years as a tragic form of behavior. Williams, however, would not see this as liberation. To his mind, the reason for adultery is the pursuit of "Beautiful Thing"; it is both cause of and symbol for poetry, not a social pastime but a Promethean transgression. Like all Promethean endeavors—like poetry itself—it is both torment and joy, damnation and salvation; as Doc tells Myra in *A Dream of Love,* "When a man, of his own powers, small as they are, once possesses his imagination, concretely, grabs it with both hands—he is made! Or lost, I've forgotten which . . ." (*DL*, 200). Consequently, the split: on the one hand, it seems, the adulterer would shrink back, put out the fires for the sake of home; on the other hand, he would plunge ahead, "steal" the fire, driven by his *daimon:*

> Beautiful thing
> —intertwined with the fire. An identity
> surmounting the world, its core—from which
> we shrink squirting little hoses of
> objection—and
> I along with the rest, squirting
> at the fire . . .

—and then the voice, inexorable, terrible: "Poet. / Are you there?" (*P*, 120).[10]

For the poet is "the maker," in the double sense of the word. He discovers his language by entering into the body of his experience—

literally, physically; his poetry is erotic.[11] Adultery is both cause and
symbol of his creative behavior. A theological sin and (more to Williams's concern) a primordial transgression, its opposite nonetheless is
not sanctity but divorce, and all that Williams means by divorce, a
condition in which "the language is missing" and we die without contact, "incommunicado" (*P,* 11). As Williams writes in *Paterson,*

> Divorce is
> the sign of knowledge in our time,
> divorce! divorce!
>
> (*P,* 18)

Fighting against divorce, for the sake of his own survival and the survival of humankind, the poet, "the maker," has only one choice:

> I must
> find my meaning and lay it, white,
> beside the sliding water. . . .
>
> (*P,* 145)

But, one might ask, why adultery? Could not the pursuit of "Beautiful Thing" be carried on just as fruitfully, and with much less human
pain, through fornication? For Williams there is nothing, nothing except nothingness, outside the condition of marriage. Surveying Williams's poetic career, one finds that marriage is, in fact, his deepest and
central metaphor, the wellspring of his art and of his life. In chapter 4
I discuss the significance of Williams's marriage to Floss; suffice it here
to quote Doc, from *A Dream of Love.* "I died when I walked upon the
grass," he tells Myra, his wife. "I died in everything. I died when I was
born. . . . From which you once rescued me—hence my devotion"
(*DL,* 201). The sentiment seems extreme unless one sees that marriage, like adultery, is for Williams powerfully symbolic. Whereas adultery is a statement of man's freedom, an assertion of desire independent
of social order, and therefore an assertion of art, marriage is a statement
of man's presence in the world, a promise of his commitment to the
world, without which commitment there would be no art and no one
to be free. Marriage creates identity because it creates "the first wife,"

the initial and essential acknowledgment of the other. As Williams writes in *Paterson,*

> [T]he snow falling into the water,
> part upon the rock, part in the dry weeds
> and part into the water where it
> vanishes—its form no longer what it was:
>
> the bird alighting, that pushes
> its feet forward to take up the impetus
> and falls forward nevertheless
> among the twigs. The weak-necked daisy
> bending to the wind . . .
>
> (*P,* 23)

—these things are reflected in marriage; like the wife, they are "the other." To be wed to her is to be wed to them, to enter into the dance revealed by all existence.[12] It is, furthermore, to become a poet, aware of the way "events" dance "two / and two with language which they / forever surpass . . ." (*P,* 23). For she, "the first beauty, complex, ovate," is the "flower within a flower" among the rocks, the site of the first embrace of "Beautiful Thing" (*P,* 22). Whatever she may think, whatever the world may think, adultery pays her homage; it is the testament of desire, the violent refreshing that keeps the dream of love first dreamed in her, and because of her, alive.[13]

Whatever one does think of Williams's theories about adultery, one must admire his reasons for writing *A Dream of Love.* Two passages from *Paterson* beautifully express what seem to be these reasons. The first passage has to do with the subplot, with Doc's pursuit of "Beautiful Thing" in his tryst with his typist, Dotty Randall. Out of fear, as Williams says,

> we die in silence, we
> enjoy shamefacedly—in silence, hiding
> our joy even from each other
>   keeping

> a secret joy in the flame which we dare
> not acknowledge. . . .
>
> (*P*, 121)

This silence, however, cannot be a choice for the poet. When he reveals his "secret joy," it is not for its prurient interest, not for self-advertisement, but because to conceal his experience is to betray "The language." The language itself is "Beautiful Thing"; to fail to pursue it and bear witness to the pursuit is to

> make a fool of myself, mourning the lack
> of dedication
>
>   mourning its losses,
> for you. . . .
>
> (*P*, 121)

And the second passage has to do with the main plot, with Doc's attempts, in the play's last act, to reveal himself to Myra and bring her understanding into his dream of love. Like the first, it is both an acknowledgment of what happens and an affirmation of what the poet knows to be necessary and true. "For what is there but love," Williams writes,

>   love, that stares death
> in the eye, love begetting marriage—
> not infamy, not death
>
>   tho' love seem to beget
> only death in the old plays, only death, it is
> as tho' they wished death rather than to face
> infamy. . . .
>
> (*P*, 106)

A Dream of Love is an "old play," in which love begets "only death." Yet it is a new play too, in which Williams faces "infamy" in the service of a love "begetting marriage." In the play's last act, the question rests with Myra (as in life it rested with Floss), and as one reads the play, the question rests with oneself: Will we condemn ourselves to the old dispensation, thereby condemning both Doc and Williams, or will we be able, by grace of the imagination, to enter into the new? For it is a desperate venture in art as well as in life: to confess to "infamy," grounds for divorce, in the hopes of strengthening marriage. Its significance is domestic, but not entirely. Williams's venture in *A Dream of Love* answers Emerson's injunction to the poet to "tell us how it was with him"; metaphorically, it is also Rousseau's venture in *The Confessions*. But though it may be true that "the experience of each new age requires a new confession," Emerson's conclusion that all men will gather around the poet and "be the richer in his fortune"[14] does not automatically follow. "Is all poetry evil?" Doc Thurber cries to Myra, seeing the divisiveness the pursuit of art has brought to his own life (*DL*, 127).

There is courage in Williams's attempt to answer this question by writing *A Dream of Love*. In many ways the play is an attack upon himself, in his character as Doc Thurber. It reveals, as the *Autobiography* does not, the intensity of the conflicts, both between writing and medicine, and between writing and marriage, that were part of Williams's experience and that influenced his behavior. It reveals, as the *Autobiography* does not, the nature of his relationship with Floss—both the depth of their love for each other and the depth of their problems. "More than a little false . . . a hell of a lot more!" Doc says at one point in the play's last act, sick at heart over the dream of love he and Myra have shared, referring bitterly to the poem which the play quotes and from which it derives, "Perpetuum Mobile" (*DL*, 193). The strength of the play is that it can show, as a poem cannot, what it means from moment to moment to live with a dream of love which can only be revealed in the "perpetuum mobile" of tenderness and bitterness, communion and isolation:

> *Doc:* Don't read. Talk to me awhile, I'm restless. What have you been doing?
> *Myra:* Reading—what else? Aren't you going into the office to write?
> *Doc:* Lay off, darling. I don't always go out there in the evening.
> *Myra:* Pretty nearly always. Don't you—when you can?

Doc: You know, you look tired. Why don't you take a vacation for yourself? You need it.

Myra: Not without you.

Doc: That's ridiculous.

Myra: No. It's not ridiculous. I shouldn't enjoy myself without you. [*There is a pause.*] Perhaps you'd like to get rid of me, darling—for a week or so?

Doc: That's an idea.

Myra: Then you'd be free. Free! To do as you please. Isn't that what you're living for?

Doc: I'd still have my practice of medicine.

Myra: Give it up. You've always resented it.

Doc: I have.

Myra: Because you've always resented me.

Doc: You're wrong.

Myra: I interfere with you.

Doc: That's right. How is anyone ever going to live with anyone else unless he interferes with him? So what? That has nothing to do with it.

Myra: Everything.

Doc: You have to take it out of me, don't you? Don't I work hard enough for you?

Myra: For me?

Doc: Who else?

Myra: Oh my dear husband, what a fool you are—and how lovable and transparent.

(*DL,* 110–11)

Painful and unfinished as it is, the conversation becomes still more painful once one realizes that, even as he talks to and reassures his wife, Doc Thurber cannot wait to get away to Dotty, with whom he has planned a liaison the following afternoon. He is a good man though beleaguered, but, as Williams bravely reveals, he is also a liar, a coward, a hypocrite, and a nervous wreck—in short, a normal adulterer—dedicated to preserving the convenient but deadly split between appearance and reality. Though he appears to be honest with Myra, in fact he cares more about protecting himself from her, telling her just enough to keep her at bay, than about finding a common ground on which they could meet openly and, surrendering pretense, begin to know each other. Consequently, he exacerbates her dependency on him, which he both desires and fights. She neither has him nor has lost him; he both loves her and does not. She reads the poem he wrote her in the first days of their marriage ("I lie here thinking of you"), mourns for him and adores him, waits for him to come home, spars with him when he does, tells him he is her life ("I get angry at you. I feel lonely, neglected. But I don't blame you. Ever. I love you. And that's my life"), and thinks that if he died she might be happy (*DL*, 126). His poetry is her tyranny; she is privileged, not to be herself, but to be a symbol, the "idea" of the wife; as she perceptively tells him, "it's never been wholeheartedly me. It's always been something else— someone else where I was concerned" (*DL*, 123).[15] And though Doc may be right in his eventual self-defense, when he comes to Myra after his death to gain her understanding, that does not mean that Myra is wrong when she accuses him of selfishness and betrayal. "One marriage!" may be the goal, and even the reality deep beneath the pain, but Doc and Myra are as much divorced as married throughout their married life (*DL*, 127).

Doc offers, early on, to give up writing. "Right here I'm happiest," he tells Myra, "—if that's what we want. Here there is at least the possibility of contentment and peace" (*DL*, 127). But of course this is not a choice, for poetry is the pursuit of "Beautiful Thing," and to abandon the pursuit would be an absolute betrayal. There remain, then, two alternatives: Either the other characters must learn to see that they share Doc's quest, that, in Emerson's sense, "they are all poets," and that what Doc wants is what they want, or he must resign himself to "divorce" from both wife and world, to isolation and failure. This is why he insists, when he comes in a dream after his death, to Myra, that his quest and his adultery were both essential and universal:

> A man must protect his price, his integrity as a man, as best he is able, by whatever invention he can cook up out of his brains or his belly, as the case may be. He must create a woman of some sort out of his imagination to prove himself. Oh, it doesn't have to be a woman, but she's the generic type. It's a woman—

even if it's a mathematical formula for relativity. Even more so in that case—but a woman. A woman out of his imagination to match the best. All right, a poem. I mean a woman, bringing her up to the light, building her up and not merely of stone or colors or silly words—unless he's supremely able—but in the flesh, warm, agreeable, made of pure consents. (*DL,* 200)

This is why he insists, furthermore, that "Every man is like me. . . . I'm just like everybody else." It is his averageness, not his specialness, that makes him both "proud" and "right" (*DL,* 209).

But though Doc and, through him, Williams need desperately to be average, in order to be right,[16] both the other characters and the dramatic action of the play itself suggest the impossibility of arriving at either this or the opposite conclusion. The question of averageness or normalcy has little to do with actions and everything to do with reasons, and takes us back for a moment to "Perpetuum Mobile": Do people really do what they do—rob banks, wage war—"for love"? Or, in terms of the play, do people commit adultery invariably "for love"? Doc's lover, Dotty, seems to understand him; his dream of love seduces her; but what about Doc's rival, the Milkman: Does he act "for love"? He would like to get rid of his wife, blow her "into the middle of the Pacific Ocean," for she, presumably, has been catting around—but would he like this "for love"? He would like to marry Myra and make her "happier than [she] has ever been," for in order to build his business and reclaim the property "they" took away he needs to improve his image—but has this to do with love? (*DL,* 159, 199). The characters all speak, but unless they can speak truly—unless, that is, they are "poets" and aware of themselves as "poets"—there is no way to determine whether or not they participate in the poet's dream of love, and therefore no way to determine whether that dream is illusion or deepest truth.

Actions speak louder than words, one says. In *A Dream of Love,* however, the other characters' actions serve not to clarify the poet's position, but to make it more confusing. At the heart of the play—but offstage, where it belongs, in the imagination—there occurs an action profoundly symbolic, in terms of private autobiography. Doc dies in bed with Dotty, having been just about to embrace "Beautiful Thing."

Williams, as playwright, kills him off, thereby killing off as well his own further chances for pretense or evasion. There he is, naked, dead; he is caught in the act of selfhood and revealed to all the world in the truth of nature.[17] The question thus becomes, when Doc returns in the play's last act to explain himself to Myra, whether she or the others who listen will be able to meet him, likewise naked, or whether they will reject him and persist in remaining clothed.

This is the question, finally, for which Williams has no answer. Myra, at least, seems healed. Though it may be part of the play's agony with language, that her healing takes place not because of Doc's words, but because she is granted a vision—a dream of Doc together with Dotty, and can, as it were, put her hands in the wounds, still, she seems at last to understand her husband. In the play's last scene, after the dream, she is able to leave the kitchen where she has hidden since Doc's death. Passing through the door, she ends the play; she goes forward, one presumes, into wholeness, and in her own way will further the dream of love.

One cannot be sure of the others: the maid Josephine, the Butcher Boy, the Milkman, all of whom, with Myra, witness Doc's seduction of Dotty. Here I must quote at length, for the climax of the play reveals a terrible indecision about what the world thinks of its poet, about whether it will turn out to be salvation or damnation to have written *A Dream of Love*.[18] Doc has been speaking to Dotty, who is aroused not by his advances but by his convictions concerning art—the passion of the Greeks, and the absence of contact in poetry in our day:

> *Dotty* [*with complete conviction*]: All right, darling.
> *Doc:* All right what?
> *Dotty:* I love you.
> *Doc:* You mean you know what I'm talking about?
> *Dotty:* Yes.
> *Doc:* You mean you understand what I'm after?
> *Dotty:* Yes.
> *Doc:* And it doesn't make you wanna puke?
> *Dotty* [*shaking her head violently*]: No. It makes me want to love you, my darling, until I'm deaf and blind and . . .
> *Doc:* You angel out of heaven, it can't be.

Dotty: Yes. Now! Yes, yes, yes, yes!

[He takes her in his arms. Her slip falls from her shoulder. There is a sudden darkness pierced by flashes of light. At the same moment the other figures on the scene break into a unison chant of: Yes, yes, yes, yes, yes, yes, yes, yes! which suddenly changes into the sound of machine-gun fire, running from right to left, low at first, but with increasing intensity. The figures from the bench rush to the center of the stage as if joining in an attack. The Butcher Boy leads the way, bearing an American flag. The Milkman has a shotgun and Josephine is beating a drum. Offstage, a fife is playing Dixie. There are pistol shots, and flashes of light through a general darkness. The attack succeeds, with cheers! Then a final explosion—not too near—followed by silence and darkness lit by a flickering light, as of a conflagration.

There is no curtain as the scene ends. When the lights come up again, all evidence of the hotel room has vanished]

(*DL,* 221–22)

Never mind about the silliness of the diction, or the echoes of Molly Bloom. Though this may not be great drama, the anguish of making confession has never more clearly been shown. Perhaps, as one critic says, the stage directions evoke a "triumphant, black-humored scene," in which drums and flags symbolize intercourse.[19] Or perhaps they evoke a blacker scene, in which, at the moment of revelation, the others for whom the poet has dreamed rush to gun him down.

For it seems that one would have to surrender one's ego entirely in order to understand all that Williams means by *A Dream of Love.* The fact of Myra awakens a song:

> I lie here thinking of you—
>
> the stain of love
> is upon the world!
> Yellow, yellow, yellow
> it eats into the leaves,

smears with saffron
the horned branches that lean
heavily
against a smooth purple sky . . .
                    (*DL*, 125–26)

And the fact of Dotty awakens a song:

            As the rain falls
            so does
                        your love
            bathe every
                                    open
            object of the world—

            In houses
            the priceless dry
                                    rooms
            of illicit love
            where we live
            hear the wash of the
                                    rain—

            There
                        paintings
            and fine
                        metalware
            woven stuffs—
            all the whorishness
            of our
                        delight
            sees
            from its window
            the spring wash
            of your love
                        the falling
            rain . . .
                        (*DL*, 165–66)

But I think it is significant that, when Doc's voice speaks Dotty's poem, Myra, not Dotty, is in the room. The poem could be for Myra; Myra's poem could be for Dotty; and what, after all, does it matter?

When Williams's son grew up, Williams noticed a look in his son's eyes that he had seen

> often enough
> > in the mirror,
> a male look
> > approaching despair—.
> It made him think of Robert Burns, whose
> > Jean forgave him
> > > and took him to her heart
> > > > time after time
> when he would be
> > too drunk
> > > with Scotch
> or the love of other women. . . .

And what he wrote of Robert Burns makes one think of *A Dream of Love,* and the gunfire at the end, and the poems for Myra and Dotty:

> What was he intent upon
> > but to drown out
> > > that look? What
> does it portend?
> > A war
> > > will not erase it
> > > > . . .
> Flow gently sweet Afton
> > among thy green braes—
> > > no matter
> that he wrote the song
> > to another woman
> > > it was never for sale.
> > > ("Address," *PB,* 144–45)

4

A World Lost:
"Philip and Oradie"

During the years around 1905—while studying medicine at the University of Pennsylvania, and later, while interning at the French and Child's Hospitals in New York City—Williams worked on his first long poem. This poem, which was never completed and never titled, I will call after the names of its hero and heroine "Philip and Oradie." In his *Autobiography,* written more than forty years later, Williams describes both the poem and its fate. The poem, he writes, was modeled on Keats's *Endymion,* and "recounted in blank verse a tragic story." When the narrative "Induction" begins, the young prince Philip has just married Oradie, the "chaste and lovely lady" of his desire, but while the wedding party is still at its celebrations, before the marriage can be consummated, someone adds poison to the communal cup and all the celebrants except Philip die. He is rescued by his old faithful nurse, who discovers an antidote to the poison; then, while still in a trance, he is abducted to a "foreign country."

In Williams's remembered account, the poem properly begins at this point, when the prince awakens from his slumber. He finds himself alone, lying in a comfortable place among the trees, quite in the open, with torn branches on all sides of him and leaves, ripped from their hold, plastered in fragments upon the rocks about him. Unfortunately, though, he didn't recognize the place. No one was there to inform him of his whereabouts and when he did begin to encounter passers-by, they didn't even understand, let alone speak his language. He could recall nothing of the past.

Then, to compound the confusion, the narrative shifts to a secondary dream, the inspiration for which was Boecklin's "Insel des Todes." The prince envisions himself "transported to that dire place in a boat—" and "at this point the poem bogged down." Despairing at treating the dismal scene in his chosen medium, heroic couplets, Williams retreated to the main story line, which, he says, meandered off into landscape descriptions and segments of adventure, and recounted in endless detail "the aimless wandering . . . of the young prince in his effort to get back home again as well as to discover what had happened to him" (*A*, 58–60).

In 1905, Williams gathered up his courage and took his manuscript of the poem to Arlo Bates, his brother Ed's English professor at the Massachusetts Institute of Technology, wanting to know "whether or not, to his mind, I should quit medicine and write." Bates's reactions were mixed: He praised Williams's "sensitive appreciation of the work of John Keats's line and form," and concluded that perhaps in twenty years, given persistent effort, Williams's writing might amount to something (*A*, 54–55).[1] Kindest of all—and most depressing—was Bates's suggestion that he and Williams were imaginatively akin. He too wrote poems, he said; when he had finished them, he put them in a drawer and closed it. But despite Bates's reactions, or perhaps in part because of Bates's reactions, Williams continued to work passionately on his poem during weekends and into the night over the next few years. Then, as he tells it, "in disgust, one day, perhaps through my impatience with my 'heroics,'" he tossed the manuscript into the furnace (*A*, 60).

At this point in the story, however, mysteries arise. Williams may well have tossed part, or most of, "Philip and Oradie" into the furnace, but he did not destroy the whole poem. Eventually the poem went to his friend Viola Baxter, and thence to the Beinecke Library at Yale.[2] What remains of the poem (approximately twenty handwritten pages) does not weigh three pounds, as Williams writes the manuscript did, and could not have taken years to write. On first thought one might assume that Williams destroyed the long, meandering account of Philip's travels that he speaks of in the *Autobiography* as the poem proper but neglected to burn the "Induction." It is true that "Philip and Oradie" covers much the same ground as Williams's description of the "Induction": Philip's arrival back home with Oradie, the marriage, the poisoning, Philip's rescue by his nurse. But one problem with this assumption is that the extant "Philip and Oradie" begins before Philip's birth and ends, as far as I can tell, with his death in a "foreign country"; in plot, tone, and psychological development, it seems to be complete in its few pages. Another problem is simply that the extant poem differs significantly from Williams's remembrance of it in the *Autobiography.* There seem to be two poems, in fact: the poem Williams wrote while he was in his twenties, just deciding to be a writer, and the poem he recalled forty years later.

Although these two poems overlap, yet they are different. "Philip and Oradie" itself begs to be read as the veiled autobiography of the potential artist. It was inspired by *Endymion,* Keats's own early poetic autobiography; like *Endymion,* too—indeed, like practically all Keats's poems—it struggles with a conflict nearly every artist since the advent of Romanticism has perceived: the conflict between a life of art, or thought, and a life of action, and the opposed claims of each.[3] Though Williams nowhere states this, I think "Philip and Oradie" was also inspired by *Hamlet,* which spoke so strongly to the Romantics (as it speaks to us still) as the archetypal dramatic expression of this conflict, both as the conflict exists within a single soul and as it is divided and externalized among antagonists.[4]

But the striking thing about "Philip and Oradie"—and the thing entirely lacking in Williams's recollections—is its strong element of autobiographical family drama, which its conventional literariness cannot obscure. Williams's description of the poem in the *Autobiography* implies that the "Induction," which takes Philip through the wedding and poisoning and up to the point of his awakening in a foreign country, is insignificant—is background merely—and that the poem truly begins with his adventures while finding his way back home. But no matter how much of the poem may have been destroyed or never written, the fact remains that the material covered in the extant "Philip and Oradie" (which is approximately the material in the "Induction," as it is described in the *Autobiography*) is by no means insignificant, even though Williams may later have felt it was. Instead, it represents his first major attempt to arrive at a sense of his identity through writing. Transposed, Philip's world is Williams's, as Williams experienced it in his twenties: There is a prince, intrinsically a poet, who lives misunderstood in dreams and solitude; there is a father, a man of action, who denies and fears his son because he envies him; there is a mother, herself an artist but held captive by her husband; there are woods into which the prince escapes, in which he wanders alone with his own nature; and somewhere beyond the woods, or within the woods perhaps, as a reward for the lonely quest, there is a bride.

The autobiographical nature of these equations becomes apparent, of course, only when one knows both the poem and the context in which it was written. And even given such knowledge, the poem tends to obscure the equations, in part because it is so conventional, so entirely imitative of popular nineteenth-century derivations from the Romantics, particularly Keats. It is awkwardly written, shamelessly poetical, and hopelessly derivative, as its first few lines make abundantly clear:

> When chivalry like summer's crimson fruit
> From blossom, April's flimsy pride and all
> The ripening seasons, burst at length full frocked
> Resplendent on her prime, when kings were young
> And liegemen bold ambitious and full oft
> Of equal blood with sovran lived a knight
> Don Pedro was he clept, prince of Navarre. . . .
>
> [Here, and henceforward, I follow the original in spelling and punctuation.]

The language itself strengthens one's inevitable and incorrect impression that the characters and situations are not felt but come undigested from Keats, Shakespeare, and a thousand melodramas. Prince Philip, for instance, reads like an inadvertent caricature of the Romantic poet. He is a mama's boy, whose birth plunges his mother, Beatrix, into a "flooding-o'er wild ecstasy." As he grows up, he learns to care little for his father's world of doughty action; instead, he prefers to wander in nature breathing "the strength of freedom from a hill" or to sit and listen to stories. His father, Don Pedro of Navarre (otherwise called Agramont), is every adolescent's Oedipal dream of a father; he is too stupid to be evil, but heavy enough to do a lot of damage. Primarily he loves

> in eager toil,
> Defiant, still to bruise those heraldries,
> Though forty years of heyday wasting war
> Had grated up his front.

When not grating up his front, he spends his time plotting against Philip; his "pate" has "grown dull from frequent cudgelings," and he is easily persuaded to believe Philip wants to seize his power (whereas all Philip really wants to do is flee to Italy with his bride and his mother). Married to such a man, Beatrix languishes in "grief and lonliness"; she is a woman of gentler climes who whiles away the hours telling stories of her past happiness to Philip:

> She told of foreign kingdoms o'er the sea,
> Of sands that shone like sheeted gold—of waves
> And calm, of auzure skies so pure and deep
> No clown so low but sang in witless praise
> At magic morn's uncloaking. . . .

Philip's father is the "warp of history"; his mother, the "woof of faery dreams." Like Philip, she is intrinsically a poet, held captive in the world of action. And though Oradie is present as a symbol in the poem, as are the woods in which Philip wanders for more than a year and a day when he is forced to leave his mother, as a character she is practically nonexistent. She is

> . . . such a maid as truth alone can tell
> More seemly on this world hath never breathed,

and at one point Philip announces rather rudely to his father that he has found "A bride too pure for Agramont, I ween," but that is all we learn about Oradie. Next thing we know, she is murdered.

The murder scene is the high point in the poem. Philip knows full well that Don Pedro wants to kill him and Oradie at their wedding celebration; consequently, he keeps "fing'ring at / His blade" and pouring Oradie's wine out on the floor. Thwarted again and again in his wicked machinations, Don Pedro at last has a moment of genius:

> "To Agramont ye'll drink.
> Ye all, then all shall drink to Agramont!"

This is Williams's cleverest stroke; Philip has no choice but to commit suicide, in effect, swearing fealty to his father. It is also unintentionally funny; so boundless are Don Pedro's idiocy and ire that in order to kill one son he has to poison sixty people. Beatrix sinks, Oradie sinks, and since he has drunk the toast, Don Pedro sinks, too. The room fills up with "guttural gurgles, groans and sighs," and the party is over.

Such life as remains continues eventful after the murders. Servants dash off "with mouths of chronicle" and are never seen again. Philip's faithful nurse, who has been on the lookout for just such an opportunity, lugs him away to a silken couch and labors to save him with the antidote; then, at midnight, she despairs of his life and totters "with a single moan quick dead." At this point Philip begins to dream. His dreams seem important—this may be the passage inspired by the "Insel des Todes," though it is not in heroic couplets—but their symbolic content is obscure. The universe turns phantasmagorical: At first Philip sees "Cleft heaven . . . with earth and Hell conjoined," and "fumes upon the nauseous stinking air"; then calm returns, with "zephyrs sweet and dapper pixies"; then hell returns once more. This vision gives way to a sort of astral travel; Philip floats above his couch while "hush lipped forms" press round "to gaze at him." This in its turn gives way to normalcy:

> . . . night still it seemed
> Was just a simple night in May and dawn
> Not yet by many a dusky hour near.

Again he experiences astral travel:

> Then rising on his elbow up, in awe,
> He looked if he could fathom the intent
> Of this aerial journey and beheld
> A veil of filmy gold, a quivering mist
> Hung on the east before him into which
> He entered suddenly and black closed round.

Whereupon, he sleeps.

The poem ends quickly thereafter. Philip awakens, rides off on his "palphrey," and begins to wander. Neither he nor Williams seems to know quite where he is going:

> North and to east and enless steady course
> He pointed out and followed fervently.
> But his black eyes told nothing w[h]ere he went
> Nor knew he by whatever other sense
> But journeyed like a tufted seed upon
> Controlling summer winds.

His horse dies, but "shoeless" he continues to wander. Then at last, he sinks down one morning "within a pleasant leafy nook" and, to all appearance, dies:

> He lay him down and soon how soundly slept
> A dreamless loutish slumber and the day
> Climbed up and up in wondrous garb and birds
> Sang near about and he alone was dead.
> Ah! what a year long journey had he come
> Poor youth, how sore a way meets here it's end.

Philip would seem at this point to be dead as dead, and the story would seem to be over. This is not, however, quite the end of the poem:

> For fully day was spread when there out rang
> An eager treble-chaunting roundelay,
> Lightly sounded forth the country song
> And quivering in the wanderers heavy ear
> Forbad more sleep and brought his night to close.

One way to account for this perplexing double ending would be to conclude that Williams had so thoroughly lost control of his poem that he was no longer paying attention to the ordinary meanings of words. This may well be true, but there is, I think, another explanation too, an explanation that shows how Williams began to become a Modernist poet.

Williams wrote "Philip and Oradie" during a difficult period of transition in his life, a period he later described as "heart-breaking" in many ways.[5] He had only the vaguest notion of what he wanted to do, or what he could accomplish, and the conflicting pressures upon him and within him were severe. To begin with, though he was studying medicine as a special student at the University of Pennsylvania, having entered the medical program immediately after he left Horace Mann, he was by no means convinced that medicine was what he wanted. He did want to please his family, however—wanted that very much—and his family pushed him in that direction. His father, English by birth and temperament, and a practical businessman, expected both Williams and his younger brother, Edgar, to become financially stable and to remember (or possibly to repay) the sacrifices he had made for their education both at private schools in Europe and later at Horace Mann. His mother's motives were different: She had an adored older brother, Carlos Hoheb, a surgeon in Puerto Rico, and she expected at least one of her sons to honor him by becoming a doctor. Williams followed the family's plans for him, but it was not easy. Though he lived on campus, he had little time to meet the other students, to take the humanities courses that might benefit him as a poet, or to read the books that those whom he most admired—Ezra Pound in particular—urged incessantly upon him.

Then too, Williams was full of high-flown ideas regarding moral behavior. He internalized his puritanical, middle-class upbringing with a nearly religious fervor: As he reports in the *Autobiography,* he decided "in late childhood or early adolescence . . . to be perfect" (*A,* 27). Perfection, as he then conceived it, was a highly visible grace; essentially it meant being so good inside that he would not have to be dishonest. Above all, it meant making his parents proud of him by doing what they wanted and by fighting off the lust that threatened to burn him "to a cinder" (*A,* 47). Neither was easy to do. Keatsian poethood called him; he longed to succumb gloriously both to poetry and to passion; but something held him back. In the case of poetry, the impediment was medicine; in the case of passion, it was the grand nebulous plan. "Dear Ed," he wrote his brother in November 1906:

> I am not even remotely cynical. The truth is I am troubled with dreams, dreams that merely to mention is too daring, yet I'll tell you that any man can do anything he will if he persists in daring to follow his dreams. To do what I mean to do and to be what I must be in order to satisfy my self I must discipline my affections, and until a fit opportunity affords, like no one in particular except you, Ed, and my nearest family. From nature, Ed, I have a weakness wherever passion is concerned. No matter how well I may reason and no matter how clearly I can see the terrible results of yielding up to desire, if certain conditions are present I might as well never have arrived at a consecutive conclusion for good in all my life, for I cannot control myself. As a result, in order to preserve myself as I must, girls cannot be my friends. (*SL,* 13–14)

At the time he wrote "Philip and Oradie," then, Williams knew very little about women. He had plenty of experience with Venus—with his dreams of romantic love—and medicine was teaching him the tough real world of the venereal, where unwed mothers cat-fought on the hospital floor and he fell in love once "with the corpse of a young negress, a 'high yaller,' lying stripped on the dissecting table" (*A,* 55). But the middle world was lacking, the world of sexual love with real women. He joined Ezra Pound on a few lascivious college rambles, at Pound's instigation, but nothing ever came of them; the girls they ogled were frightened, and Williams was too gentle to persist. He became friends with Hilda Doolittle, but she was "just one of the guys," "no hips, no nothing, just Hilda" (*A*, 68). He fell for a girl "of French descent and a college graduate, which is a combination hard to beat," gazed into her eyes one night, and wrote her a dreadful sonnet (*SL*, 11). He tried to squire a few girls around, but something always went wrong, especially, he felt, because he had no money. Most important of all, he went home to Rutherford on weekends. There he made one of a court gathered around Charlotte Herman, the brilliant young pianist of whom I believe he was thinking when he made Philip ride out of the woods with his bride.

Charlotte Herman was beautiful. Furthermore, she was an artist, passionate and strange, the unattainable *princesse lointaine* whom all the young men worshiped for her devotion to Beauty. The *Build-up*, an autobiographical novel written late in Williams's life, tells the story. Both Williams and his brother (Charlie and Fred Bishop, in the novel) fell in love with Charlotte. For a time they were content to admire her in silence, but then Edgar (Fred) won the Prix de Rome. The parents had promised that if he won, both brothers should study in Europe; therefore, "holy and pure, as their natures demanded their thoughts to be, buoyed aloft on wings of song, nevertheless they were practical enough to find themselves on the brink of action" (*B*, 257). They discussed the dilemma, and agreed that Edgar (Fred) should go and propose for them both. He did, and his own suit was accepted:

> "Fine," said Charlie and then, disgracefully, he flung his arms about his brother's neck and went mad. Fred was embarrassed, loosened himself from his brother's hold and fled. Charlie thought the earth had dissolved under his feet. He hadn't foreseen the sweep of his emotional reaction or the wreckage it would cause. Had Fred been decent enough about it? He had. He had done everything one man could do for another, under the circumstances. In fact the perfection of his behavior only added to the effect. And yet something had come to an end. It was a deeper wound than he should ever thereafter in his life be able to sound. It was bottomless. (*B*, 259)

A great deal came to an end when Charlotte rejected Williams. For one thing, his naive belief in filial solidarity was shattered—as, I imagine, was his equally naive belief in the happy consequences of self-abnegation. But deeper things still were broken. Charlotte was nearly the only one to admire his early poems; she thought they were beautiful, and that a poem "should be beautiful" (*B,* 238). She understood his passion, which was, like hers, to "show the world something more beautiful than it has ever seen."[6] She felt, as he did, that in Rutherford the people were small—"they see their little neighborhood"—and shared his desire to see the world, "to contemplate and, in all humbleness of mind, wonder at even greater things" (*SL,* 14). For her to accept his offer of marriage would have seemed only natural; it would have been a powerful validation of his "Keatsian" image of both himself and his poetry.

It might have been a dreadful marriage. The last thing Williams needed, to develop as a man or as a poet, was a marriage conceived in the realms of faery. He needed what he got: Flossie, the kid sister, to whom he proposed about three days after Charlotte's rejection. Unlike Charlotte, Flossie was "hard as nails," a "rock" on whom he could build; unlike Charlotte, she was both practical and enamored (*A,* 130, 55). She had been in love with him, had watched him paying court to her sister, and had felt rejected. Now, "having found out what love is, having been rejected, and what it could do, with their eyes open, [they] could and would face it together." He did not love her, but he would will himself to love her, not with a "romantic love, but a love that with daring can be made difficultly to blossom. It is founded on passion, a dark sort of passion, but it is founded on passion, a passion of despair, as all life is despair" (*B,* 262). However complicated this sounds, it worked for Williams. It was not what he thought he wanted—but then again, perhaps it was what he really did want; otherwise, why had he sent Edgar to propose to Charlotte for him? Flossie accepted him in 1909; they were married at last in 1912, and blossomed "difficultly" until his death more than fifty years later.

When Williams was working on "Philip and Oradie," of course, all this lay in the future. Then, he was still rushing home on weekends to listen to Charlotte's piano. It is wish fulfillment, not history, that impels his account of Philip's marriage with Oradie—and wish fulfillment perhaps, or a dark and sure self-knowledge, that makes him kill Oradie off before the consummation. For the parallels are there: Oradie, like Charlotte, is the poet's dream, the Romantic image, the quest for which spelled death for Philip and a kind of death for Williams. After Oradie's murder, and after Charlotte's rejection, the poem truly begins. It begins, however, in a memory of loss: "April's flimsy pride" becomes "a passion of despair, as all life is despair." For Oradie, like Charlotte, is the *princesse lointaine,* the still-unravished bride.

Medicine and morality, poetry and passion: These warred within Williams when he was in his twenties. They correspond closely to the conflicting temperaments of his father and his mother—conflicting temperaments which troubled Williams and which, together, formed him. Williams's father was morality, English to the bone. Though she insisted fiercely on morality in bringing up her children, Williams's mother was passion.

Williams's father, William George Williams, was born in England to Emily Dickinson Wellcome, of a man whose identity remains uncertain. At the age of five he sailed with his mother to New York; when she married (or married again), he went to live with his parents in Puerto Rico. There he grew up, "by the sea / on a hot island." He "learned / to play the flute—not very well"; one night a fellow amateur flautist, Carlos Hoheb, introduced him to his sister. Soon thereafter William George Williams and Raquel Hélène Hoheb sailed to New York and were married. They settled in Rutherford, New Jersey, where Elena raised two sons and William George earned a living working for Florida Water.

Williams's father was an English gentleman who never renounced his British citizenship. He loved culture, Arnoldian culture—he read to his sons from Shakespeare, the Bible, and Paul Laurence Dunbar, and paid Williams to read *The Origin of Species* and *The Descent of Man,* a dollar apiece. He was away a lot, sometimes for a year at a time, selling Florida Water in Latin America; when he came home, he told exciting stories of riding "muleback over Costa Rica / eating pâtés of black ants." But, though the stories were exciting, somehow he was not. He was a good man, a mild man—only once did Williams see him enraged, when he forced his son to eat a tomato—who did whatever he did from a sense of duty:

> . . . being an Englishman
> though he had not lived in England

desde que avia cinco años
he never turned back
but kept a cold eye always
on the inevitable end
never wincing—never to unbend—
God's handyman
going quietly into hell's mouth
for a paper of reference—
a British passport
always in his pocket—
. . . . .
and the Latin ladies admired him
and under their smiles
dartled the dagger of despair—
in spite of
a most thorough trial—
found his English heart safe
in the roseate steel. Duty
the angel
with which whip in hand . . .
("Adam," *CEP,* 371–74; *CP,* 407–10)

On the surface, Williams's father would seem to be totally unlike
Philip's father, the dastardly Don Pedro of Navarre. In fact, he *was*
unlike Don Pedro; this Williams recognized in later life. Nevertheless,
Don Pedro is a portrait of Williams's father, as Williams saw him at the
time. A curious anecdote in the *Autobiography* helps to establish the
connection; that the incident described took place ten years after
"Philip and Oradie" was written, and that Williams remembered it
even in his sixties, indicates the depth of the conflict and its power to
disturb him:

I'll never forget the dream I had a few days after he died,
after a wasting illness, on Christmas Day, 1918. I saw him coming down a peculiar flight of exposed steps, steps I have since
identified as those before the dais of Pontius Pilate in some
well-known painting. But this was in a New York office building, Pop's office. He was bare-headed and had some business

letters in his hand on which he was concentrating as he de-
scended. I noticed him and with joy cried out, "Pop! So, you're
not dead!" But he only looked up at me over his right shoulder
and commented severely, "You know all that poetry you're writing. Well, it's no good." (*A*, 14)

This is a dream merely; in real life Williams's father seems to have been
pleasant about his son's poetry, at least if the poetry remained an avo-
cation. He welcomed Ezra Pound into the home and corrected all the
printing mistakes in Williams's first book, the Keatsian *Poems* of 1909.
But by 1918 Williams was writing poems his father would not perhaps
have liked—the experimental poems of *Al Que Quiere!*—and besides,
dreams speak truth to the dreamer. The thing Don Pedro in "Philip
and Oradie" shares most strongly with the father in this dream is a lack
of imagination. Both the knight, who finds his identity in waging war,
and the English businessman, who finds his in doing his duty, live
according to their stations; they have no sense of poetic passion, of an
inner self that must challenge the world of action in its need for self-
expression. Consequently, both men misunderstand and reject their
sons; and as a consequence of this, metaphorically speaking, both men
die. The story of Philip's childhood is sketchy; we may conjecture,
however, that Philip proves himself soon after birth to be an unwilling
knight: he

> gave no heed
> To wars account, refused all tutors and
> Instead would bide a live long summer's day
> A fawning milk-sop by his mother's side.

A rupture takes place; apparently the father orders the son to leave his
mother, for "From that time forth these boon friends met no more."
Instead of pining away, however, or hanging around his father, Philip
goes off to the woods, where he wanders long alone and whence he
returns with his bride. He follows his own path, enters the woods of
his own nature,[7] and in doing so attains a state of wholeness that enables him to return to the world of action. But the father cannot release
him; though Philip asks specifically to be allowed to live in Italy (a

conventional symbol for the world of art) with his wife and mother, Don Pedro believes that Philip will overthrow him. Viewed in this context, these melodramatic lines take on a poignant significance:

> Throughout the castle burst the news! the news!
> How Philip had returned and how, Good God!
> Audacity did eat himself with rage
> At thought of this unthroning; at his side
> A lady, thing unknown. . . .

Don Pedro has a "lady"—Beatrix, named perhaps for the Beatrice in Dante,[8] and an adequate muse for any man—but he does not know his lady. He has no recourse but to kill the son who threatens his own power; in the event, he also dies.

In *Spring and All,* published in 1923, Williams wrote, "poetry does not tamper with the word but moves it . . ." (*SA,* 149). It stands "between man and nature as saints [or Christ] once stood between man and the sky . . ." (*SA,* 112). That is to say, poetry does not change life, it does not come to bully or usurp the world of action, as Don Pedro fears Philip will; rather, it redeems life, "by showing the individual, depressed before [his experience], that his life is valuable—when completed by the imagination. And then only" (*SA,* 107). There is sorrow then, as well as anger, in Williams's dream that his father stood on the steps before the dais of Pontius Pilate on the Christmas Day he died. For, in Williams's view, his father thought of art as divorced from action, as culture and tradition, not passion and life; he read Shakespeare and did his duty. He did not see the truth when it stood before him; therefore, though his son cried, "You're not dead!" like Don Pedro he did die.

> . . . he was driven
> out of Paradise—to taste
> the death that duty brings
> so daintily, so mincingly,
> with such a noble air—

that enslaved him all his life
thereafter—

("Adam")

Williams's hurt, then, seems to have gone much deeper than merely the understandable but arrogant hurt at his father's rejection of "that poetry you're writing." He felt the pain normal to young adulthood, which arose in his case from the conflict between needing to find his own direction and wanting to please his father. He felt as well a less usual pain: He had something important to give, which his father could not accept; this rejection hurt both his sense of self-confidence and his chances of communion with his father. In "Philip and Oradie" he describes Philip as knowing "By truths sheer grace his father not at all." That does not trouble Philip, but with regard to his own father it troubled Williams.

The similarities between Don Pedro and Williams's view of his father appear more clearly still when one sees Williams's father through the colored glasses of Williams's feelings for his mother. His parents' marriage was not entirely unhappy—"she enjoyed the love of her husband, I am sure," Williams writes in the manuscript of *Yes, Mrs. Williams;* "she gave him love. I am sure of that"—but theirs was "a house built out of disappointed hopes," and the disappointed hopes were Elena's.[9]

The story of Williams's mother influenced him profoundly; he told it again and again throughout his life. She was born, perhaps in 1847, perhaps in 1855, in Mayagüez, Puerto Rico, of a lineage half French, out of Martinique, and half "mixed breed." As a young girl, she went to Paris to study art, but after three years returned to Puerto Rico. The reasons for her return remain unclear: Perhaps there was no money; perhaps there were difficulties with the family with whom she was staying; there seems to have been a love affair with a Spaniard, which ended when he told her that he had upheld her honor by jilting another woman. In any case, Elena's return to Puerto Rico ended her glory in life. She married "on the rebound" and settled down in Rutherford, a captive of necessity, a woman of her time.[10]

Williams's mother was a good deal tougher than Philip's mother Beatrix. In a way, her life succeeded. She was quite eccentric, given to depressions, to trances in which she communed with the dead, to passionate bouts of nostalgia. At times she would behave like an ordinary American middle-class wife and mother, but then she would be off in imagination, to Mayagüez, Paris, bitterness: Hers is the voice in *Kora in Hell* "eating, eating, eating venomous words with thirty years' mould on them and all shall be eaten back to honeymoon's end" (*K*, 62). She was, to Williams's mind, intrinsically an artist, "seeing the thing itself without forethought or afterthought but with great intensity of perception"; she lived, as a result, in "an impoverished, ravished Eden but one indestructible as the imagination itself" (*K*, 8, 7). She was what she was with intensity; this was her perfection. It inspired Williams to write for her:

> All this—
>
>   was for you, old woman
> I wanted to write a poem
> that you would understand.
> ("January Morning," *CEP*, 165; *CP*, 100)

But though Elena was tougher than Beatrix, she was no less lonely. Both she and Beatrix lived through their sons—and here the likeness between them becomes prescient and uncanny. For Williams as a child was not primarily in his mother's charge; she took care of Edgar, and he was taken over by Grandma Wellcome, who had followed her son to Rutherford from Puerto Rico. Williams was always close to his mother, alternately tormented and delighted by her, but the bond between them deepened as they grew older. Between 1924 and her death in 1949, Elena lived with Williams and Flossie; for much of this time she was bedridden, and to keep her occupied Williams began working with her on a translation from the Spanish. While they worked, he jotted down things she would say, along with his own thoughts about her; this mass of notes gradually took form as *Yes, Mrs. Williams* (1959), Williams's moving attempt to retrieve his mother from silence and show the difficult beauty of her life. Had he been able to express his sense of Beatrix when he was in his twenties, he might have described her plight as he later describes his mother's:

... [S]he stands bridging two cultures, three regions of the world, almost without speech—her life spent in that place completely out of her choice. . . . So gross, so foreign, so dreadful, to her obstinate spirit, that has neither submitted nor mastered, leaving her in a *néant* of sounds and sense—Only her son, the bridge between herself and a vacancy as of the sky at night, the terrifying emptiness of non-entity. (*Y, MW,* 94)

"How mad to have thrown him over," Williams's mother would say again and again, referring to her Spanish lover. Both she and Beatrix should, perhaps, have married somebody else—someone, as Hamlet says,

> so loving to my mother
> That he might not beteem the winds of heaven
> Visit her face too roughly.

Elena seemed made, as was Beatrix,

> For unrestrained clear mirth, for all the world
> To gaze upon and turn refreshed away
> As they had drunken of a crystal spring. . . .

But instead, it remained for the sons to try to rescue their mothers, Philip by planning to take Beatrix far from the alien country, and Williams by writing again and again for and about Elena, becoming the bridge that stood between her and silence, until, at the age of 93 or 102, she died.

In a letter to Marianne Moore, written in 1934, Williams describes the inner changes that made possible what she saw as an "inner security" in his work:

> It is something which occurred once when I was about twenty, a sudden resignation to existence, a despair—if you wish to call it that, but a despair which made everything a unit and at the same time a part of myself. I suppose it might be called a sort

of nameless religious experience. I resigned, I gave up. I decided there was nothing else in life for me but to work. . . . I
won't follow causes. I can't. The reason is that it seems so much
more important to me that I am. Where shall one go? What
shall one do? Things have no names for me and places have no
significance. As a reward for this anonymity I feel as much a
part of things as trees and stones. Heaven seems frankly impossible. I am damned as I succeed. I have no particular hope save
to repair, to rescue, to complete. (*SL*, 147)

"I won't follow causes. I can't." Williams never says much more about
this "sudden resignation to existence"; he does not try to find its well-
springs in certain events of his life. Even if he found them, such causal
connections would be too simple—and searching the past again and
again would merely usurp the presentness in his life. The heart mur-
mur doctors discovered when he was in his teens probably had something to do with it; it put an end to his dreams of excellence in sports
and made him start to turn inward, toward books, toward art, away
from the world of action. Surely, Charlotte Herman had much to do
with it: Her rejection meant his failure, the failure of both what he was
and what he most wanted to be. His only way out of that failure was
to resign, suddenly, to his existence—to dry his tears and go propose
to Flossie, who, loving him as she did, would help him "blossom" in a
"passion of despair." And then there were the tensions with his parents,
and the wars within himself. As it turned out, Williams was the son of
both his father and his mother: He wanted *both* medicine and morality,
and poetry and passion, and realized fairly early that in order to fulfill
all the needs of his own nature "there was nothing else in life for me
but to work."

I think, too, that "Philip and Oradie" had a great deal to do with
this "nameless religious experience" that gave birth to an inner security. The most important thing about "Philip and Oradie" is that it was
a failure, and showed its poet to be a failure, in a fundamental way.
Williams recognized this, and either literally or figuratively tossed the
poem into the furnace. Had he not done so, had he held on to "Philip
and Oradie," there would never have been what we know as William
Carlos Williams. For "Philip and Oradie" is not just a poem with auto-

biographical elements, a poem in which one can recognize certain real people and events in the poet's life. It is Williams's first attempt to write his autobiography, to come by means of art to a sense of his inner standing. Philip *is* Williams, as Williams perceived himself to be during this early state of his life.

If we look at Philip as Williams, and at "Philip and Oradie" as autobiography, we can see that, at the beginning of his career, Williams was trying to write out of a defunct conception of selfhood and, in consequence, of the function of poetry and the nature of the poetic. In "Philip and Oradie" he strikes a posture of loss and longing borrowed from the Romantics, who in turn had borrowed it from medieval Christianity. He equates the attainment of wholeness, or true selfhood, with the possession of an unpossessable *princesse lointaine,* and represents himself as wandering prince in search of the ideal. Like the boy in Joyce's story "Araby"—and indeed like many Romantic poets and autobiographers—he envisions himself as bearing the "chalice" of the self through an inimical universe (represented by Don Pedro and his cohorts), a "throng of foes," toward a holy consummation.[11] And because of this self-dramatization, like the boy, he arranges for himself a double kind of failure: failure both to attain fulfillment and to make contact with reality, with the flawed but possible sources of selfhood that lie everywhere at hand.

Williams's description of the poem in his *Autobiography* seems to indicate that the failure of "Philip and Oradie" enabled him, in time, to see the causes of that failure. No longer is the poem primarily an Oedipal family drama, nor even a story of the persecuted prince. Instead, it becomes in Williams's recollection a poem about language—specifically, about "poetic" or what he called "Keatsian" language and its corresponding vision, and about the failure of that language and that vision.[12] Williams's description of the poem in the *Autobiography* emphasizes what happens to Philip *after* rather than before he awakens in a "foreign country"; what he describes is quite unlike what seems to happen in the extant poem. Essentially, in Williams's recollection, he has lost his language because he has lost the world that would answer to that language. After the cataclysmic loss of all that would serve to define him, the prince awakens to his naked condition. He has neither family, bride, nor social estate to help him answer the questions, How did I get here? Where is my home? and Who am I? Like the child in Wordsworth's "Ode: Intimations of Immortality," he has suffered a birth which is a "sleep and a forgetting";[13] and, though Williams first says that the prince can "recall nothing of the past," he then refines the point to allow for the quest for identity: "—he had not been able to recall the details, merely 'sensed' them: That there had been a beautiful bride, a father, a mother; that a disastrous event of some sort had occurred." And so, like Wordsworth's child "trailing clouds of glory,"[14] he sets off through the woods, "homeward or seeking a home that was his own . . ." (*A,* 60).

"The language . . . the language!" Williams implores in *Paterson* (*P,* 12). If the prince in "Philip and Oradie" is doomed after his awakening by the absence of a true language, Williams as poet is doomed throughout "Philip and Oradie" by the presence of a false language. In the simplest sense this is true; as I have remarked, the poem is full of archaisms, inversions, bombast, stock conceits, every sort of "poetical" diction:

> —then her child! He came!
> He came, he came! Ye faint ribbed mid-May skies
> Whence, whence this flooding-o'er wild ecstasy,
> That we may sip, we too, of that deep well?

It is true in a deeper sense as well. To adopt a "poetical" language he must adopt a "poetical" vision, and this vision closes the poem up, again and again, just where it should open. Nothing has a chance to strike fire, to come to life, to surprise the poet, for he has already determined where his alter-ego stands in relation to it all and, consequently, what it all means and must accomplish. Don Pedro, for instance, threatens to become interesting:

> Oh I could sing
> Of his brave deeds until the barking throng
> Cloyed with flat peace would fly like midnight birds
> Into the sudden flame and hell of passion
> Heedless of torment toppling kingdoms down—

But the poet pulls back at once:

> But to what end? For they were impious all
> Nor fit a tongue's report. . . .

Philip's birth, too, might have been interesting; birth was certainly something the young intern knew plenty about. "But no," he writes, just as he starts to wonder about Beatrix's ecstasy:

> . . . for now imagination flings
> With puzzling Beatrix through that infancy
> When here, in short, there grew an upright boy. . . .

Again and again this happens; Williams must keep cranking up the story and propelling it along, for he must keep Philip on his quest— first for the selfhood he briefly attains when he falls in love with Oradie, then (as implied in the *Autobiography*, at least) for the selfhood he would have regained had he got back home to his castle. There is no time, given this vision of the self and of the nature of the "poetic," to look at things, take pleasure in things, make contact with experience. Kipp's woods, for instance, which Williams describes so lovingly in the *Autobiography*, are here, all right—transmuted, they are the woods in which young Philip wanders—but we do not see what Williams saw, for he could not see it either, not in his guise as Philip. And everyone but the poet must die along the way—even Oradie, even the faithful old nurse—for selfhood, in such a vision, is solipsistic. It can never be found in surrender "to existence."

In 1917, Williams published *Al Que Quiere!*. One of its poems, "The Wanderer," had been written before the others; Williams had worked on it for several years (*CEP*, 3–12; *CP*, 108–17). "It is actually a reconstruction from memory of my early Keatsian *Endymion* imitation that I destroyed, burned in a furnace," he reports in *I Wanted to Write a Poem*. "It is the story of growing up" (*IWW*, 25–26). "The Wanderer" is indeed a reconstruction from memory of the "*Endymion* imitation," but the remembering self has undergone sea changes. For, if "Philip and Oradie" may be called Williams's venture into the Keatsian realms of the egotistical sublime, in "The Wanderer" the poet dies into life; he is baptized into "knowledge enormous"[15] in the filthy Passaic River:

> Then the river began to enter my heart,
> Eddying back cool and limpid
> Into the crystal beginning of its days.
> But with the rebound it leaped forward:
> Muddy, then black and shrunken
> Till I felt the utter depth of its rottenness
> The vile breadth of its degradation
> And dropped down knowing this was me now.
> But she lifted me and the water took a new tide
> Again into the older experiences,
> And so, backward and forward,
> It tortured itself within me
> Until time had been washed finally under
> And the river had found its level
> And its last motion had ceased
> And I knew all—it became me.
> And I knew this for double certain
> For there, whitely, I saw myself
> Being borne off under the water!

"The Wanderer" is generally described as ushering in the concepts of the self, the function of poetry and the nature of the poetic which, for Williams, were to endure. But it is "Philip and Oradie" that ushers in "The Wanderer," and this is the meaning at last of that perplexing double ending. Philip is dead and stays dead, and along with him dies Williams's early self-conception. But, as always in Williams's career, "A / world lost . . . beckons to new places" (*P*, 78). For, from this defeat a song arises, a simple "country song," a "treble-chaunting roundelay," and this song, about which nothing more is said, is something new in the poem. It arises only *after* the prince has died and is the sound of life going on, the sound of other voices. And the song awakens a new man, a man who will learn to listen. This man, "the wanderer," will learn that while there are no answers to the riddle of the self, the self is

not the only thing that matters. He will seek his self-reflection not by
gazing into a pool but by polishing his language, so that, over a lifetime
of endeavor, it may become strong enough to serve as a bridge between
people and their silence, and clear enough and clean enough to answer
the wanderer's question: "How shall I be a mirror to this modernity?"[16]

There is a happy ending, therefore, to "Philip and Oradie." It is not
unusual for young people to want to get rid of their parents; some
people say that one is never fully adult, never fully autonomous, until
both parents have died. The deaths of Beatrix and Don Pedro may
have been essential in this respect; Oradie's death as well, and even the
death of the faithful nurse, seem to speak to a need for solitude and
longing on the part of the young poet. But the happy thing in Williams's case is that he was able to kill off Philip. And once Philip is
gone, the other characters, who have been sacrificed to his quest, come
intensely back to life. The faithful old nurse appears first; she metamorphoses at once into the Muse of "The Wanderer,"

> . . . old
> Forgiveless, unreconcilable;
> That high wanderer of by-ways
> Walking imperious in beggary!

and appears in several poems as Grandma Wellcome. Beatrix and Don
Pedro go through many changes in the course of fifty years; when we
last see them they are the dying old woman of *Yes, Mrs. Williams,* the
"father" on the subway in "Asphodel," and the "dried wafer only" of
"The Sparrow." Oradie is everywhere; she becomes Beautiful Thing,
Williams's name for the "thing of beauty" which is

> . . . a joy for ever:
> Its loveliness increases; it will never
> Pass into nothingness. . . .[17]

And the woods, Kipp's woods, or the woods of his own nature, especially their flowers, and what they taught Williams to know of flowers—Williams wanders through these woods in a hundred poems, for
the rest of his life.

Making Something of Oneself:
"Pastoral," "Love Song,"
"Queen-Ann's Lace,"
"The Crimson Cyclamen"

H ere is a poem from the book William Carlos Williams's father
would probably not have liked, *Al Que Quiere!:*

Pastoral

When I was younger
it was plain to me
I must make something of myself.
Older now
I walk back streets
admiring the houses
of the very poor:
roof out of line with sides
the yards cluttered
with old chicken wire, ashes,
furniture gone wrong;
the fences and outhouses

built of barrel-staves
and parts of boxes, all,
if I am fortunate,
smeared a bluish green
that properly weathered
pleases me best
of all colors.

No one
will believe this
of vast import to the nation.
        (*CP,* 64; *CEP,* 121)

Modest as it is, this poem serves well nonetheless to illustrate the development and changes that took place after "Philip and Oradie" in
Williams's ideas regarding the sources and function of writing, the nature of the self and of its relationship to the world, and, consequently,
the possibilities open to autobiography. The desires to be outwardly
successful and inwardly complete seem to have guided Williams into
his twenties: Outward success, "to *make* something of myself," would
probably have meant to become a famous doctor in New York City,
while inner completeness, "to make something of *myself*," would certainly have meant to be able to finish his first attempt at poetic self-
creation, "Philip and Oradie."[1]

Judged in this light, "Pastoral" would seem to bear witness to what
adolescents often think are the wages of adulthood: compromise and
failure. "Older now," the speaker has ended up in Rutherford, neither
in New York City nor in the "Keatsian" realms of faery; besides, he is
not even in his office working to get ahead, but "stealing"[2] again, stealing time from medicine and writing to wander through the city "admiring the houses / of the very poor." He seems quite content, but in
terms of his early dreams, a little pitiful and humbled; the brokenness
of the lines, the aimlessness of the journey, make him appear to be as
imperfect and unfinished as the neighborhood he wanders, with its
roofs "out of line with sides / the yards cluttered." And Lady Fortune
now—or her more modest counterpart, "being fortunate"—grants not
the fame, glory, and immortality which great poets of the past were

wont to seek, but something entirely different: an evidence of death, of man's rootedness and poverty in a physical world of change and decay, the "bluish green" of time "smeared" on the shabby buildings. The speaker would seem to be right: In a country such as ours, with its enormous fear of death, and its corresponding emphasis on size, success, and cleanliness as the measures of salvation, no one is apt to believe either this small poem or its vision of small life to be "of vast import to the nation."

And yet, consider the line again, "make something of myself." Neither the speaker nor the people of his world as he presents it in this poem have *made* something of themselves, as it was Franklin's desire to do, nor have they made something of *themselves,* as it was Rousseau's: They have attained neither a state of invincible success nor a condition of inviolable completion. But only the terms of the expectations preordain the failure, for an alternative remains. What Williams is seeking here—and what he learned to seek in all his writing after the failure of "Philip and Oradie"—is to "make something *of* myself," to make something out of himself, to bring a world to birth by surrendering to reality and its processes of creation. Seen in this light, "Pastoral" bears witness not to compromise but to a triumph and serenity made possible only by failure. Losing oneself, one finds oneself. Losing the dreams of faery or of fame in New York City, one finds the world as it truly is: not merely impoverished, rotting, dying, but also rich beyond measure, tough and enduring, and very much alive. Like the girls gone wrong and the boys out of line whom Williams praises so highly in his *Autobiography,* the "furniture gone wrong" and the "roof out of line" bespeak despair, perhaps, but also the eccentricity, the willingness to live, to use and be used, that constitutes their "perfections."[3] And the

> bluish green
> that properly weathered
> pleases me best
> of all colors

—this stain or smear from the heart of things no longer seems just the shadow of death. It is also a trace of "Beautiful Thing," as Williams would come to call it,[4] the "color" given off by things when they are embraced by the imagination. Man does not make it, neither can he destroy it; it comes from the earth and is the patina of her poverty and beauty. It teaches man himself—but only if he is "fortunate." And fortune consists, paradoxically, of failure. As long as man desires to *make* something of himself or to make something of *himself*—desires invincible success, as did Franklin, or inviolable completion, as did Rousseau—he is condemned to blindness and therefore to isolation.

"He thought he kept the universe alone. . . ." This line, from Frost's poem "The Most of It,"[5] could serve as epitaph for many of the poets over the past two hundred years, among them Williams's Philip. It expresses a belief which, even after exorcising Philip, Williams continues in part to share; "Pastoral" is, after all, "of vast import to the nation." And the reason it is important is that "no one / will believe this"—that, in twentieth-century America, the poet nearly does keep the universe alone. Still, though this tragic and heroic (and essentially Romantic) conviction may be true, it comes to seem too simple. When man is reborn as a wanderer, surrendering the self, he begins to discover that everything in the universe participates in its keeping. When he begins to make something *of* himself, to enter into the processes of creation, he becomes part of the universe. Poems, like flowers or facts,[6] emerge from the fecund and unfinished, and find their "counter-love" in life, in the myriad phenomena which offer up again and again "original response." Discovering this plenitude even in his poverty, man discovers at last that the universe keeps him too. There is nowhere he needs to go, and nothing he needs to long for, for he is at home already. His wandering, therefore, is not a quest, but a journey of celebration; and in this celebration, if he sees Frost's mysterious buck or Williams's bluish-green smear, he can pay it its proper homage: He can say with joy, not regret, "And that was all."

There is a happy irony in all this, which adolescents like Williams's Philip tend not to see. Desiring to *make* something of oneself or to make something of *oneself* means, essentially, desiring to *be* something—in the case of the former, to be a famous doctor, perhaps, or a Pulitzer prize-winning writer; in the case of the latter, to be a "found" and completed soul. The desire to be something, however, can create a path riddled with snares—the snare of the overweening ego, or of the paralyzed present, or of the predetermined future—all of which can prevent one from becoming what one has decided to be. But desiring to *do* something, to make something *of* oneself, enables one to forget about oneself and get about one's business. And then it happens, delightfully, that one makes *something* of oneself, reveals or creates a self that could never be known beforehand, but which emerges inexorably in the processes of creation. This self has the authority of springing from both itself and the things of the world; consequently, it is complete at every step, as much an "all" as the smear on the weathered buildings. Insofar as they are not already paralyzed, people hunger for this authority, which teaches them their own. No wonder, then, if, as happened with Williams, greatness and fame eventually follow. But even if they do not, something more important does: a selfhood like the tapestry in *Paterson, V,* a selfhood which is the pattern formed by a lifetime of creation, and which is a thing of beauty because every detail was woven with beauty. This is a selfhood of art, the lasting space in which a man can live even as he is dying—but only if, as Thoreau says, "the material was pure, and his art was pure,"[7] every step of the way.

Purity enables the artist to perceive and reveal the world's perfection. When speaking of Williams, however, one must clarify these terms, for as we have begun to see with regard to the weathered houses, he thinks of both purity and perfection in unconventional ways. Perfection, to his mind, is the quality things or people cannot avoid possessing, of being utterly themselves.[8] Purity is the intensity of devotion that allows one to surrender oneself in response to this perfection, to plunge without care for the self into the fecund ground of experience. Considered in this way, purity is by no means a naive or passive condition, and purifying oneself by no means a simple matter. It is a kind of sainthood of what Williams calls damnation, a discipline of surrender enjoined and made bearable by passion.[9]

That Williams arduously worked to purify and intensify his powers of self-surrender, so that he might enable an object or a person to reveal its perfection, becomes clear if we look at two versions of a poem which, like "Pastoral," appeared in *Al Que Quiere!.* The version often anthologized is "Love Song"; it is a reworking of a poem entitled, in *The Collected Earlier Poems,* "First Version: 1915." The two versions read as follows:

First Version: 1915

What have I to say to you
When we shall meet?
Yet—
I lie here thinking of you.

The stain of love
Is upon the world.
Yellow, yellow, yellow,
It eats into the leaves,
Smears with saffron
The horned branches that lean
heavily
Against a smooth purple sky.

There is no light—
Only a honey-thick stain
That drips from leaf to leaf
And limb to limb
Spoiling the colors
Of the whole world.

I am alone.
The weight of love
Has buoyed me up
Till my head
Knocks against the sky.

See me!
My hair is dripping with nectar—
Starlings carry it
On their black wings.
See at last
My arms and my hands
Are lying idle.

How can I tell
If I shall ever love you again
As I do now?
(*CP*, 53–54; *CEP*, 173–74)

Love Song

I lie here thinking of you:—
the stain of love
is upon the world!
yellow, yellow, yellow
it eats into the leaves,
smears with saffron
the horned branches that lean
heavily
against a smooth purple sky!
There is no light
only a honey-thick stain
that drips from leaf to leaf
and limb to limb
spoiling the colors
of the whole world—

you far off there under
the wine-red selvage of the west!
(*CP*, 107–8; *CEP*, 174)

It is not entirely unfair to say that the most important line of the "First Version" is "See me!" Though this poem purports to be a love poem, its emphasis shifts midway from concentration on the beloved to observation of the effects of *eros* as it transfigures the self. As Williams discovers here, the fact that one is watching oneself means that the process has failed: "I am alone," he writes, just when he should be most in contact, most fully given over to "the stain of love," the fluidity of imaginative connection. Wishing to plunge ahead, he has in effect two choices: He can fall into the pit of physiological description—which, mercifully, he does not do—or he can rise into the etherealized inane— which he accomplishes with abandon. The head knocking against the sky, the hair being carried by starlings, all the while dripping with nectar, the arms and hands lying idly by—the image is less that of a transfigured lover than that of Prufrock's John the Baptist. The last few lines arise from this dilemma and suggest an odd reversal. By trying to declare his love absolute in the present moment, Williams inadvertently opens the door to the chill winds of time and failure: Indeed, he may *not* love the woman again as much as he does now.

Such things happen, but that is beside the point. "What is time but an impertinence?" Williams asks in *The Great American Novel* (213). The important thing is not that love may pass—as indeed it will, for everyone—but that it be surrendered to completely in the moment, the "eternal moment in which we alone live." "To refine, to clarify, to intensify" this moment is the purpose of art for Williams, and is beautifully accomplished in the revision of the poem (*SA, 89*). In "Love Song," as opposed to "First Version," the emphasis remains where it belongs: on the beloved, who, though absent, is for the moment so charged a presence in the poet's imagination that to think of her makes the world become "yellow, yellow, yellow." "There is no light," only "the stain of love" called up by the poet's surrender. Becoming part of the world, he is consumed and transfigured as the world is consumed and transfigured: eaten, smeared, covered "from leaf to leaf / and limb to limb." Deepening and intensifying, the "stain" and the surrender create at last an order to countermand nature's order, "spoiling" or washing over the colors of the world—which colors the stain of love seems even to have called from darkness, since the sun has already set and according to nature's law the world should be colorless, night.

In "Love Song," as opposed to "First Version," Williams trusts and therefore surrenders to his language, which is to say he trusts and therefore surrenders to his love. No longer does he feel compelled to stand apart from and comment upon the process of transformation; he does not say, "See me!" simply because there is no longer a separate self to see. Instead, he *becomes* the process of transformation: Lying "here thinking of you," he becomes his thought, and his thought becomes his language, and his language becomes the stain of love, and the stain of love is the fact of the beloved; there is no longer any aloneness, any gap between the speaker and his audience, the poet and his beloved, or the poem and the world. Into such perfection "time does not enter";[10] the poem ends, therefore, not with the poet's suspicions about the passage of love but with the image of an absence which is, paradoxically, absolute presence: "you far off there under / the wine-red selvage of the west!" The presence this expresses is known because trusted, trusted because created, created because surrendered to; it is both the cause and the effect of the processes of creation. Once there, it is discovered to have been there all along; it is "Beautiful Thing," and its stain is love, or the bluish green that colors the shabby houses. But the burden is on the poet: He must surrender the self again and again to its creation, for "Beautiful Thing" can be discovered in no other way.

In no other way? Having written that, I realize suddenly that, as sometimes happens in critics' attempts to come to a sense of Williams, I have just said something which is both true and untrue. On the one hand, Williams makes absolute claims for the power and necessity of poetry; in *Spring and All,* for instance, he remarks that without poetry, without its power "to repair, to rescue, to complete" (*SL,* 147), "no man could suffer the fragmentary nature of his understanding of his own life . . ." (*SA,* 112). This is not because poetry helps us to escape from our lives, for it does not. Rather, it helps us to enter our lives, to endure them because we embrace them. It

> gives the feeling of completion by revealing the oneness of ex-
> perience; it rouses rather than stupefies the intelligence by
> demonstrating the importance of personality, by showing the
> individual, depressed before it, that his life is valuable—when
> completed by the imagination. And then only. (*SA,* 107)

The value of life, and of one's own life, is the "news" to be gotten from poems; as Williams says simply in "Asphodel, That Greeny Flower,"

> . . . men die miserably every day
>   for lack
> of what is found there.
>
>   (*PB,* 161–62)

Williams's belief in the power of poetry to reveal the value of reality is intense and absolute. Yet on the other hand, he also clearly believes that reality does not need poetry in order to be, as it is, replete with value.

> so much depends
> upon
>
> a red wheel
> barrow
>
> glazed with rain
> water
>
> beside the white
> chickens
> (*SA*, 138)

One possible meaning of this little poem is that so much depends upon the poet's ability to perceive the value of the "red wheel / barrow" on which so much depends. This is not, however, the only or the most important meaning. The red wheelbarrow needs neither poem nor poet. It is simply itself; it has its own existence, its own plenitude and significance, perfectly independently of William Carlos Williams. It is the reality upon which the poem depends. Just so, one feels when reading Williams's poetry, with the old jaundiced woman, the poor old woman eating her plums, the black woman with the marigolds, the schoolgirls sucking candy:[11] They do not need the poem for they are themselves the poem. They enter and depart from Williams's poem, and the moment of intersection of reality with language becomes a moment of contact, and therefore an "eternal moment" of celebration; but the value of their lives does not depend entirely on his language. The fact of their existence is the poem of their existence, "the poem which their lives are being lived to realize" (*A*, 362).

Their lives, but also Williams's.

If this apparent contradiction indicates confusion in Williams's thinking, it is a fertile confusion. Believing the poet to be essential to reality enables Williams to retain a deeply Romantic faith in the supremacy of the imagination and the redemptive power of poetry. Conversely, believing the poet to be inessential to reality enables him to move beyond the solipsism and *hubris* that plague both Romanticism and his own early "Keatsian" effort, "Philip and Oradie." He can believe both that what he does in writing a poem is supremely important, and that what everything in the universe does is supremely important. This doubleness of conviction gives him both an unshakable pride and a deep humility—both the faith to persist in writing, and the openness to the world, the exuberance for the world, to replenish the persisting. More than anything else, I think, it is this double conviction which accounts for Williams's tutelary position among many of the serious poets of the past few decades. They have learned from his example (or found verification therein for what they believed already) that poetry can "be made of anything—provided it be seen, smelt, touched, apprehended and understood to be what it is—the flesh of a constantly repeated permanence" (*SL,* 130). Poetry and the world support and affirm each other, for "Beautiful Thing," the "constantly repeated permanence," inheres in both the world and the poem.

If "Beautiful Thing" inheres in both the poem and the world, then the poem becomes not only an effort "to repair, to rescue, to complete" that which is lost or fragmented, but also—and simultaneously—a "flowering" or a "dance" which participates in and celebrates the wholeness intrinsic in both itself and the world. This, it seems to me, is the most difficult and the central paradox in Williams; it is the paradox his critics encounter when they labor to discover whether there is "absence" or "presence," ontologically speaking, at the center of his vision.[12] Williams's language indicates both. He remarks in the Prologue to *Kora in Hell,* for instance, that "Rich as are the gifts of the imagination bitterness of world's loss is not replaced thereby. On the contrary it is intensified, resembling thus possession itself" (*K,* 18). Here, absence is central; the world is lost and cannot be recovered. The naive assumption of an innate correspondence between the self and the world, or between language and reality, which men possessed in an age of belief—and which Williams possessed before the failure of "Philip and Oradie" and the consequent death and rebirth of the self discussed in chapter 4—has been broken; there is no longer an overarching structure which would give the universe meaning. The self can become creative, can complete itself by means of the imagination, rather than succumb to the fragmentary nature of its experience, but the fact remains nonetheless that this creative endeavor issues from and into bitterness and despair, because it cannot bridge the gap between what the self creates and the world as it is, independent of the self and its efforts at creation. Loss is absolute—so absolute that it can, in a sense, bottom out, if entered into fully, and so come to resemble possession. Only, however, to resemble it.

But then, to resemble possession seems to *become* possession when, in *Spring and All,* Williams writes that the poem, the gift of the imagination, is "not a removal from reality," not an imaginative "possession of that which is lost." Rather, it is "a dance over the body of [one's] condition accurately accompanying it" (*SA,* 149). Williams's example in this passage is John of Gaunt's speech from *Richard II,* and the example is instructive. To describe England as

> This royal throne of kings, this scept'red isle,
> This earth of majesty, this seat of Mars,
> This other Eden, demi-paradise,
> This fortress built by Nature for herself
> Against infection and the hand of war,
> This happy breed of men, this little world,
> This precious stone set in the silver sea . . .

when, in fact, England is infected and plagued by war and John of Gaunt himself is un-Edenically dying, is not simply to elegize, nor is it to idealize. "Fact" is not the only fact; the self is also a fact, as are the flowerings of the imagination. John of Gaunt is creating an imaginative construct, a poem, which does not resemble possession, but *is* possession; and in so doing, he is in possession of himself. As is Shakespeare in possession of himself, though he is nowhere apparent; he has become John of Gaunt, who is nothing but the dance of his words. "World's loss" may be the body of their condition, but above this body the dance spins free: "The play written to be understood as a play, the author and reader are liberated to pirouette with the words which have sprung from the old facts of history, reunited in present passion" (*SA,* 149).

The poem, too, is written to be understood as a play: it is a dance, a *jeu,* which springs free from our condition and in its freedom reveals us to ourselves. Here the paradox is most intense, for the poem is based in the reality which is "world's loss," yet in springing free it enacts the process of possession. And this possession, being neither an attempt to escape reality nor an attempt to change it, can be of no other thing than just that lost world. "A world lost" becomes, by the agency of the poem, not simply a world irretrievable but also "a world unsuspected," that "beckons to new places . . ." (*P,* 78; *PB,* 73). To suspect it is to imagine it; to imagine it is to affirm it; and to affirm it is to "move" it— not in the sense of tampering with or changing but in the sense of causing to quicken, to bring to the surface its unaroused beauty and life. Once moved, however, the world declares itself to have needed no moving, to have been complete and self-awakened all along; thus it frees and affirms the poem, just as the poem, by affirming the world, has enabled it to reveal itself as free. In a central passage from *Spring and All,* Williams struggles to express his sense of this interrelation between dependency and freedom; he succeeds, not in discursive argument but by means of an image. Poetry, he writes,

> affirms reality most powerfully and therefore, since reality needs no personal support but exists free from human action, as proven by science in the indestructibility of matter and of force, it creates a new object, a play, a dance which is not a mirror up to nature but—
> As birds' wings beat the solid air without which none could fly so words freed by the imagination affirm reality by their flight. (*SA,* 149–50)

Just so, the paradoxical nature of absence and presence can be expressed most clearly in an image. Consider once again, for instance, the final lines of "Love Song": "you far off there under / the wine-red selvage of the west!" This image cannot be reduced to discursive paraphrase, simply because it embodies or unites "in present passion" two seemingly mutually exclusive perceptions: both an absence so keen that it makes itself felt as a presence, and a presence so remote that it can be intuited only in the energy of the poem's final lines, only at the moment of total self-surrender. Furthermore, two seemingly mutually exclusive conclusions follow. On the one hand, one could say that the

radiance or nakedness at the center, "under the selvage," is there only
when the poem *makes* it there—when, by getting there, the poem creates it. But on the other hand, what is "the stain of love" but a track—
like blood—to follow, to trace the stain to its source beneath the fabric
of creation, which source like the sun must be there already? This, of
course, is the failure of "First Version": it remains on the periphery,
never surrendering to its clues, never plunging to its center. Given the
poem's peripheral stance (or peripheral peregrinations), it is inevitable
that the poet should worry that he might not love the lady again as
much as he does "now." And his worry betrays the fact that he is remaining peripheral; not quite loving the lady, he has not completely
made it or "gone over."

Loving the lady, quite simply, is the answer. It is the poet's privilege,
not to solve the paradox—for, of course, the deeper he goes, the more
it reveals itself as insoluble—but to embrace it, possess it, surrender to
it completely, and so come to know it as a paradox. Or perhaps now
we need another word, for "paradox" implies the agonies of logic,
which the poem goes beyond. Loving the lady, the poem and the poet
enter into the fertile grounds of mystery. For the lady is any other, and
whatever her earthly form—be she old jaundiced woman, or poor old
woman eating the plums, black woman carrying marigolds, schoolgirls
sucking candy, or even just the wheelbarrow, or the smear on weathered houses—the other is "Beautiful Thing," in every moment broken
and most whole.

Everything that the failure of "Philip and Oradie" enabled Williams to
discover regarding the sources and function of writing, the nature of
the self and of its relationship to the world, and the consequent possibilities open to autobiography, is present in a poem written around
1919 and published in *Sour Grapes:*

Queen-Ann's Lace

Her body is not so white as
anemone petals nor so smooth—nor
so remote a thing. It is a field
of the wild carrot taking

the field by force; the grass
does not raise above it.
Here is no question of whiteness,
white as can be, with a purple mole
at the center of each flower.
Each flower is a hand's span
of her whiteness. Wherever
his hand has lain there is
a tiny purple blemish. Each part
is a blossom under his touch
to which the fibres of her being
stem one by one, each to its end,
until the whole field is a
white desire, empty, a single stem, a cluster
flower by flower,
a pious wish to whiteness gone over—
or nothing.

(*CP*, 162; *CEP*, 210)

This poem is so fully a flowering, so rich and seamless an act of participation, that it is difficult to know exactly where or how to start talking
about it. But to begin with, to see how far Williams has come in his
understanding of the source of poetry, one might consider for a moment the short shrift he made of Kipp's woods in "Philip and Oradie,"
and then compare that with the loving care with which he has ob-
served the Queen Anne's lace. His observation of the flower, which
enables him to equate it with the process of desire, has been painstak-
ing and perfect: Like the nervous system of the human body, the
Queen Anne's lace branches off a central stem, and each of the branching stems branches in turn into others. Each of these small stems opens
into an aggregate of flower; what appears to be a single flower is in fact
composed of a cluster of flowers, each round and white and, when seen
together, helping to make up the larger orb of white. The "tiny purple
blemish" at the center of the orb, which is in fact two or three purple
flowers, is the only mark of differentiation. Then, each orb which is a
flower made up of hundreds of flowers is also a part of the larger orb
opening off the branching bundle of stems; and again in turn, this

larger orb is a part of the plant's whole circle, the circle of whiteness, flower within flower within flower, issuing from the single stem. And to see a field of Queen Anne's lace, in which the flower of each plant seems to merge with every other, as if all the stars gathered together to form a "white desire"—this is indeed to see the earth entirely "to whiteness gone over."

Or, to see the sources of William's poem, one might consider the other half of his indivisible metaphor, the lady. Oradie was remote; she was the *princesse lointaine,* purely a creature of the escapist imagination. But this woman—who is she not? Like the Queen Anne's lace, she springs up everywhere; those less ardent than Williams often mistake her for a weed and, thinking her common, fail to learn her rampant beauty. She is every woman, a possible woman, in whom there is "no question of whiteness"; she would never serve as muse for an adolescent (and essentially misogynist) poetic imagination. Some readers have even concluded that the image of "a purple mole / at the center of each flower" implies that her body is badly blemished. This, of course, pushes the metaphor too far; and yet, once one knows Margaret in "The Farmer's Daughters" or the girl with the pimply face,[13] one realizes that, for Williams, were she covered with eczema it would not really matter. For her beauty lies not in what she is but in what she becomes, the way in which she flowers by surrendering herself. Her desire awakens "the stain of love"; she is so purely in contact with both herself and her lover that his touch awakens the queenly purple of agony and pride—pride at being this body, agony that the blood cannot leap beyond the skin, and so make one with the lover. Here, in this moment, there is "no question of whiteness." She and the moment are "white as can be"; one might absolutely say "her body thought."[14]

"Queen-Ann's Lace" is a beautiful celebration of sexuality, but it is also more than that. For Williams, sexual awakening and passion remains simply itself, one process among many, but it also becomes a metaphor or type for all awakenings and passions. Surrendered to desire, the woman in "Queen-Ann's Lace" remains herself, one flower, but she also makes one of a world or "field" of flowers, comprising all those who surrender. The woman who "gives herself" to the "solace" of her plums, the black woman holding her marigolds "upright / as a torch / so early in the morning," the schoolgirls "touching their avid mouths / with pink sugar on a stick": All these are whole in their surrender to the moment, no matter how seemingly trivial the objects of their passion. The old jaundiced woman too is whole, but hers is the wholeness of torment: Moaning "I can't die / I can't die," she has surrendered but has not yet been possessed; the ecstasy of her desire makes her seem "Elysian," but she has not "gone over."

How beautifully, toward the end, the language of "Queen-Ann's Lace" grips down and begins to awaken. For, of course, "Queen-Ann's Lace" is not just a flower or a woman; it is also a poem. And like the woman he describes, the poet becomes whole, and reveals himself to be whole, as he enters into the body of his passion. Like Shakespeare in *Richard II,* he is nowhere to be seen: He is neither the flower, the woman, nor the object of her desire. Yet he is everywhere too, for in the flowering of his language he is becoming the poem, and the poem is becoming himself, all of himself there is to become, "a pious wish to whiteness." This is the choice he has: to hold himself back at the last, or to surrender absolutely. Either way there is "nothing." But between the "nothing" of failure and the "nothing" of self-surrender, what a difference there is—what a plenitude has come.

"Root, Branch & Flower." The image of one's life as rooted in infancy, branching throughout youth, and coming to flower in adulthood has lain for centuries at the heart of autobiography. It has proven to be a fertile structural device both for public autobiographers, like Franklin, and for private autobiographers, like Wordsworth and Rousseau. The organic metaphor is beautiful, seemingly all-embracing and all-uniting; however, to make it the pattern for the story of one's life is to adopt two assumptions which, as one sees in the case of Williams's *Autobiography,* are dangerously confining. The first assumption is that the past, from birth to the narrative present, was incomplete—was root, branch, or bud merely to the present flowering, and contingent upon this flowering for its meaning, its perfection. And the second, conversely, is that the narrative present is complete, can be complete— that the autobiographer can attain to a condition of full-blownness and rest in this static perfection while he traces the evolving patterns of his life. It matters little, at this point, whether his desire is public—to portray an invincible success—or private—to portray an inviolable completion—for both desires are absolute. And, as autobiographers have increasingly discovered, both desires are impossible. Life, by virtue of its continuation, always branches off from the single long-stemmed rose of one's autobiography.

The organic metaphor abounds in Williams's writing, from his earliest poems to the beautiful, late "Asphodel, That Greeny Flower." As "Queen-Ann's Lace" demonstrates, however, his characteristic use of it reveals two assumptions entirely opposite to those underlying its use in the *Autobiography.* The first of these assumptions is that every act, every moment of one's experience, is complete. "Everything exists from the beginning," Williams declares in *The Great American Novel;* consequently, in terms of autobiography, there can be no such thing as partial selfhood leading to perfect selfhood, as a root or branch leads inexorably to flower (*GAN,* 158). Every moment of one's experience reveals a plenitude of rooting, branching, flowering: the infant, the adolescent, the old jaundiced woman do not depend for their selfhood upon what they will be or what they were, but—like the woman in "Queen-Ann's Lace"—only upon what they are, in the complex presentness of their perfection. And the second assumption, simply, is that nothing is complete, because nothing is ever finished. Time is absolute; even God, to Williams's thinking, is "composition and decomposition,"[15] flowering and dispersion. Life, like literature, is "nothing . . . but change" (*K,* 13). It is nearly true to say of Williams, as Whitman said of himself, that he accepts time absolutely. Even in Williams, however, one finds at times a Keatsian longing for endings, a longing for death in art, and a consequent despair at surviving ecstatic completions and entering once again into the cycles of change.

> Now more than ever seems it rich to die,
>   To cease upon the midnight with no pain,
>   While thou art pouring forth thy soul abroad
>   In such an ecstasy . . . ,

Keats writes in the "Ode to a Nightingale," in a heartbreaking prayer for apotheosis. "I too have heard the nightingale sing in the rose-arbor," Williams quietly remarks, in a handwritten draft of the *Auto-biography.*[16]

One of Williams's fullest expressions of both the ecstasy and the despair occurs in a passage from *The Great American Novel,* a passage which describes a moment of flowering so acute that the self seems finally finished. This is a moment of "little death" attained not in sexual fulfillment—as it is in "Queen-Ann's Lace"—but in that most kindred fulfillment of finding oneself gone over into the body of one's writing:

> And approaching the end of the novel in his mind as he sat there with this wife sleeping alone in the next room he could feel that something unusual had happened. Something had grown up in his life dearer than—It, as the end. The words from long practice had come to be leaves, trees, the corners of his house—such was the end. He had progressed leaving the others far behind him. Alone in that air with the words of his brain he had breathed again the pure mountain air of joy—there night after night in his poor room. . . .
>
> That which had been impossible for him at first had become possible. Everything had been removed that other men had tied to the words to secure them to themselves. Clean, clean he had taken each word and made it new for himself so that at last it was new, free from the world for himself—never to touch it—dreams of his babyhood—poetic sweet-heart. No. He went in to his wife with exalted mind, his breath coming in pleasant surges. I come to tell you that the book is finished. (*GAN,* 166–67)

"I come to tell you that the book is finished." Here is the moment of selfhood toward which conventional autobiographies, including Williams's *Autobiography,* aspire. Here is the static perfection, the condition of full-blownness. "I have added a new chapter to the art of writing," Williams tells his wife. "I feel sincerely that all they say of me is true, that I am truly a great man and a great poet." He has, in this moment, *made* something of himself and made something of *himself;* public and private desires have converged and both been realized. *Consummatum est.* But as always in Williams's writing, consummation consumes itself to issue in new beginnings. "What did you say, dear, I have been asleep?" his wife drowsily replies (*GAN,* 167). And so the cycles continue to turn. The moment of perfect selfhood is not the end of the life; nor, coming as it does only partway through a book written partway through his life, can it be the final word of Williams's auto-biography.

Or, I should say, autobiographies. For making something *of* himself, creating something out of himself, allows Williams to go beyond this nostalgia for endings and see the organic metaphor as standing for the completeness of being perpetually unfinished. Every moment is "It, as the end." Rootedness is complete: Hence, "By the road to the con-tagious hospital," pulls back continually—back from "spring ap-proaches," back from the presence of the "cold, familiar wind," back from the promise of "wildcarrot leaf"—and down, down into earth, into a space one seldom thinks of either in nature or oneself but which, once seen, awakens awe for its beauty:

> But now the stark dignity of
> entrance—Still, the profound change
>
> has come upon them: rooted they
> grip down and begin to awaken.
>
> (*SA*, 96)

The profound change is "Still": It is always and unmoving. "Now" is not simply a moment in March but the space of all beginnings. The process of gripping down and beginning to awaken occurs not only in this poem, not only in the book entitled *Spring and All,* but every time something is born. Life, like death, is "contagious." And so, in the moment of "Spring and All," the imagination catches life and gives birth to a poem. This poem, complete and unfinished, is one expres-sion of the self's inner standing, one autobiography.

Just so, branching is complete. "I must tell you / this young tree," Williams writes in "Young Sycamore." And that's what the poem does: It enacts in language, *tells* us, "this young tree."[17] Rising from earth, "bending forward" at the end into inexpressible air, the poem, like the sycamore, is nothing but branching,

> dividing and waning
> sending out

> young branches
> on all sides—
> (*CP,* 266; *CEP,* 332)

The poem never ends—that is, according to one's expectations—but leaves one dangling from the "eccentric knotted / twigs" that are its series of relative and adverbial clauses, waiting for something to happen, wondering, "Tell me what?" But that is the point. In its process lies its wholeness. Unfinished, yet at the same time fully a statement of *haecceitas,* are the phrase and the living object, "this young tree." The urgency of "must," furthermore, makes Williams's position clear. Once again he is pushing toward a sense of his inner standing and offering one, as well, a new sense of one's own. Once again he is writing an autobiography.

Most poignantly of all, perhaps, flowering is complete. In a late poem Williams writes,

> The rose fades
> and is renewed again
> by its seed, naturally
> but where
> save in the poem
> shall it go
> to suffer no diminution
> of its splendor
> ("Poem," *PB,* 39)

Life and death are not art, and never will be. Yet this poem, once again, reveals the nostalgia for endings, for the perfect and undiminished rose. It reveals as well the fear of endings; an old man's poem, it stems from his knowledge of the difference not only between art and life but also between roses and humans. Roses fade; humans know they fade. Issue and art, man's "seed" (as in Shakespeare's sonnets), provide only partial consolation for his awareness that he himself is not "renewed."

Yet if one surrenders both the nostalgia for, and the fear of, endings, one discovers a space in which death becomes irrelevant. This is the space of love and of artistic creation, in which art, nature, and human experience reunite "in present passion," and flowering, once begun, is absolute. It is the subject of "The Crimson Cyclamen" and the space in which Williams wrote this beautiful elegy for his friend, the painter Charles Demuth (*CP*, 419–26; *CEP*, 397–404).

"The Crimson Cyclamen," written around 1935 and published in *Adam & Eve & The City*, seems a bridge between the earlier, shorter poems like "Queen-Ann's Lace" or "A Pot of Flowers" and the longer, later poems, particularly "Asphodel, That Greeny Flower." Tighter and less profuse than "Asphodel"—Williams confines himself here to describing one process only, the growth and flowering of the cyclamen—it manages nonetheless to suggest the whole course of a life. Or does it? One cannot equate the poem's beginning with Demuth's beginning, nor its ending with his ending. Perhaps, after all, it suggests only one flowering and dispersion, one ecstatic arc of creation. Yet it does not read like "Queen-Ann's Lace." It begins sooner, in the infancy of the plant,

> . . . when the first
> pink pointed bud still
> bowed below . . . ,

and goes on longer, past maturity and passion, into the plant's old age in which

> . . . the color
> draws back while still
> the flower grows. . . .

To read it moves one profoundly; though one learns nothing at all about the "facts" of the situation, one feels at the end that nothing about Demuth, about Williams's feelings for Demuth, or about the crimson cyclamen remains to be said.

And this is true. Nothing remains to be said. For insofar as "The Crimson Cyclamen" is "about" anything, it is about what it comes to mean, in terms of one's experience, to be an artist. To be an artist is not to *be* anything. It is to change, to become, to embrace, to create. Therefore the poem describes neither Williams nor Demuth, but a plant in Williams's living room. Or rather, it describes—and enacts—what Williams and Demuth shared through their lives as artists: the process of perceiving and entering into the life of a plant in a living room, and so creating a new plant, from the imagination, by means of words or paint.

Demuth's painting of a plant, "Tuberoses," hung in Williams's living room.[18] Williams's poem "A Pot of Flowers" translates this painting into words:

> Pink confused with white
> flowers and flowers reversed
> take and spill the shaded flame
> darting it back
> into the lamp's horn
>
> petals aslant with mauve
>
> red where in whorls
> petal lays its glow upon petal
> round flamegreen throats
>
> petals radiant with transpiercing light
> contending
> > above
> the leaves
> reaching up their modest green
> from the pot's rim
>
> and there, wholly dark, the pot
> gay with rough moss.
>
> > > (*SA*, 96)

And then, "The Crimson Cyclamen" echoes "A Pot of Flowers." It grows, that is, not only from a plant but also from a poem and a painting, from an artistic connection reaching far into the past: "Pink confused with white" becomes "White suffused with red / more rose than crimson." Echoes it with a difference, however, for whereas "A Pot of Flowers" captures a single moment and responds to a single painting,

"The Crimson Cyclamen" celebrates a lifetime that was painting, responding to all the paintings that were a life.

Williams met Charles Demuth "over a dish of prunes at Mrs. Chain's boarding house on Locust Street" while still a medical student at Penn (*A, 52*). Perhaps their friendship began as a cyclamen plant begins, with leaves "of logic"—with lively but abstract discussions about the meaning of art and life. Perhaps not, too, though at the time Williams was fond of writing essays with titles like "Beauty and Truth,"[19] and these lines from "The Crimson Cyclamen" seem a wonderful description of "Philip and Oradie":

> Such are the leaves
> freakish, of the air
> as thought is, of roots
> dark, complex from
> subterranean revolutions
> and rank odors
> waiting for the moon—.

Whether or not one feels a biographical connection, this, for Williams, is where thought begins: in

> a pattern more
> of logic than a purpose
>   . . .
> an abstraction
> playfully following
> centripetal
> devices. . . .

Thought begins here not only in youth but also in the creative act: One plays around the edges, entertains the possibilities. But then, in a decade, in a moment, "it begins that must / put thought to rest"; passion "is loosed" in love or art and "The flower / flows to release."

At the moment of flowering each poem begins; hence, looking back at the first two stanzas of "The Crimson Cyclamen," one finds that it does too. These stanzas form a poem in themselves, resembling "A Pot of Flowers," one "painting" or image cluster of perfection:

White suffused with red
more rose than crimson
—all acolor
the petals flare back
from the stooping craters
of those flowers
as from a wind rising—

And though the light
that enfolds and pierces
them discovers blues
and yellows there also—
and crimson's a dull word
for such play—
yet the effect against
this winter where
they stand—is crimson—

It is miraculous
that flower should rise
by flower
alike in loveliness
as though mirrors
of some perfection
could never be
too often shown—
silence holds them—
in that space. And
color has been construed
from emptiness
to waken there—.

If "The Crimson Cyclamen" ended here, it would resemble as well the passage quoted above from *The Great American Novel;* it would describe one moment, but one moment only, of imaginative possession.

But Williams presses further: not, this time, into the abrupt intrusion of loss ("What did you say, dear, I have been asleep?"), but into the space of possession itself. Moving forward, the poem circles back, to enact its own creation. From leaf to flower it flows until it finds, once again, its ecstasy: each word,

> each petal
> by excess of tensions
> in its own flesh
> all rose—
>
>   . . .
>
> answering
> ecstasy with excess
> all together
> acrobatically
>
> not as if bound
> (though still bound)
> but upright
> as if they hung
>
> from above
> to the streams
> with which
> they are veined and glow—
> the frail fruit
> by its frailty supreme
>
> opening in the tense moment
> to no bean
> no completion
> no root
> no leaf and no stem
> but color only and a form—.

This is the moment of "It, as the end." But it is not the end, can never be the end; beautifully, gravely, the poem continues:

And the flowers
grow older and begin
to change, larger now
less tense, when at the full
relaxing. . . .

The question is simply put: What happens to the woman after "Queen-Ann's Lace"? What happens to the artist after he has spent himself, gone to "nothing" in his passion? For passion can be triumph but also despair; it "rises above thought" but is likewise

> . . . soonest to wither
> blacken
> and fall upon itself
> formless—.

And the answer is simply found, both in the cyclamen and in a little more intimate look at the woman's body. Passion gives life, not death. The self, the flower, endures, opening into peace. Nothing can take away the knowledge of its passage through plenitude into plenitude, through ecstasy into repose.

Charles Demuth died "frail" of diabetes. In the *Autobiography,* Williams writes,

> Dr. Allen opened a sanatorium for the dietary treatment of diabetes at Morristown that year. Demuth was one of his first patients. His intake was reduced to the caloric minimum. The result was frightening.
>
> . . .
>
> Insulin came in just the nick of time to save Charley from dissolution, but he was careless and died later while on his way home to Lancaster, either from lack of insulin or an overdose: I was never able to get the answer. (*A,* 152)

But in the space of "The Crimson Cyclamen," this frailty, this death, becomes irrelevant. The frailty by which Demuth lives was the frailty of art, of passion, of losing the self to discover the self. Such frailty is

delicate, not weak; and it is lasting. The "day" of the cyclamen "rises,"
and, as in a woman's body,

> . . . the color
> draws back while still
> the flower grows
> the rose of it nearly all lost
> a darkness of dawning purple
> paints a deeper afternoon—
> The day passes
> in a horizon of colors
> all meeting
> less severe in loveliness
> the petals fallen now well back
> till flower touches flower
> all round
> at the petal tips
> one flower—.

In this space, which is not just the space of art but also the space of a
poet and a painter, flowering is absolute. Their lives have become an
arc of creation; the arc has become their lives. "A Pot of Flowers"
moves downward, affirming the earth from which we spring. But "The
Crimson Cyclamen," flowering, is its response and its companion.
Rooted in the elegiac "winter," it expands to encompass at last both
Williams and Demuth in the space of love and creation, the space of
their inner standing. Perfect and unfinished, it is a prayer, an affirmation, a testament to a friend, and a discovery of a self. Profoundly
it is an autobiography.

6

A Song of a Man and a Woman: "Asphodel, That Greeny Flower"

"The / theme is difficult," Williams writes in "The Orchestra,"

    but no more difficult
        than the facts to be
   resolved. Repeat
     and repeat the theme
        and all it develops to be
   until thought is dissolved
     in tears.

             (*PB,* 81–82)

There is a "theme" in "Asphodel, That Greeny Flower." Over and against this theme are "facts to be resolved." Both, in their ways, are "difficult," for the facts, in the largest sense, are death, and the theme is love. There is movement toward a goal: not straightforward movement, like an arrow's, but, as these lines suggest, fugal and incremen-

tal, flowing, shifting, swooping, circling movement. And there is the
goal itself: a state of feeling, or colloquy, in which "thought is dissolved / in tears." When thought dissolves in tears, the soul, as Shakespeare says, "delivers weeping."[1] The facts which in one sense can
never be resolved *are* by this means resolved, for pain brings forth joy,
blindness brings forth vision, and the knowledge of loss and death
brings forth an unshakable sense of possession in the renewal of love.
Such is the burden of "Asphodel," Williams's greatest poem, and his
fullest, deepest, most beautiful autobiography.

Williams wrote this long love poem to Flossie during a time of nearly
overwhelming crisis in his life. He began the poem on March 1, 1952,
writing on a menu at the New Weston Hotel while on vacation with
Flossie in New York City, and he worked on the poem—which origi-
nally he thought of as the fifth book of *Paterson*—for almost two years.
During these years his health, which had begun to break with his heart
attack in 1948 and strokes in 1949 and 1951, continued to deteriorate.
He suffered another major stroke in August 1952, while staying with
friends, the Gratwicks and the Abbotts, at Gratwick Highlands in up-
state New York; and he knew he could expect further strokes—any
one of them possibly fatal—at any time from then on.[2] His mental
condition was likewise precarious. Depression had been intensifying
during the past few years; it was exacerbated both by the recent stroke
and by the imbroglio surrounding Williams's appointment as Poetry
Consultant to the Library of Congress. Finally, on February 21, 1953,
Williams was admitted to a private mental hospital in Queens, where
he underwent psychiatric treatment until his release on April 18. The
Library of Congress affair continued throughout the summer. The position was first offered, then, with allegations of Communist sympa-
thizing, withdrawn, then offered again contingent on further loyalty
investigations, which were conducted but never evaluated so that the
year's term was up before Williams ever served; and the injustice of it
all tormented Williams with feelings of rage, powerlessness, and humiliation.[3] Most painful of all, perhaps, the old uneasy balance between
confession and deceit in Williams's marriage to Flossie finally gave way.

All of Williams's writing is autobiographical, and adultery recurs as
a theme at least as early as *Kora in Hell*, which was published in 1920.
A Dream of Love, in particular, is so thinly veiled a confession that its

veils merely advertise its nakedness. It is hard to see, therefore, how Flossie could have thought Williams faithful until the years around "Asphodel." But apparently she did—or perhaps, as the line "I don't care—so long as I have my garden"[4] that Myra speaks in *A Dream of Love* suggests, she just repeatedly deflected a full awareness of the situation. There are ways of confessing, furthermore, that conceal even as they reveal. But now the threat of death intensified Williams's need for Flossie to know him, once and for all, in all the truth of his nature, and he began the barrage of specific, detailed accounts of infidelity which at last compelled her full belief.[5] The process must have been immeasurably painful for them both; needing Flossie to hold firm now more than ever, Williams must test her, prove her, by buffeting and shaking her. "Having your love / I was rich," he tells her in "Asphodel." "Thinking to have lost it / I am tortured / and cannot rest." The threats both of physical death and of the death of love are right at the center of "Asphodel." Both the strength and the fear present in this part of the Williamses' marriage are movingly described in these lines from another late poem, "For Eleanor and Bill Monahan":

> . . . I have seen the ivy
> >   cling
> >   to a piece of crumbled
> wall so that
> >   you cannot tell
> >   by which either
> stands: this is to say
> >   if she to whom I cling
> >   is loosened both
> of us go down.
>
>   (*PB*, 84)

Williams himself had expressed the extent of the wrong his infidelities did Flossie when, planning *A Dream of Love,* he had written,

> . . . for the first time in his life [Williams's persona Doc Thurber] sees the implications and the fact of monogamy (the whole man and the man whole).

He SEES—and the light it casts through and through his life is brilliant—He stands in amazement before it . . . before her, her life given; desperately assailed by the tragedy of her life.[6]

But at the time of *A Dream of Love,* Williams was not ready for this vision. He needed not to see Flossie, but to make Flossie see him; therefore, instead of coming around to Myra's view and embracing monogamy, Doc Thurber leads his wife, in the dream sequence after his death, to an imagined witnessing and acceptance of his adulterous liaison with Dotty Randall. With the writing of "Asphodel," however, Wiliams moved toward the deeper communion of regenerated marriage. Now, in "Asphodel," though there is still self-justification, there is also a new and moving attempt to see Flossie as she is, and a heartfelt plea for forgiveness:

> It is winter
> > and there
> > > waiting for you to care for them
>
> are your plants.
> > Poor things! you say
> > > as you compassionately
> pour at their roots
> > the reviving water.
> > > Lean-cheeked
> I say to myself
> > kindness moves her
> > > shall she not be kind
> also to me?   At this
> > courage possessed me finally
> > > to go on.

Touching bottom, Williams found new strength. He began to make what he called the longest journey, the journey to love; and he could write to Flossie from the hospital, "I really feel as if I had just been married."[7]

With "Asphodel, That Greeny Flower," Williams comes closest—perhaps as close as the post-Augustinian autobiographer can—to bridging the gap between private and public autobiography. He does this, however, by changing the terms of the quest. Rather than enact a search for his inner standing, as the private autobiographer traditionally does (and as Williams himself does in *A Dream of Love*), he gives himself over to the process of creation and enacts the self in its fluidity. Rather than offer a life history fit for imitation, as the public autobiographer traditionally does (and as Williams himself does in his *Autobiography*), he finds a way of speaking so that, though he has no programmatic answers, he can address his public with authority. Here, too, the emphasis shifts from product to process; he gives us not a pattern, but a voice. The voice we hear in "Asphodel" is intensely personal and individual, yet it is also the voice of a wisdom figure. It is hesitant and troubled, yet it is also clear, calm, and profoundly reassuring. It is so deeply private that it becomes public, so deeply rooted in the local that it becomes universal.[8] It is much more honest than the voice of the *Autobiography,* much more willing to admit doubt, weakness, guilt, confusion, and even occasional meanness; for this reason, its affirmations carry tremendous weight. It is much less defensive and anxious than the voice of *A Dream of Love;* for this reason, its confessions and discoveries seem more inclusive. So fully is Williams present in his poem, and with such natural dignity, that he leaps the barriers of the self. One thinks while reading "Asphodel," this describes the circle of experience. This is what it feels like to be human.

The sense of universality is important, for "Asphodel" has a strongly public dimension. Though neither partisan nor programmatic, it is political. Like Thoreau, Williams questions the value of what we have come to call the news; his comment that we do not find the "news" we need in "what passes for the new" echoes Thoreau's reflection in *Walden* that newspaper news is gossip merely, and that the proper object of our knowledge is "what that is which was never old."[9] Nevertheless, the man who wrote "Asphodel" was a man who read the papers. Though some of Williams's allusions—to Homer, to Columbus, to the witchcraft trials at Salem, to Melville, Cézanne, and Darwin—span the centuries, others—to Juan Perón's burning of the "priceless Goyas," to the execution of the Rosenbergs—specifically date the

poem and ground it in the tensions of the early 1950s. The allusions
have in common Williams's lifelong championship of freedom of imagination and expression. From *In the American Grain* to *Paterson* to
"Asphodel" his conviction remains unchanged. Oppression, suppression, repression: These deal death.

> All suppressions,
> from the witchcraft trials at Salem
> to the latest
> book burnings
> are confessions
> that the bomb
> has entered our lives. . . .

Expression alone is life. Without it, "We come to our deaths / in silence."

William Blake writes, "Every honest man is a Prophet he utters his
opinion both of private & public matters/Thus/If you go on So/the
result is So/He never says such a thing shall happen let you do what
you will."[10] In this sense, "Asphodel" is not only political but also pro-
phetic. The near fusing of private and public in "Asphodel" allows the
poet's fate to seem both particular and exemplary; his struggle in his
personal life to understand and affirm the theme of love in the face of
the facts to be resolved both exemplifies and participates in the
struggle between love and death to which all of human history has
come. "Asphodel" is one of the first great works of art of the nuclear
age. "I am reminded," Williams writes,

> that the bomb
> also
> is a flower
> dedicated
> howbeit
> to our destruction.
> The mere picture
> of the exploding bomb
> fascinates us

> so that we cannot wait
>   to prostrate ourselves
>   before it. We do not believe
>   that love
>   can so wreck our lives.

Williams's sense of the conflict between the theme, or love, and the facts to be resolved, or death, closely resembles Freud's description of the struggle between *eros* and *thanatos,* for it is not simply the fact of death against which love does battle, but, as the lines I have just quoted make clear, the fascination with death, the desire to wield death and the desire to die. At the end of *Civilization and Its Discontents,* Freud writes:

> The fateful question for the human species seems to me to be whether and to what extent their cultural development will succeed in mastering the disturbance of their communal life by the human instinct of aggression and self-destruction. It may be that in this respect precisely the present time deserves a special interest. Men have gained control over the forces of nature to such an extent that with their help they would have no difficulty in exterminating one another to the last man. They know this, and hence comes a large part of their current unrest, their unhappiness and their mood of anxiety. And now it is to be expected that the other of the two 'Heavenly Powers', eternal Eros, will make an effort to assert himself in the struggle with his equally immortal adversary. But who can foretell with what success and with what result? [11]

As Williams advises himself in "The Orchestra," "Say to them: / 'Man has survived hitherto because he was too ignorant to know how to realize his wishes. Now that he can realize them, he must either change them or perish'" (*PB,* 82).

But here the problems become complex. If, as Freud suggests, aggression and self-destruction are instinctual and immortal desires— if *thanatos* goes as deep in the human psyche as *eros*—and if, as Williams suggests, man must either change his desires or perish, what is to be done? Freud added the last sentence to the passage I have quoted in 1931, when the threat Hitler presented had begun to be apparent;[12] Williams wrote "Asphodel, That Greeny Flower" at the height of the Cold War; and humanity's chances of survival have not improved since then. Must we simply consent to perish?

At every level the answer lies with *eros*. It is contained in the lines from "The Orchestra" with which this chapter begins: "Repeat / and repeat the theme / and all it develops to be."[13] It may seem at first that love is over and against death, but this is to say, conversely, that death is over and against love. Such a formulation gives death dominion, for life and love always end in death, fullness is always swallowed up in emptiness. A brief comparison of two poems, one early and one late, will illustrate my point, and reveal the change that takes place in Williams's thinking about the conflict between death and love. The early poem, "Death," which Williams wrote about his father, powerfully expresses the anger and despair that come when one realizes the powerlessness of love against death, the otherness and nothingness of death, the shamefulness of the lifeless body:

> He's dead
> the dog won't have to
> sleep on his potatoes
> any more to keep them
> from freezing
>
> he's dead
> the old bastard—
> He's a bastard because
>
> there's nothing
> legitimate in him any
> more
>   he's dead
> He's sick-dead
>   he's
> a god-forsaken curio
> without
> any breath in it

He's nothing at all
   he's dead
shrunken up to skin

   Put his head on
one chair and his
feet on another and
he'll lie there
like an acrobat—

Love's beaten. He
beat it. That's why
he's insufferable—

   because
he's here needing a
shave and making love
an inside howl
of anguish and defeat—

He's come out of the man
and he's let
the man go—
       the liar

Dead
   his eyes
rolled up out of
the light—a mockery

      which
love cannot touch—

just bury it
and hide its face
for shame.
(*CP,* 346–48); *CEP,* 78–79)

The bitterness this poem expresses cannot be gainsaid, and there is courage in its relentless insistence on the body. "The body makes love possible," Galway Kinnell has remarked;[14] we like to think in terms of fine abstractions, but if there were no bodies, there would be no love. In one sense, death *does* end the possibility of love. To say, however, that death beats love, and that each individual death beats love, is to condemn all human experience to futility. As Williams's line breaks suggest, not only love but also each act of "making love" becomes "an inside howl / of anguish and defeat." To my mind, furthermore, there is something childish and obsessive about "Death." Its tone suggests that of a child furious with his parents for turning out to be fallible and human; and it does seem cruel to heap insults upon a corpse simply because the poor mortal had the temerity to die. "He's dead / the old bastard," Williams writes; "He's a bastard because . . ." And in the space between stanzas the hidden feeling rushes in. *Timor mortis conturbat me.* He's a bastard because he died.

Such revulsion and anger may be luxuries of youth; they were not, at any rate, sufficient answer for Williams in his eventual struggle to come to terms with his own failing body. "The Descent," the poem in triadic lines that began as just one of many passages in *Paterson, II* but which later leapt out at Williams to show him a new direction in both content and form,[15] expresses a different sense of death and love:

> The descent beckons
>   as the ascent beckoned.
>   Memory is a kind
> of accomplishment,
>   a sort of renewal
>   even
> an initiation, since the spaces it opens are new places
>   inhabited by hordes
>   heretofore unrealized,
> of new kinds—
>   since their movements
>   are toward new objectives
> (even though formerly they were abandoned).
> No defeat is made up entirely of defeat—since
> the world it opens is always a place
>   formerly

                                       unsuspected. A
world lost,
                a world unsuspected,
                                beckons to new places
and no whiteness (lost) is so white as the memory
of whiteness   .

With evening, love wakens
                though its shadows
                                which are alive by reason
of the sun shining—
                grow sleepy now and drop away
                                from desire   .

Love without shadows stirs now
                beginning to awaken
                                as night
advances.

The descent
                made up of despairs
                                and without accomplishment
realizes a new awakening:
                                which is a reversal
of despair.
                For what we cannot accomplish, what
is denied to love,
                what we have lost in the anticipation—
                                a descent follows,
endless and indestructible   .
                                (*P,* 77–79; *PB,* 73–74)

"The Descent" marks an important turning point in Williams's understanding of the sources and function of poetry. Throughout his early and middle years, Williams was preeminently a man of action, and his poetry one form of that action, oriented toward the present and celebrating the relations between the poet and his world. "Good Christ what is / a poet," Williams asks in the early "The Wind Increases," and answers,

> a man
> whose words will
>   bite
>   their way
> home—being actual
>
> having the form
>   of motion
>   (*CP,* 339; *CEP,* 68)

All the forms of action in the poem are aggressive and sexual. The wind harries the earth, tosses the trees and tulips. Inspiration, riding the wind, begins to torment and caress "the tortured / body of thought." "Love" begins to "flow" and "blow." Nature quickens the poet, and his poem, "gripping the ground," ascends like the sap in a tree all the way "to the last leaftip" and arches there ecstatic in expression. This tactile, restless, energetic, and extroverted desirousness is the characteristic mode of many of Williams's early and middle poems; his words, like an animal's or a lover's teeth, "bite / their way home." With "The Descent," however, action has begun to fail him, and he is tempted by the belief common to men in a society that equates action with virility, the belief that his life becomes worthless once his sexual, physical, and mental powers have started to decline.

Williams's late poems are grounded in inaction and the recurring terror of powerlessness, yet they are for many readers among his most life-filled and powerful work. How can this be so? "The Descent" contains the answer, in what it shows of Williams's awakening sense of the power of both memory and love, not to overcome death, but to make death and its foreshadowing diminishments, though inescapable, also somehow irrelevant. Loss becomes its own New World. The mind, which would know the ground of its being, seeks to know this too, and so "A / world lost" becomes as well "a world unsuspected" and "beckons to new places." The past is "a world unsuspected" because it is gone; the present is "a world lost" because the self that could act in it is gone. But the past can be entered by memory, which can itself become a form of creative action, since to remember something is not simply to live the past again but rather to live something new and different—the mingling of past-as-remembered and present-as-remembering. Not only can memory be a form of action; it can also lead to further action. It can engage the imagination in its movement "toward new objectives"—new desires to enter into the truth of another's experience, or to seek the truth of one's selfhood, such as we see in "Asphodel," in the poet's desire to find and know both his wife and himself more deeply and fully than he has ever done before. The past, which has seemed gone, floods back; the present, which has seemed empty, fills; the self, which has seemed powerless to act, reveals itself as powerful in acting. "Love without shadows stirs now," and the poet, reawakened, enters, embraces, and fecundates his life.

"Love without shadows" is love without desire. Other of Williams's late poems—most notably "Asphodel" itself, *Paterson, V,* "The Desert Music," "Address," and "To Daphne and Virginia"—speak of the torments and complications, the beauty and ubiquity, of desire, but for the moment, in "The Descent," Williams rests in a serenity much like T. S. Eliot's when, in *Four Quartets,* Eliot writes,

> This is the use of memory:
> For liberation—not less of love but expanding
> Of love beyond desire, and so liberation
> From the future as well as the past.[16]

Memory awakens love—not the imperious, needy love which is desire, but a gentler love, which does not need because it has, and therefore soars free of time. What it has is not the thing that was in the past, but the thing that *is* in the memory, not "whiteness (lost)" but "memory of whiteness." As Williams remarks in "To Daphne and Virginia," such a love is infinitely "penetrant," like a "healing odor" (*PB,* 77–78). Or, like heat and light, it washes around things; it becomes the fluid medium in which everything, past and present, is suspended. This love is the theme of "Asphodel." Again and again the poem repeats its theme, allowing the concept of love to blossom and flow until, in the metaphors of the poem, there is nothing left outside its flowering waters.

In the awakening of love lies the only "reversal / of despair." "Everything left over that wasn't done or said—," Williams writes to himself on an early draft of "Asphodel"; and then below that he adds the words "*at ease.*"[17] The final lines of "The Descent" reveal the magnitude of the autobiographer's task; in order to be "at ease," he must retrieve not less than everything. For he who would save his life, their warning is unmistakable:

> For what we cannot accomplish, what
> is denied to love,
>> what we have lost in the anticipation—
>>> a descent follows,
> endless and indestructible   .

In 1897, William Carlos Williams, his mother, and his younger brother Ed traveled to Europe to spend a year in Switzerland and Paris, while Williams's father set up a factory in Buenos Aires for the manufacture of Florida Water. The boys were sent to school at the Château de Lancy, near Geneva, and there Williams became a collector of flowers, which he pressed to save "between the leaves of a copybook." Fifty years later, writing his *Autobiography,* he returned to the memory of those flowers: "my greatest joy was . . . the *ruisseau,* the icy-clear mountain brook running beside the soccer field, and the flowers growing about it, that spring, before the fields had been mowed. There I first became acquainted with the native yellow primrose, so delightfully sweet-scented. The green-flowered asphodel made a tremendous impression on me" (*A,* 29).

But *Kora in Hell,* published in 1920, contains Williams's first allusion to asphodel. "To the sick their sick," he writes. "For us   heads bowed over the green-flowered asphodel. Lean on my shoulder little one, you too. I will lead you to fields you know nothing of. There's small dancing left for us any way you look at it" (*K,* 48). The reference is moving. If "little one" is Flossie, then "small dancing left to us" reveals the sadness Williams already feels about their troubled marriage. Adjacent lines, in which Williams refers to struggling "with ants for a piece of meat" and to "a mangy cur to swallow beetles and all," and concludes, "Oh let him have it. Find a cleaner fare for wife and child" (*K,* 48), seem to allude to Eliot, whom Williams scorns in the Prologue to *Kora in Hell* as a "fumbling conjurer" and a "subtle conformist," but whose poetry, even as Williams writes, is drawing critical acclaim as "'the very fine flower of the finest spirit of the United States'" (*K*, 24–25). The "explanation" which follows the asphodel improvisation makes Williams's drift more clear:

> *A man who enjoyed his food, the company of his children and especially his wife's alternate caresses and tongue lashings felt his position in the town growing insecure due to a successful business competitor. Being thus stung to the quick he thinks magnanimously of his own methods of dealing with his customers and likens his competitor to a dog that swallows his meat with beetles or maggots upon it, that is, any way so he gets it.*
>
> *Being thus roused the man does not seek to outdo his rival but grows heavily sad and thinks of death and his lost pleasures thus showing himself to be a person of discernment. For by so doing he gives evidence of a bastard sort of knowledge of that diversity of context in things and situations which the great masters of antiquity looked to for the inspiration and distinction of their compositions. (K, 48)*

Surliness mars this passage; neither its bitterness nor its self-hatred shows Williams in his best light. But beyond that, what I take Williams to be getting at, with reference to his "business" of both love and art, is a determination to sink to the very ground of his despair—to grieve, bowed over the flower that grows in hell; to think of "death and his lost pleasures." Merely to attempt to outdo one's rivals dooms one to the arena where the wounded fight the wounded. Merely to attempt to maintain an illusion of happiness dooms one to the chambers where the sick lie by the sick. But if, somehow, the descent can be completed, and the grieving self find the fields of death, of which it knows nothing, but senses something, then perhaps the sources of life can be renewed.[18]

Asphodel is not mentioned in the first, handwritten drafts of Williams's *Autobiography*. But then the sentence about the asphodel by the *ruisseau* appears, to be expanded in the poem several years later:

> When I was a boy
> > I kept a book

> to which, from time
> to time,
>   I added pressed flowers
>   until, after a time,
> I had a good collection.
>   The asphodel,
>   forebodingly,
> among them.
>   I bring you,
>   reawakened,
> a memory of those flowers.
>   They were sweet
>   when I pressed them
> and retained
>   something of their sweetness
>   a long time.

It is as if, unbeknownst to Williams himself, his remembering the flower in the *Autobiography* offers him a clue as to where he must eventually go. As a public autobiographer, Williams tries to outdo his rivals and maintain the appearance of happiness. But what he knows in *Kora in Hell*—and forgets in the *Autobiography*—stands him in good stead when he turns in a season of grief to explore the hint unguessed in the *Autobiography,* the hint offered by the "poor / colorless thing," the greeny asphodel.

In several important ways, the structure of "Asphodel, That Greeny Flower" resembles the structure of the Ignatian meditation, as Louis Martz describes it in *The Poetry of Meditation*.[19] The essence of meditation is its systematic awakening and directing of emotion for purposes of devotion. As systematized by Saint Ignatius, it utilizes the three functions of the mind—memory, understanding, and will—in what is essentially a three-part exercise, with composition leading to analysis and thence to colloquy. Psychologically, the process is ingenious. The devotee begins by "remembering" one aspect of that which is doctrinally true about the nature of God, the nature of man, and their interrelationship, and attempts to establish the felt reality of this truth by means of a composition of place, a dramatic projection of the self into a setting appropriate for the meditation. This is the first prelude. In the second prelude, he anticipates the desired result of the entire meditation, in petitioning for the awakening of emotion according to his subject. To hold any idea fixed in the mind leads naturally to active analysis; memory gives way to understanding, and the devotee investigates the personal ramifications of doctrinal truth. Man's sin, God's mercy and justice, man's reliance on the former and fear of the latter take on added emotional impact. Analysis flows spontaneously into colloquy, the free outpouring of devotion in a total direction of the will toward God. Man speaks to God in this final stage, hoping that God will respond.

"Asphodel, That Greeny Flower" is not, of course, a Christian poem, and Williams was not influenced by methods of religious meditation. Nonetheless, like the Ignatian meditation, "Asphodel" aims systematically to awaken and direct emotion, enabling the poet to seek redemption by aligning himself with what he conceives of as truth. Religious meditation is guided by doctrine. Williams, in contrast, follows the Romantics in affirming his own experience rather than any doctrine or dogma as the only sure ground of knowledge; therefore, he takes guidance, not from doctrine but from the connections that memory establishes with his own deepest self. Religious meditation is directed toward an unmoved mover, the principle of being, God. "Asphodel," in contrast, is directed toward Flossie. It is not that Williams conceives of Flossie as God, but rather that he attaches absolute importance to marriage. As "Philip and Oradie," *A Dream of Love,* and *Paterson* all reveal, for Williams, to live unwed or divorced is to live absented, unfertilized and unfertilizing, languageless and issueless. In Williams's own self-conception, it seems as if his identity is absolutely tied to his being married—at times, in fact, as if he only began to exist when he got married.[20] To him, to marry is to become present to the world, to engage with the world, to acknowledge and affirm the reality of existence. Though at times Williams clothes Flossie with divinity, he does not make her his God; he remains fully aware that she is "a woman / ... and [has] to face / the problems which confront a woman." But if the world is all there is, and if marriage represents being in the world, then to reestablish contact with the "first wife" is to reestablish contact both with all otherness and with the ground of one's own being. That is why marriage, though sometimes hell, is for Williams the only state of grace. And that in turn is why, in a working title, he called this poem which celebrates marriage, his flower which grows in hell, "The River of Heaven."[21]

> Of asphodel, that greeny flower,
>   like a buttercup
>   upon its branching stem—
> save that it's green and wooden—
>   I come, my sweet,
>   to sing to you.

With these words, Williams begins his poem and his composition of place. He begins to create the voice that will be his—that will be *him*—for the duration of the poem, and to create and project himself into a setting appropriate for the purposes of his meditation. Already, and in several different ways, he performs the characteristic act of the poem: the act of joining and uniting disparate entities; the act, in short, of marrying, with the poet as both minister—he who joins—and bridegroom—he who offers himself up for joining. Public and private modes of address, for instance, join in the coupling of the formula for beginning an epic, "Of asphodel, that greeny flower . . . I sing,"[22] with the lyric, intensely personal announcement, "I come, my sweet / to sing to you." Or look at this same sentence in another way. It is made of a core statement, essentially two lines of unrhymed iambic tetrameter—"Of asphodel, that greeny flower, / I come, my sweet, to sing to you"—parted and penetrated by the wistful, hesitant, dogged, somewhat literalistic prolongations and qualifications of "like a buttercup / upon its branching stem—/ save that it's green and wooden." Subtly the poet joins traditional and experimental prosody, classical and local allusion, past and present, imagination and reality, the melodies of poetry and ordinary speech. And the asphodel itself is both a real and an imaginary flower: both a lilaceous plant closely related to the daffodil, the leaves of which, according to the *Oxford English Dictionary,* afford good nourishment to southern European sheep, and the poets' immortal flower, mentioned by Homer, and after him, Milton, Browne, Pope,

Tennyson, Carlyle, Ruskin—the flower which covers the Elysian meads. "I saw it / when I was a child," Williams writes, referring to his early trip to Switzerland; it comes to him from life, and yet it comes from art as well, and places Williams firmly within the Western literary tradition.

Above all, I think, the mention of asphodel comes from the moment in Book XI of *The Odyssey* when the knowledge of life and the knowledge of death are wedded, and the passion for life is consequently most acute: the encounter between Odysseus and Achilles. Odysseus has sailed with his ships to hell to seek Teiresias, who, once he has drunk of the blood of a sacrificial ram and ewe, will prophesy the outcome of Odysseus's homeward journey. Innumerable shades crowd around, each seeking to drink and thereby to be released to tell his story. Of these, Achilles steps forth. "Was there ever a man more blest by fortune / than you, Akhilleus?" Odysseus asks him, and continues,

> Can there ever be?
> We ranked you with immortals in your lifetime,
> we Argives did, and here your power is royal
> among the dead men's shades. Think, then, Akhilleus:
> you need not be so pained by death.

Achilles' answer, however, is absolute:

> Let me hear no smooth talk
> of death from you, Odysseus, light of councils.
> Better, I say, to break sod as a farm hand
> for some poor country man, on iron rations,
> than lord it over all the exhausted dead.

He asks then about his son, and he is so proud of what Odysseus tells him of Neoptolemos's skill and courage in battle that he goes off without speaking,

> striding the fields of asphodel,
> the ghost of our great runner, Akhilleus Aiakides,
> glorying in what I told him of his son.[23]

With bitter clarity we see what it means *to live,* and what, in this classical vision, it means to die. In his composition of place, Williams puts himself in the way of Achilles' anguish; he stands back from life in order to see and prize it. For like the asphodel, life comes cheap for the living,

> but the dead see,
> > asking among themselves:
>
> What do I remember
> > that was shaped
> > > as this thing is shaped?

We see the dead through art; we see the great Achilles, so full at heart that he cannot speak; and "our eyes fill / with tears."

Like *The Odyssey,* "Asphodel" does not end here; like Odysseus, the poet turns from the dead to begin his long journey homeward to love. The knowledge of death creates a sense of urgency—

> There is something
> > something urgent
>
> I have to say to you
> > and you alone

—but stronger than fear or bitterness, stronger than death itself, is what the asphodel "will be telling." At this point in the poem, however, not only death but the death of love threatens the poet's authority; "too weak a wash of crimson" colors the asphodel to make it "wholly credible." He must therefore find a way to renew both his own and his wife's devotion, if he is to speak convincingly of "love, abiding love." Here again his procedure resembles that of Ignatian meditation: As in the second prelude, he anticipates the result of the entire process by giving himself an image which expresses his goal. At this point the image is vague—

> I have forgot
> > and yet I see clearly enough
> > > something

central to the sky
which ranges round it

—but I think the vagueness is justified. The center is there, and yet,
because the poet has "forgot," neither it nor its significance can be
directly apprehended. It resonates, nevertheless:

An odor
springs from it!
A sweetest odor!
Honeysuckle! And now
there comes the buzzing of a bee!
and a whole flood
of sister memories!
Only give me time,
time to recall them
before I shall speak out.
Give me time,
time.

The first three sections of "Asphodel," then, emerge from the flood of
remembering; they give him "time." In the "Coda," the colloquy, he
speaks out. Memory has reawakened feeling, and feeling pours forth
in a magnificent testimony to love, imagination, and light. Everything
comes full circle at the end; that early, mysterious image is that of
Flossie,

a girl so pale
and ready to faint
that I pitied
and wanted to protect you,

standing beside his own youthful self "so intent . . . before my vows"
at the moment of their wedding. This, "forgot," is the image from
which the poem made of memories arises, and the image the poem
retrieves. By the end all of life ranges round it; it is the wellspring of
Williams's existence, the act that centers the sky.

The final element in this initial composition of place is poetic form, for the place being composed is, of course, inseparable from the poem being written. "Asphodel" is written in what Williams called the variable foot and the triadic line. In *I Wanted to Write a Poem*, Williams speaks of the importance the variable foot came to have for him once he discovered it in "The Descent." He argues that it gave him a way of writing verse that was neither bound by dead metrical conventions nor "free," but rather "ordered," "altered" to suit "our new relativistic world," and "just simply variable, as all things in life properly are" (*IWW*, 82). The variable foot is difficult to pin down, except to say that we recognize it visually, not audially, as forming one of the three stairsteps of the triadic line.[24] That, however, is the most important thing about it: It exists only in context, in relation. It is one element in a recurrent wholeness, neither fixed—since its length can vary from one syllable ("time," "to," "love") to at least twelve ("I'm filled with the fading memory of those flowers")—nor free—since there would be no variable foot were there no triadic line. It is flexible and changing, always responsive to the larger whole of which it makes a part.

But it is not sufficient to say that, whereas the foot is partial and dependent, the line is whole and free. Consider these lines, for instance:

> We lived long together
>   a life filled,
>   if you will,
> with flowers. So that
>   I was cheered
>   when I came first to know
> that there were flowers also
>   in hell.
>   Today
> I'm filled with the fading memory of those
> flowers. . . .

None of these feet is a complete sentence; none is independent. But three—"We lived long together," "I was cheered," and "I'm filled with the fading memory of those flowers"—are potentially complete sentences, and nearly all the rest are units of syntax, thought, or feeling. "That there were flowers also" is an exception; "also" seems to obtrude; but then one sees that, joined to the line, it gains a double meaning: There were flowers also in *hell,* and there were also *flowers* in hell. Both readings quietly emphasize Williams's faith that beauty springs from loss and grief, so that the "world lost" becomes the "world unsuspected" and "beckons to new places." And finally, the foot reading "with flowers. So that" both pleases as a sport and reminds one of dependence; like the poet at this moment, it is situated right in the middle of things, and looks for its significance on what has gone before and will come after.

Were Williams to insist on the self-sufficiency and freedom of the triadic line, he might lineate the passage quoted above this way:

> We lived long together
> > a life filled, if you will
> > > with flowers.
> So that I was cheered
> > when I came first to know
> > > that there were flowers also in
> > > > hell.
> Today I'm filled
> > with the fading memory
> > > of those flowers. . . .

Instead, just as the variable foot plays off against the triadic line, the triadic line plays off against the sentence. The two establish a counterpoint, and interweave in every conceivable way. They begin together—"We lived . . ."—but then the sentence spills over the boundaries of the triadic line and must hurry to catch up—"with flowers. So that. . . ." Next, the sentence finishes one foot short of the triadic line; there is a strong pause, emphasized by the caesura, on the two short feet—"in hell. / Today . . . "—and then the melody begins to swell with the new triadic line, with the grave, slow poignancy of "I'm filled with the fading memory of those flowers. . . ."

What Williams does in "Asphodel" with the variable foot, the triadic line, and the sentence is an infinitely more complicated version of the pattern of self-sufficiencies and interdependencies he establishes with the metaphor of the flower in "Queen-Ann's Lace." The feet, the lines, the sentences: Each is like a small floweret of Queen Anne's lace, self-expressive and whole, yet dependent on its relation to all the others, just as the small branching flowerets merge and blend to form, first an orb, then a cluster, then a field of flowers. J. Hillis Miller writes of "Asphodel" that everything in it seems to happen simultaneously.[25] It is as if, when one begins to read the poem, a "sweet-scented flower" is poised, and as one reads, it opens, and opens, until by the end, to quote from "Queen-Ann's Lace," the whole field is a "white desire," a "pious wish to whiteness" (*CEP,* 210; *CP,* 162). Even the way the poem looks contributes to this effect: Without anxiety, without a need either to back up against the left-hand margin in defense against an encroaching emptiness or to give the illusion of defeating that emptiness by inking in the whiteness with great hewn blocks of speech, it opens itself up back and forth across the page. Filling the space, it composes the place. It seems drawn, as it were, with a free hand; it moves in its space *"at ease."*

Though it is true that everything in "Asphodel" seems to happen simultaneously, it is also true that as one reads it one is made aware of incessant change, one thing endlessly giving way to another. Like *Four Quartets,* "Asphodel, That Greeny Flower" gives the impression of ceaseless meditation; selfhood in it must be continually reenacted, continually won. Eliot seeks selfhood beyond the flux of experience; for him, true being inheres in the "point of intersection of the timeless / With time."[26] But Williams posits no still point; for him, selfhood *is* the fluid body of its experience. For Eliot, time must be made to reveal timelessness; for Williams, it must be made to reveal time*full*ness, the fullness of being in time. Just as the flower (and by extension the garden) becomes emblematic for the way in which "Asphodel" blossoms, all in a simultaneity, to fill up the space, so too the sea becomes emblematic for the way in which it moves in a stately measure to fill up the time. This effect of memory, thought, and speech as fluid and unceasing, as swirling, shifting, flowing, hesitating, building and breaking, playing freely but also always pressing forward, is the strongest effect of the triadic line. The poem covers the page like waves of the sea; and while it may be true, as some critics have suggested, that

Williams found this descending, stairstep line congenial in the time of his own descent,[27] still, the effect of the recurring pattern of lines, as of the sea, is not one of death alone but also one of eternal movement and continuity.

The flower (or garden) and the sea emblematize the spatial and temporal effects of Williams's triadic line; they are also two of the major symbols in the first three sections of "Asphodel, That Greeny Flower." (The other is the bomb, and in the "Coda" they are all subsumed in light.) Each has a rich history in Williams's poetry. He refers to flowers and uses metaphors of flowering many times, from the early "Portrait of a Lady," "The Flowers Alone," "The Locust Tree in Flower," or "Chicory and Daisies" (*CP*, 129, 365, 379, 65; *CEP*, 40, 90, 93, 122) to the flower-strewn fields of the Unicorn in *Paterson, V.* At least one early poem, "Flowers by the Sea," joins flowers and sea in a way that points toward the oppositions, metamorphoses, and complementarities of the two in "Asphodel":

> When over the flowery, sharp pasture's
> edge, unseen, the salt ocean
>
> lifts its form—chicory and daisies
> tied, released, seem hardly flowers alone
>
> but color and the movement—or the shape
> perhaps—of restlessness, whereas
>
> the sea is circled and sways
> peacefully upon its plantlike stem.
>   (*CP*, 378; *CEP*, 87)

Williams's references to the sea are less frequent though they are important, and include the early "The Sea-Elephant," "The Sea," and "There are no perfect waves," and the late "The Sound of Waves" and "The Birth of Venus" (*CP*, 341, 222, 292; *CEP*, 71, 275, 298; and *CLP*, 171, 189). What these poems share is the sense that, as "The Sea-Elephant" has it, love is "from the sea"; therefore, Williams's rejection of the sea at the end of *Paterson, IV* is at first glance surprising. Death, however, proves to be the problem.

At the end of *Paterson, IV,* Williams turns back from the sea; in what
was to be—until the addition of *Paterson, V*—the poem's final moment, the poet heads inland toward life, followed by a dog. Echoing
Whitman and Homer, he has described the sea as

>   Thalassa
> immaculata: our home, our nostalgic
> mother in whom the dead, enwombed again
> cry out to us to return   .
>   the blood dark sea.
>   (*P,* 202)

But he turns from it nonetheless. Partly, as critics have pointed out, he
turns back in this gesture from Europe, renouncing his own nostalgic
longing for the great "enwombed" dead who, like Homer himself, ex-
ert so strong a pull on the American artist.[28] Partly he turns back from
the "dream of / the whole poem . . ." (*P,* 200). And partly he turns
back from thoughts of death, toward a reassertion of struggle, shape,
identity. For all these reasons the turn seems entirely praiseworthy until one realizes how much anxiety there is in the rejection of the sea.
The poetic voice divides into a voice of passionate longing and a voice
of self-preservation, and again and again the second cuts across the
first, insisting, "The sea is *not* our home. . . . the hungry sea / is not
our home! . . . No! it is not our home. . . . It is NOT our home" (*P,*
201–2). It seems the ego is struggling desperately against a descent
into "losses / and regrets," against the desire to lay the self down, even
though it senses that surrender can lead to replenishment (*P,* 201).
"Turn back I warn you," the fearful voice cries out; turn back from
yourself as an image of pain,

> from the shark, that snaps
> at his own trailing guts, makes a sunset
> of the green water. . . .

But then another thought emerges, soothing and reassuring:

> lullaby, they say, the time sea is
> no more than sleep is   .   afloat
> with weeds, bearing seeds.
>
> (*P,* 200)

The conflict expressed in these passages is between two different no-
tions of identity. The first, threatened by the sea, seems dominated by
the ego and oriented toward control; in it, the self must be preserved
as a discrete and embattled entity. The second is paradoxical: Hunger
for the sea is indeed a hunger for death, but it is also a hunger for
wholeness and completeness which has nothing to do with the dream
of monumentalization, the "dream of the whole poem." "You will come
to it," the poet tells himself, "the blood dark sea." And with the subsequent line break, the tone suddenly shifts:

> . . . the blood dark sea
> of praise. You must come to it. Seed
> of Venus, you will return   .   to
> a girl standing upon a tilted shell, rose
> pink.
>
> (*P,* 202)

In a lovely accession of feeling, the image for the self becomes not shark
devouring itself but "Seed / of Venus." In touch with and quickened
by *eros,* it is both begetter and begotten of Beautiful Thing. As the
delicate modulations of the passage suggest, though, love depends on
death: To "return to a girl" the self must first of all "return." Then,
acknowledging the infinitude of the unknowable, acknowledging also
its own fragility, it finds itself buoyed up nonetheless, sustained by its
submission to the waters.

> The female principle of the world
>   is my appeal
>   in the extremity
> to which I have come . . . ,

Williams writes in a poem composed around the same time as *Paterson,
IV,* and "Asphodel, That Greeny Flower" ("For Eleanor and Bill

Monahan," *PB,* 86). But in *Paterson, IV,* he finally cannot overcome his terror of self-surrender, and hence of Venus in her guise as the Sirens. "The / song is in your / ears," he tells himself; therefore, "Put wax . . . in your / ears" (*P,* 201). Brave but doomed he turns inland to fight the good fight—and thereby enacts the divorce he has so deplored throughout the poem. Male turns from female, psyche from *anima,* lover from Venus; and if, as Joseph Riddel suggests,[29] the "blast" with which *Paterson, IV* closes is a blast of sperm from the body of its final protagonist, one "John Johnson," it seems to the point that John Johnson is being hanged for murder, that his seed goes nowhere, and that his death takes place on the dominant female landscape of *Paterson I* through *IV,* the appleblossomed slopes of Garrett Mountain.

"You must come to it. . . ." Williams comes to the sea sooner than he might have guessed, for his first attempt to write a sequel to *Paterson, IV* was, of course, the poem that became "Asphodel, That Greeny Flower."[30] He comes to it, furthermore, willingly. In "Asphodel," as in the lovely and largely neglected poem "The Birth of Venus" (*CLP,* 189–91),[31] it is not the fact of death, or even the longing for death, that is the enemy; Williams's sense in both poems is that repression numbs humans' ability to love and that, in their desperate attempts to revive feeling, they dedicate themselves increasingly to violence and destruction.[32] The bomb stands as sign and adequate symbol of this phenomenon in "Asphodel"; in "The Birth of Venus," it is the Second World War. "But why must we suffer / ourselves to be so torn to sense our world?" Williams asks in "The Birth of Venus":

> We do not have
> to die,
> in bitterness and the most excruciating torture, to feel! We
> can
> lean on the wall and experience an ecstasy of pain, if pain
> it must
> be, but a pain of love, of dismemberment if you will, but a
> pain
> of almond blossoms, an agony of mimosa trees in bloom, a
>
> scented cloud!

It is not that nature and *eros,* both represented by the sea, are free from violence and death, nor that such freedom would be desirable.[33] Just the opposite. But when *eros* has not been numbed, when the senses are quick, one does not need strong stimulants to summon up the presences of Venus and Dionysus. Even the little things—almond, cloud, mimosa—feed the awareness of beauty and the awareness of death which, as Wallace Stevens remarks, is the "mother of beauty."[34] Therefore, Williams concludes,

>   I wish we
>   might
> learn of an April of small waves—deadly as all slaughter,
>   that we
> shall die soon enough, to dream of April, not knowing why
>   we have been
> struck down, heedless of what greater violence.

"Asphodel" grows from this deeper sense of selfhood, rejected with so much disquietude in *Paterson, IV.* Now, instead of spelling annihilation,

>   The sea alone
> with its multiplicity
>   holds any hope.

The sea holds hope because it is a metaphor both for infinite depth and for inexhaustible desire. In an important and difficult passage from the second section of "Asphodel," Williams writes,

>   . . . if I have come from the sea
>   it is not to be
> wholly
>   fascinated by the glint of waves
>   The free interchange
> of light over their surface
>   which I have compared
>   to a garden

should not deceive us
      or prove
              too difficult a figure.
The poem
      if it reflects the sea
          reflects only
its dance
      upon that profound depth
          where
it seems to triumph.

He has been talking about the "deaths" he suffered at the hands of the "world's niggardliness," and has concluded, simply, "I was lost / failing the poem." That is to say, the poem saves him, but only if he serves it well; they are reciprocally dependent. To serve and take his identity from the measures that incarnate Beautiful Thing is to "come from the sea," and differentiates the poet from the landlocked with whose living death he has been surrounded. But he acknowledges too that his measures can catch only the "glint of waves," the "free interchange / of light over their surface." A poem can be likened to a garden; language can be described as flowering, and flowering as dancing, for the play of language, the dance, and the garden flowering all form roughly horizontal patterns, like the glint of light on waves. A poem, however, cannot be likened to the sea; though language can be borne up by and can bear witness to the presence of "profound depth," it cannot reveal it directly, just as the surface of the water cannot reveal the depths directly, since the depths become surface once they surface. Language can imply but cannot plumb either the depths of nature or the depths of the mind. The poem, therefore, only "seems to triumph." The thought may be bleak, but it may also be sustaining; it confirms human contingency, but it also gives limitless depth to existence. It gives as well a sense of both terror and safety. Discussing the oceanic feeling in *Civilization and Its Discontents,* Freud quotes from Christian Dietrich Grabbe, "We cannot fall out of the world. We are in it once and for all."[35] Or, as Stein says to Marlow in Conrad's *Lord Jim,* "A man that is born falls into a dream like a man who falls into the sea. If he tries to climb out into the air as inexperienced people endeavour to do, he drowns—*nicht wahr?* . . . No! I tell you! The way is to the destructive element submit yourself, and with the exertions of your hands and feet in the water make the deep, deep sea keep you up."[36] Turning inland in *Paterson, IV* was like trying to climb out. With "Asphodel," Williams submits himself. He does not fail the poem, and the poem, in turn, does not fail him. Sustained by the deep, deep sea, it becomes both swimmer and the waves that hold him—both self and the site of its preservation in autobiography.

Primarily, though, the sea in "Asphodel" is a metaphor not of depth but of desire. "The sea! The sea!" Williams writes,

> Always
> > when I think of the sea
> there comes to mind
> > the *Iliad*
> > > and Helen's public fault
> that bred it.

"Helen's public fault," in Williams's mythopoeia, is the original act of "stealing" and sexual transgression that ruptured a state of order and wholeness and gave birth to art, to consciousness and longing, to the poet's song of love, deceit, and war:

> Were it not for that
> > there would have been
> no poem but the world. . . .

The sea is the realm of this transgression, and plays off against the garden, the realm of marriage. In the first two sections of "Asphodel" they divide much of human experience between them, and each accrues intense symbolic significance. "Asphodel" begins as a celebration of marriage and a poem of the garden; Williams's memories range for several pages over a life "filled, / if you will, / with flowers," and he seeks to bring, "reawakened, / a memory of those flowers" to his wife. As a boy he kept a book of pressed flowers; now, though the sweetness and color of them have long been gone, they retain—and here the metaphor shifts, suddenly, to what remains of sexual passion in this forty-year-long marriage—they retain

>   . . . a curious odor,
>   a moral odor,
>   that brings me
>   near to you.

That, in turn, leads to memories of the time when odor and color were new, and thoughts of courtship culminate with an image of sensual wealth in the consummation of marriage:

>   There had come to me
>   a challenge,
>   your dear self,
>   mortal as I was,
>   the lily's throat
>   to the hummingbird!
>   Endless wealth,
>   I thought,
>   held out its arms to me.
>   A thousand topics
>   in an apple blossom.
>   The generous earth itself
>   gave us lief.
>   The whole world
>   became my garden!

And then, ominous, beautiful,

>   But the sea
>   which no one tends
>   is also a garden. . . .

Marriage, which an instant before seemed fulfillment, now seems closure. Fulfillment itself seems closure. And all the little rituals—the gardening, the tending—seem pathetic and self-conscious when set against the wild, vast sea. "I have seen it / and so have you," Williams says to Flossie, "when it puts all flowers / to shame."[37] If the garden is closed, the sea is open. If the garden is stasis, the sea is change. Life in the garden is rooted and orderly, lawful, nurturant, bonded; life on the sea is wandering, guilty, lawless, careless, and free. Marriage, which was supposed to be the finest flower of life, becomes instead a type of death, if it marks the end of the story, the assumption of final, permanent, and promissory feelings and identity.[38]

This is not, of course, all there is to marriage, nor to Williams's handling of garden imagery in "Asphodel, That Greeny Flower," one of the few great love poems in English written not for a mistress but for a wife. The fact remains, however, that the sea and what it symbolizes rescue the poem from premature closure; for good or ill, Williams's poem in celebration of marriage quickly encounters the problem of desire. Nor does it ever resolve it. In a way, the poem does transcend the problem of desire, for both sea and garden represent types of love, and their opposition fades beside the greater opposition which pits love against the bomb:

> There is no power
> so great as love
> which is a sea
> which is a garden—
> . . . . .
> Few men believe that
> nor in the games of children.
> They believe rather
> in the bomb
> and shall die by
> the bomb.

But the magnitude of the second conflict does not cancel the painfulness of the first. As Paul Mariani writes, thinking specifically of Williams's relations with Flossie, "Williams's life . . . was both a vindication and a personal tragedy."[39] In the soaring, affirmative strains of the "Coda," it is easy—but mistaken—to forget the tragedy.

Relations between a man and a woman are always a "riddle," as

Williams says, both to themselves and to any outsider (*P,* 106). And I do not want to intrude on the delicate ground that was a marriage. Within "Asphodel" itself, however, a certain failure of imagination occurs in Williams's conception of marriage and of Flossie. In his handling, the story of Helen of Troy resembles that of the Fall from Eden, in that it becomes an initial act, a radical beginning, a plunge into consciousness, guilt, and death, and, since it issues in beauty and art, a *felix culpa.* There is one difference, though, that goes right to the heart of Williams's poetry: In the story of Eden, the act of sexual transgression takes place within the circle of marriage, whereas in the story of Helen it takes place as a breach of the marriage contract. Williams has his myth of the garden, in the myth of Demeter and Persephone, or Kore: and it may seem preposterous to fault him for *not* conceiving of Flossie as sexually guilty, like Eve; but what Eve offers, as Demeter and Persephone do not, is an image of woman, married and faithful, but nonetheless sexually aggressive and sexually tempting. The man Eve seduces is, after all, her husband. Demeter is mateless, the Mother, and Persephone, in the configuration so dear not only to Williams but to some of his male critics, is the "Virgin" who is "whored."[40] Williams refers at one point to a woman within himself.[41] As a figure for the *anima,* the inner female ground to which the male aspects of the psyche descend for their completion, and as a figure for the "radiant gist" or "Beautiful Thing" which the imagination discovers and releases in its penetration of reality, the Kore (or "core")[42] that so dominates Williams's writings is both moving and fruitful. As a figure for actual women, in the way he conceives of Kore, it is very problematic. For one thing, it makes a woman's sexual maturity seem a degradation rather than a fulfillment of nature; to lose her virginity is, in this view, to be whored. For another, it makes the woman entirely passive; she is made, she is changed, and the man, be he Pan or Pluto, remains essentially unchanged but does the making and the changing.[43] Then too, *pace* Freud, the man does not desire the Demeter, the Mother, and he desires the Virgin only once. Then, once she is "whored," he refreshes his desire for her (if he has married her) by seeking out unconquered fields. Williams refers to this pattern obliquely when he writes, to Flossie,

I cannot say
> that I have gone to hell
>> for your love

but often
> found myself there
>> in your pursuit.

I do not like it
> and wanted to be
>> in heaven. Hear me out.

And in an essay from the 1930s, "The Basis of Faith in Art," he asks his brother, "Did it ever occur to you that a marriage might be invigorated by deliberately breaking the vows?" "That is impossible," his brother says. He replies, simply, "Nothing is impossible to the imagination" (*SE,* 188).

In "Asphodel" the configuration I have been describing receives its clearest exposition in the last few pages of Book I. Williams has been speaking of the sea, the *Iliad,* and "Helen's public fault"; his thought reaches a momentary conclusion with the lines I have already quoted: "The sea alone / with its multiplicity / holds any hope." He turns then to consider his own immediate condition—the strokes, the mental illness, the estrangement from Flossie, all of which are suggested by "the storm." This time it

has proven abortive
> but we remain
>> after the thoughts it roused

to
> re-cement our lives.

In the lines which follow, he acknowledges the need to rediscover a sense of fruitfulness, of harmony and order:

> It is the mind

the mind
> that must be cured

> short of death's
>
> intervention,
>
> and the will becomes again
>
> a garden.

The lines are both universal in their recognition that, as Williams later writes, "The measure itself / has been lost," and intensely personal. In order to re-cement his own life, he must find common ground with Flossie; he must explain himself truly to her and gain her understanding; and—as in *A Dream of Love*—he cannot do this by falsifying the problem of desire. At one point in *A Dream of Love,* Myra asks Doc, referring to his death *in flagrante delicto* with Dotty Randall, "Suppose you had found me in such a position?" "You couldn't be in such a position," he replies. "You've got *me!*" (*DL,* 209). Now, in "Asphodel," he is a great deal more gracious:

> All women are not Helen,
>
> I know that,
>
> but have Helen in their hearts.
>
> My sweet,
>
> you have it also, therefore
>
> I love you
>
> and could not love you otherwise.

These lines constitute a gallant (and courageous) tribute to Flossie's autonomous sexuality. The lines that immediately follow, however, cast them in a rather different light:

> Imagine you saw
>
> a field made up of women
>
> all silver-white.
>
> What should you do
>
> but love them?

To acknowledge Flossie's desire now seems less a tribute to her than a plea for her imagined complicity. "The storm" seems now to contract, to refer simply to any given act of illicit passion—"The storm bursts /

or fades!"—and there is truth but also callousness in Williams's next remark: "it is not / the end of the world."

In the passage that follows, the poem again turns graciously toward Flossie:

> Love is something else,
> > or so I thought it,
> a garden which expands,
> > though I knew you as a woman
> > > and never thought otherwise,
> until the whole sea
> > has been taken up
> > > and all its gardens.
> It was the love of love,
> > the love that swallows up all else,
> > > a grateful love,
> a love of nature, of people,
> > animals,
> > > a love engendering
> gentleness and goodness
> > that moved me
> > > and *that* I saw in you.

The tribute is so generous, and the *caritas* of which Williams speaks is so fine and rare a thing, that one feels like a boor for noticing that the woman being described no longer resembles Helen. She has become Demeter—nurturant, maternal—and though she sounds wonderful, she does not sound exciting. One *would* feel like a boor, that is, except that Williams beats one to it. In lines which may register a legitimate complaint, but which seem both cruel and churlish, he takes a shot at Flossie's virginity and goodness:

> I should have known
> > though I did not
> > > that the lily-of-the-valley
> is a flower makes many ill
> > who whiff it.

This is nasty but all too human. It shows clearly the price the split into virgin and whore exacts from a man as well as a woman. "You make me sick," it is a fancy way of saying, "for being better than I was, for making me worse than you."

Williams's final formulation of the interdependency between marriage and adultery takes place near the end of Book I. "You understand," he tells Flossie,

> I had to meet you
>   after the event
> and have still to meet you.
>   Love
>   to which you too shall bow
>   along with me—
>   a flower
>   a weakest flower
> shall be our trust
>   and not because
>   we are too feeble
> to do otherwise
>   but because
>   at the height of my power
> I risked what I had to do,
>   therefore to prove
>   that we love each other
> while my very bones sweated
>   that I could not cry to you
>   in the act.

But what does this actually mean? What, specifically, is the significance of the second "because"?—"We shall trust love, not because we are old and weak, but because I committed adultery"? If there is logic here, it is a bleak and bitter logic. Adultery may have kept the marriage alive, periodic escapes to the sea may have alleviated claustrophobia and stagnation in the garden, but how does the very act of betrayal "prove / that we love each other"? And if his "very bones" were sweating—if it was truly Flossie whose name he wanted to call—why didn't he just go home?

"Heart-mysteries there," as Yeats remarks.[44] Conjecture leads off indefinitely, into the realm of repressions, compulsions, fears, idealizations, temperamental disinclinations, and yet remains only conjecture. One thing is certain, though: Asphodel does grow in hell. Book I comes through enormous pain to end on a note of faith, for though the life may not always have proven the love (no matter what Williams wants to argue), living the life led to writing the poem, and writing the poem does.

Book I ends by referring to the "news" to be found in "despised poems," and insists,

> It is difficult
> to get the news from poems
>   yet men die miserably every day
>   for lack
> of what is found there.

That asphodel grows in hell is part of the "news." This world, this life, is all we need of hell, and yet it is our "palpable Elysium."[45]

> Of asphodel, that greeny flower,
>   I come, my sweet,
>   to sing to you!

The conflicts are never resolved, the ambivalence and confusion are never completely cleared, the pain is never completely healed. But something can be made to flower. Even in hell, the asphodel is "greeny."

Williams's theme in Book II of "Asphodel" is death, and, as he fears, the death of love. The bomb becomes his dominant symbol; his antithesis is not between two types of love, represented by the garden and the sea, but between *thanatos* and *eros,* represented by the bomb and the poem. As is true throughout "Asphodel," Williams's musings have both personal and broadly cultural implications; his desire to "know,

what I have to know / about my own death" leads him both to a recon-
sideration of the "pinnacles" and "deaths" of his own life and to a confrontation with the problem of evil.

In "Asphodel," Williams seems unable to decide whether repression
is the product of the death wish, or the death wish the product of
repression. Like the question of the chicken and the egg, this question
may be impossible to answer. Nor does it entirely matter. But "Asphodel" arises from a very strong desire to synthesize and unify experience;
Williams's sense of selfhood seems to depend, here, upon his ability to
bring the disparate facts of his existence into a coherent vision of the
nature of life, death, and love. So strong is the impulse toward union
that, by the "Coda," Williams can write, "Only the imagination is real!
I have declared it / time without end," and by the end of Book III he
can speak of facts, flowers, and poems as "interchangeable," and aver
that "love / rules them all." But then what about the bomb? In a stun-
ning image, Williams declares that "the bomb / also / is a flower." But
if the bomb is a flower ("dedicated / howbeit / to our destruction"),
then—to follow the metaphor—it must spring from the black earth of
the unconscious just as surely as the poem does. There must be an
instinct for death as well as an instinct for love and life; as Freud reluctantly concludes in *Beyond the Pleasure Principle*,[46] the will to destruction and closure must be innate, rather than simply a secondary reac-
tion to repression. In this case, it is difficult to see how love rules all.

Thanatos may be innate, but so is *eros,* and for human history to
have arrived at the point of its own annihilation bespeaks a gradual and
terrible imbalance between the forces of death and love. Here Williams
comes down firmly against repression. The death instinct and repression go hand in hand; each magnifies and intensifies the other. "All
suppressions," Williams writes,

> from the witchcraft trials at Salem
>   to the latest
>   book burnings
> are confessions
>   that the bomb
>   has entered our lives. . . .

One thing that is repressed, of course, is *eros*. Paradoxically, though, the repression that leads to the triumph of *thanatos,* in which "The bomb speaks" but "We come to our deaths in silence," includes *thanatos* as well. We deny our awareness of the death wish even as it operates within us, and so give it increased power over us. As Jung writes in "Aion," an essay contemporaneous with "Asphodel," "when an inner situation is not made conscious, it happens outside, as fate. That is to say, when the individual remains undivided and does not become conscious of his inner contradictions, the world must perforce act out the conflict."[47] This seems a fair description of the typical modern attitude toward the psyche, and of the effect it has had on the world. "If you bring forth what is within you," Jesus says in one of the Gnostic gospels, "what you bring forth will save you. If you do not bring forth what is within you, what you do not bring forth will destroy you."[48] Repressing both love and death, we grow numb, and, as Williams says, silent. Love and death do not vanish, though; they come back at us in monstrous guise, as the world acts out the conflicts each individual has denied.

What Susan Griffin writes of the pornographic imagination in *Pornography and Silence*[49] pursues a similar line of thinking into the twisted passages of sadomasochistic sexuality. The man who tortures a woman, she argues, tortures a displaced image of his own body—and does so both because he has learned to loathe and fear it, so that he wants to destroy it, and because his numbness has grown so great that only thus can he feel it. The wish for pain and death becomes inextricably mingled with, and bears its own dark witness to, the wish for health and love. Griffin's argument reminds me of a passage from Williams's *Great American Novel,* which in turn seems central to his understanding, in "Asphodel," of the kinship as well as opposition between the poem and the bomb: "The imagination will not down. If it is not a dance, a song, it becomes an outcry. If it is not flamboyance, it becomes deformity; if it is not art, it becomes crime" (*GAN,* 200). But the conditions of modern life numb the imagination, making both love and death increasingly remote from us. The bomb, the agent of our destruction, becomes our last, most desperate creation. We worship it, we fall in love with it, for it both feeds our hunger for horror and assures us that we will die—and this we long to know for it is true, and something in us seeks the truth, no matter how we twist it or deny it.[50] The bomb gives us, as well, a sense of enormous power; as long as we can wield such weapons, we are not already dead. We play both roles in our relations with the bomb: both "male" and "female," sadist and masochist, aggressor and victim. And death gives us back the image of ourself, in what is at once the dance of Kali and the ultimate pornographic scenario:

> The mere picture
> > of the exploding bomb
> fascinates us
> > so that we cannot wait
> > > to prostrate ourselves
> before it.

Why must be come to this anguish? Williams's answer is simple: "We do not believe / that love / can so wreck our lives."

Like pornography, the bomb promises a quick trip. But as long as the urge toward life remains, its ecstasies soon grow stale:

> we are sick to death
> > of the bomb
> and its childlike
> > insistence.
> > > Death is no answer,
> no answer—
> > to a blind old man
> > > whose bones
> have the movement
> > of the sea,
> > > a sexless old man
> for whom it is a sea
> > of which his verses
> > > are made up.

Against death there is only life, and life not as a fine abstraction but as what William Blake has called "minute particulars,"[51] and Wallace

Stevens, "the particulars of rapture."[52] In Book II of "Asphodel," Williams does not simply talk about, but *enacts,* the process of pitting life against death, finding, shaping, and articulating the particulars the love for which alone defuses the bomb.[53] Book II begins in vagueness; the poem must figure out the implications of death, but even as he tries to formulate his ideas, forgetfulness and confusion, the harbingers of death itself, seem to be gaining the ascendancy:

> Approaching death,
>   as we think, the death of love,
>   no distinction
> any more suffices to differentiate
>   the particulars
>   of place and condition
> with which we have long been
>   familiar.
>   All appears
> as if seen
>   wavering through water.
>   We start awake with a cry
> of recognition
>   but soon the outlines
>   become again vague.

"No ideas but in things." But what if things fail? What if memory and sight both vanish?

As so often in Williams's writings, though, what threatens closure can be made to yield openness. The known categories, the habitual modes of thought, begin to release their hold on the mind, and either death or a descent to origins and a radical new beginning may follow. This time, the latter occurs. This, I believe, is the connection between the lines I have just quoted and the lines that follow:

> If we are to understand our time,
>   we must find the key to it,
>   not in the eighteenth
> and nineteenth centuries,

                    but in earlier, wilder,
                         and darker epochs   .

Not just the poet himself, but the whole of modern life, seems to be
approaching death and "the death of love." The key to the end lies in
the beginning; to understand the present in its monstrosity, we must
dig back through time, culture, and thought to the savage, instinctual
level where life begins. "The earth is black and it is there," Williams
writes in connection with human sacrifice in "The Destruction of Ten-
ochtitlan." "Only art advances" (*IAG,* 34). Now, in "Asphodel," he
points back beyond Romanticism and the Age of Reason to some un-
specified time, like ours in darkness and violence, but unlike ours in
that it had a creative immediacy which we seem to have lost. We must
consequently trace love and death back beyond the roots of their per-
version. We must descend to earth; it is the ground from which we
spring.
    Williams writes,

            So to know, what I have to know
                 about my own death,
                      if it be real,
        I have to take it apart.

Immediately thereafter, he makes what seems an arbitrary leap and
recalls asking a nameless young artist, "What does your generation
think / of Cézanne?" In fact, though, the need for descent, the taking
apart of death, and the mention of Cézanne are intimately connected.
In *Spring and All,* Williams laments the staleness of the present age,
and describes its art as "a plagiarism of nature," as "prose painting,
representative work, clever as may be in revealing new phases of emotional research presented on the surface" (*SA,* 111, 134). This is the
art that serves death, for it stems from a reductive and confining view
of reality. Williams contrasts it with the art of "certain of the primitives" and of Cézanne, which manifests a "realism . . . of the imagination" (*SA,* 111). This art is not lost to us, even now: "the primitives
are not back in some remote age—they are not BEHIND experience.
Work which bridges the gap between the rigidities of vulgar experi-

ence and the imagination is rare. It is new, immediate—It is so because it is actual, always real. It is experience dynamized into reality" (*SA*, 134). It seems, then, that when Williams says we must find the key to our time in "earlier, wilder / and darker epochs," he is both espousing a myth of history and—paradoxically—describing a movement which is perennially possible in the present. This is the importance of Cézanne.

Williams does not discuss Cézanne in much detail, but a writer with whom he shares many ideas, D. H. Lawrence, does, in "Introduction to These Paintings." What Lawrence writes in this essay develops Williams's line of thinking in *Spring and All,* and offers eloquent reason for Cézanne's presence in "Asphodel." According to Lawrence, Cézanne struggled all his life with the cliché. When he painted a woman or an apple, he fought against the fact that, in the present age, "We don't live in the flesh. Our instincts and intuitions are dead, we live wound round with the winding-sheet of abstractions."[54] He fought to surrender himself to the thing he painted, to feel and release the "appleyness" of an apple, to discover

> something that was neither optical nor mechanical nor intellectual.
>
> . . . . .
>
> He wanted to touch the world of substance once more with the intuitive touch, to be aware of it with the intuitive awareness, and to express it in intuitive terms. That is, he wished to displace our present mode of mental-visual consciousness, the consciousness of mental concepts, and substitute a mode of consciousness that was predominantly intuitive, the awareness of touch. In the past the primitives painted intuitively, but *in the direction* of our present mental-visual, conceptual form of consciousness. They were working away from their own intuition.[55]

Cézanne struggled to reverse this process, to recapture what Williams calls the "actual," "experience dynamized into reality." Therefore, Lawrence concludes, Cézanne was a "pure revolutionary," whose "apple rolled the stone from the mouth of the tomb."[56]

For these reasons, Cézanne presides over Book II of "Asphodel"; the painter who so influenced the Cubists (among them Williams's favorite, Juan Gris) serves as tutelary genius in Williams's dismantling of his own death into its constituent planes and pieces. To "take apart" his own death and find out "if it be real," Williams struggles against abstractions and preconceptions to discover the actual shape of his life—for death in itself is unimaginable; it becomes real or unreal only if a specific being dies.[57] What he finds, in this telling of the self, are "pinnacles" and "deaths." The pinnacles are all revelations like the "appleyness" of an apple, momentary glimpses of Beautiful Thing. As he turns his mind to the past, Williams recalls the Jungfrau shining white with virgin snow after four days of steady rain, on his trip with Flossie to Switzerland in 1924, and the gypsy girl appearing like a mirage in the overpowering heat to lead him, lost, down the "new path" from the Alhambra, on his bachelor trip to Granada in 1910. He recalls as well the "broken / pieces of a green / bottle" gleaming among cinders between "the back wings / of the hospital where / nothing / will grow," and the "scalloped curtains" blowing in upon the gaily flowered, brightly static wallpaper, billowing wild and fresh and windy "to / the sound of rain." Both life and art have redeemed him at random moments; the first two memories, of course, are of things that happened to Williams, while the second two refer to poems he made (*CP,* 453, 285; *CEP,* 343, 345).

Over and against the bomb, the fact and symbol of closure, Williams sets these moments of sudden, joyful, unexpected opening; and over and against those who lie down to the bomb, he sets those who—to echo Lawrence—have tried to roll the stone from the mouth of the tomb. The hanging of witches at Salem, the burning of books under Hitler, the burning of "priceless Goyas" with the connivance of Juan Perón: The everlasting flames give tongue to oppression and denial. But the past offers heroes as well: Homer, Cézanne, Columbus, Darwin. Homer sang of a Fall, Cézanne fought to paint an apple untouched by a Fall; these seem opposites at first, but are more truly two sides of a single desire to cherish the world's body. Columbus opened space, and Darwin, time; each thereby decentered the universe, set us wandering, and declared this world the only site of meaning.[58] Each opened his eyes, that is to say, to what was there already: "a new world," as Williams remarks in his brief remarks on Cézanne, a world where "one has freedom of movement and newness" (*SA*, 134).

Book II of "Asphodel" ends on a muted note. The artists and explorers may open "our eyes / to the gardens of the world," kindle our minds, and set us dancing "to a measure, / a new measure!" But soon enough, perennially, the world's avarice, hatred, and fear cause the garden to be despoiled and the measure to be lost. Columbus's fate governs ours, as Americans, and typifies ours, as humans. "How the world opened its eyes!" Williams writes, of the voyage

> with which I myself am so deeply concerned,
>   that of the *Pinta,*
>   the *Niña*
>   and the *Santa Maria.*
>
>   . . . . .
>   It was a flower
>   upon which April
>   had descended from the skies!
>   How bitter
>   a disappointment!

Both in American history, and recurrently, with human dreams, the glad cries of "*Nuevo Mundo!*" all too soon become, "America is lost. Ah Christ, Ah Christ that night should come so soon" (*GAN*, 181, 209).

American history has devolved from Columbus to the Rosenbergs, electrocuted for espionage even as Williams was working on "Asphodel." Their guilt has never been absolutely proved, but they remain powerful figures nonetheless for those whose lives are pervaded by death, whose faces confront one in the papers as marked for death, who give themselves over to governments in their wielding of death, and who go to death in silence under the shadow of the bomb. The Rosenbergs are one of two married couples mentioned in "Asphodel"; the Williamses are the other. Near the end of this section of "Asphodel," Williams remembers some of his own life's minute particulars:

> You know how we treasured
>   the few paintings

> we still cling to
>   especially the one
>   by the dead
> Charlie Demuth.
>   With your smiles
>   and other trivia of the sort
> my secret life
>   has been made up,
>   some baby's life
> which had been lost
>   had I not intervened.

Against death, Williams sets art. Against death, he sets skill and touch and dailiness and compassion. The section ends with his lament for the loss of poetic inspiration, but though he says there has "come an end" to the words that "came to me / out of the air," "Asphodel" itself is proof that the words and the "single image," Beautiful Thing "that I adore," still continue. "The end / will come / in its time," for death is real. But if life can be lived for life, then death can come in the fullness of time, rather than collapsing and devouring time. And for Williams, still at work on "Asphodel," it is not yet time.

Book III begins in the "winter's harshness" of an endangered marriage. Williams's past infidelities and the strain on Flossie of listening, years after the fact, to confessions of those infidelities have made "the death of love" a threat, if not already a reality.

>   Having your love
>   I was rich.
>   Thinking to have lost it
>   I am tortured
>   and cannot rest.

In Book II he has considered death—both the fact of his own impending death and the desire for death that plays so large a part in human history. Against death, he has asserted life in its minute particulars, especially the "trivia" of his marriage to Flossie. If these are to have any meaning, though, they must blossom from and bear witness to "love, abiding love." Book III is Williams's plea for forgiveness for having damaged that love. "What has been done / can be undone," he insists to Flossie; "love's year," like the natural year, can open out of winter into springtime, "if we can but find / the secret word / to transform it." Finding the secret word becomes his task, now, in "Asphodel." He has done the damage and he must work the magic, for, as he says to Flossie, "our hearts / gasp dying / for want of love."

Like Book I, this section reveals a man who is capable of striking the wrong note in his attempts at self-presentation. Something of the sort occurs near the beginning of it: Williams tells Flossie that he does not approach her "abjectly, / with confessions of my faults," for he has already confessed them, but though one can understand his desire not to cringe, it seems a bit premature to announce that he comes "proudly / as to an equal / to be forgiven." But the most notable example occurs later on, and indicates a defensive shift away from vulnerability such as also takes place in Book I. Williams refers first to the lines I have just quoted about being proud:

> I spoke hurriedly
> > in the spell
> of some wry impulse
> > when I boasted
> > > that there was
> any pride left in me.
> > Do not believe it.

Then he reconsiders:

> > > Unless
> in a special way,
> > a way I shrink to speak of
> > > I am proud.

He is in a delicate position. Without her love he is lost, and he knows it. Yet for both their sakes he must continue to believe in his own worth; he must not simply succumb to broken apologies. The way to

resolve the conflict, however, is *not* to do what he does when he says to
Flossie,

>   I call on you
>   as I do on myself the same
>   to forgive all women
>   who have offended you.
>   It is the artist's failing
>   to seek and to yield
>   such forgiveness.

It may be the "artist's failing / to seek and to yield / . . . forgiveness,"
but it is cowardly to seek this particular kind. He was, after all, *there,*
helping those women offend Flossie. It is not his place to forgive them,
nor do they owe him an apology. "It will cure us both," he goes on to
say, but I do not see how. If there is to be a cure, it must come from a
truthful presentation of the self, for what is not honestly confronted
cannot be transformed—and Williams was certainly not just the victim
of those women's offensive sexuality.

Mostly, however, Book III moves with a wonderful sensitivity and
tact. The myth of Orpheus and Eurydice underlies it. The question
confronting Williams is whether, in this time of desolation, he will be
able to move Flossie to forgive him. She has gone dead to him; she is
in her own cold hell of hurt and grief; and now he who put her there
must summon song to lead her back. In Book I, he has written,

>   I cannot say
>   that I have gone to hell
>   for your love
>   but often
>   found myself there
>   in your pursuit. . . .

In Book III, he finally does go all the way to hell for her love. "I am
tortured / and cannot rest"; "I spoke hurriedly / . . . when I boasted /
that there was / any pride left in me": Though Williams then shies

away from such admissions, the fact that he makes them at all gives this poem a rare emotional nakedness and vulnerability.

Delicately, this Orpheus does not turn to look at his Eurydice as he sings her back to earth. Instead he talks about men and male desire, for her forgiveness must be based on understanding. He explains himself by means of archetypal images, giving

> . . . the steps
>> if it may be
> by which you shall mount,
>> again to think well
>>> of me.

The image of steps suggests a hierarchy, from base to sublime manifestations of desire, but what follows is more truly a nonhierarchical dialectic, for Williams wants to lead Flossie not from brute to angel, but from winter into spring, both of them of the earth, within the realm of the simply human.[59] Phallic power and energy characterize the first figures he offers for her contemplation:

> The statue
>> of Colleoni's horse
>>> with the thickset little man
> on top
>> in armor
>>> presenting a naked sword . . . ,

and

> the horse rampant
>> roused by the mare in
>>> the Venus and Adonis.

These are figures of presence, of the animal or the centaurlike man acting in possession of his body.[60] Williams calls them "pictures / of crude force," but they are not negative images so much as images of a simplicity impossible, except at moments, to those who are not, in

Schiller's sense, "naive."[61] They are followed by the brief but haunting anecdote involving Williams's friend, the homosexual painter Marsden Hartley:

> Once at night
> waiting at a station
> with a friend
> a fast freight
> thundered through
> kicking up the dust.
> My friend,
> a distinguished artist,
> turned with me
> to protect his eyes.
> That's what we'd all like to be, Bill,
> he said. I smiled
> knowing how deeply
> he meant it.

Hartley was a man of absence and longing, "a tragic figure," "one of the most frustrated men I knew" (*A,* 171). Tormented by the ability to recognize and respond to power that he did not embody or could not directly express, Hartley painted "bursting shells" that seemed to predict World War I, "colored stars and flaming globes scattered over violent skies" (*A,* 170). In the *Autobiography,* Williams describes Hartley's bed, on the other side of a paper-thin wall from the bed of two noisy lovers. "I, too, had to reject him," Williams writes. "Everyone rejected him. I was no better than the others" (*A,* 173). Hartley emerges in Williams's writing not as weak, but as blocked and stymied, and as a "sentimental" rather than a "naive" artist.[62] In both the *Autobiography* and the published version of "Asphodel," Williams takes Hartley's statement about the train at face value, but in a manuscript of "Asphodel," Williams has written, not, "I smiled / knowing how deeply / he meant it," but, "I smiled / knowing how *little* / he meant it" (*YALC,* emphasis mine). With his longing for power and his ambivalence toward power, he is a type of the artist and one of several alter-egos for Williams—who, like Hartley, admires, thrills to, and envies, but would never consent to be, a train, a stallion, or even the *condottiere* Colleoni.

The statue and the stallion cannot speak, whereas Hartley—who remains unnamed and undescribed in "Asphodel"—is nothing but his speech. Encompassing both is the man on the subway whom Williams next describes. Neither stone nor beast, he could speak, but does not. Though Williams feels impelled to address him—"Speak to him, I cried. He / will know the secret"—he makes no effort to do so, and the man on the subway gets off, the encounter having taken place in silence.

But what is the nature of this encounter? Why, of all the faces Williams sees, should this one be unforgettable, swimming into his ken with the strange familiarity of a long-lost face in a dream? Part of this man's power lies in his ambiguity. It is hard to tell, for instance, what race he is; his skin is darker than his "brown felt hat," yet Williams specifies that his beard is black, which, if *he* were Black, would be a redundant specification. It is also hard to tell what social class he belongs to, with his "good / if somewhat worn" and "recently polished" shoes, his "heavy and very dirty / undershirt," and his "brown socks / . . . about his ankles." He is dirty enough to remind one of the earthliness of the body, careful enough of his appearance to seem dignified and willing to please. His eyes are "evasive, mild," his demeanor is gentle, yet the "worn knobbed stick / between his knees" and the "worn leather zipper case / bulging with its contents" that lies "between his ankles" associate him powerfully with male sexuality, with Pan.[63] He is local yet like an "exotic orchid / that Herman Melville had admired / in the / Hawaiian jungle," civilized yet primitive, contemporary yet ancient and ageless. He reminds Williams

> of men who left their marks
> by torchlight,
> rituals of the hunt,
> on the walls
> of prehistoric
> caves in the Pyrenees . . .

and he seems a figure from those "earlier, wilder / and darker epochs" which, as Williams has said, offer a key to our time. He reminds

Williams also of his own father, but of a father that Williams never knew, young enough to be his son:

> When my father was a young man—
>   it came to me
>   from an old photograph—
>   he wore such a beard.

At this point, categories break down; individual identity reveals the archetypal, the eternal. Briefly, time and death are abrogated, and the child and father merge to form the man:

>   This man
>   reminds me of my father.
>   I am looking
>   into my father's
>   face! Some surface
>   of some advertising sign
>   is acting
>   as a reflector. It is
>   my own.

The man on the subway enters and departs from Williams's life.

>   With him
>   went all men
>   and all women too
>   were in his loins.

He is the seed, the secret, *potentia*. Words and phrases accrue to him as one tries to say what he is: our first father, the word within the word, the great god Pan. Yet there he sits, silent and self-contained, forever surpassing the words by which one calls him.

The figure who next appears is both "all women"[64] and one particular, ordinary woman, just as the figure on the subway was both "all men" and one particular, ordinary man. The poem turns to focus now on Flossie, who seems to coalesce, conjured by love, in our field of vision. "It is winter," Williams writes,

> and there
> > waiting for you to care for them
> are your plants.
> > Poor things! you say
> > > as you compassionately
> pour at their roots
> > the reviving water.

Like the man on the subway, Flossie appears quietly but suddenly from nowhere. Desire creates her; first the plants need her, and then she is there, knowing just how to care for them. She moves with a luminous otherness; her actions are ordinary, and yet they are performed in such an attentive stillness that they seem dancelike or hierophantic. The season is winter still, but Flossie's solicitude hints that she has begun to thaw. Her gesture seems a sign directed at Williams, whose own desire he has projected on to the plants—a love sign that she may be wooed into spring's renewal. So, at least, he interprets it:

> > Lean-cheeked
> I say to myself
> > kindness moves her
> > > shall she not be kind
> also to me? At this
> > courage possessed me finally
> > > to go on.

Time, this poem, her own love have all helped to transform her from Eurydice to Demeter. "Sweet, creep into my arms," he implores. Presumably, she does so, for her forgiveness soon follows.

Williams's Orphic endeavor has been to move Flossie, to bring her out of death and make her new, but such an endeavor cannot be entirely free from projection and coercion, even though, ideally, "poetry does not tamper with the world but moves it" (*SA*, 149). In Book I, Williams writes,

> I speak in figures,
>   well enough, the dresses
> you wear are figures also,
>   we could not meet
>   otherwise.

But the poem he writes is infinitely more expressive than the dresses she wears, and he can pretend to represent her—or *believe* he represents her—in a way that she cannot pretend to represent him. There is no way of ascertaining the extent to which his image of Flossie corresponded to her actual feelings. Within the poem, furthermore, we do not see her forgive him, but are told that she has done so; she never does speak of herself. Simply put, "Asphodel" is Williams's, not Flossie's, autobiography.

If Book III is to be convincing, then, one must imagine when and why Flossie might be moved. For instance, when Williams first reflects Flossie back to herself, she is watering plants. With this image, he shares one of his most cherished conceptions of her and reminds her of a deep fund of mutual experience. Williams and Flossie were both ardent gardeners throughout their marriage; in some ways, they seem to have met most easily and shared emotion most freely over flowers and plants. In "The Stolen Peonies," for example, Williams writes of the discovery once, long ago, that a "magnificent / stand of peonies" they were raising had been stolen, and concludes,

> nothing could have
>
> brought us closer
> we had been
> married ten years.
>   (*PB,* 51–52)

Now, in "Asphodel," his references to gardening would remind Flossie of the flowers—and poems—of a lifetime. Paying homage to Flossie's passion for gardening, Williams gives the image of her as nurturer local, specific density and texture. This is the Flossie who reveals what he has called "the love of love, / the love that swallows up all else, / a grateful love." She waters her plants, and "rooted, they / grip down and begin to awaken" (SA, 95–96). She furthers the mystery of life. She has her own powerful ways to "make it new."

Williams reminds her too of the age we live in. "A trance hold men," he writes. Those in control are "dazed," and we follow them to death as "children followed / the Pied Piper." He adds, "the heads of most men I see / . . . are full of cupidity." Subtly he persuades Flossie of the moral importance of their marriage. Poet and gardener, they have sought to "breed / from those others" who are the "flowers of the race." Their union has derived enormous strength from their shared enemies and beliefs, and has had public as well as private significance. Whatever the conflicts between them, Flossie has been his partner in his struggle against the times and his search for true and everlasting values.

Finally, Williams calls Flossie "flowerlike":

> . . . you were a woman
> and no flower
> and had to face
> the problems which confront a woman.
> But you were for all that
> flowerlike. . . .

This is the last thing he says to her before she forgives him, the final word that moves her. I think I can see why. He tells her that he has found her not only good but also beautiful. He tells her that, whatever the rigors and habits of daily life, she has opened to him anew. She not only furthers the mystery but is part of the mystery: Demeter and Persephone, an identity, the one who cares for and the one who blooms.

Book III ends with what at first appears to be a barrage of sublime illogic. "Don't think," Williams says to Flossie,

> that because I say this
> in a poem
> it can be treated lightly
> or that the facts will not uphold it.
> Are facts not flowers

                              and flowers facts
          or poems flowers
                    or all works of the imagination,
                                   interchangeable?
          Which proves
                    that love
                              rules them all, for then
          you will be my queen,
                    my queen of love
                              forever more.

The passage does make sense, however, if one remembers the enthusi-
asm with which Williams views facts—"No ideas but in things"—and
the centrality, in his imagination, of flowers. A fact is a flower or a
poem because, when the mind makes contact with it, a new world
opens. A flower is a fact, as a poem is a fact. And a flower is a poem, as
a poem is a flower, because both are the process of opening—the germ
burgeoning, taking form, releasing at last the ineffable fragrance. "Asphodel" itself has embodied these equations. A fact in touch with facts,
it is also the "last flower" the poet brings. If fact and poem and flower
are "interchangeable," a unifying principle must underlie them all.
This is *eros,* which brings something out of nothing, and sets the
world to blossoming and changing. But it all depends on Flossie, for
the threat of loss has taught Williams that, without her love, all the rest
of the world would not do him any good.

> I have been very near the Gates of Death & have returned very
> weak & an Old Man feeble & tottering, but not in Spirit & Life
> not in The Real Man The Imagination which Liveth for Ever.
> In that I am stronger & stronger as this Foolish Body decays.
>   William Blake[65]

   The "Coda" to "Asphodel" is Williams's gift to Flossie, made possible by her forgiveness of him. They approach the end, the "thunderstroke," together, and tenderly he seeks to reassure her:

          Inseparable from the fire
                    its light

takes precedence over it.
Then follows
what we have dreaded—
but it can never
overcome what has gone before.

Reassuring her, he also reassures himself. Without Flossie's love, any attempt at final affirmation would be whistling in the dark; with it, though the dark remains real, the poet's voice rings with authority, soars in celebration, and nearly breaks in a quiet hymn of praise. This poem was written by a man in his seventies who had to type it with the fingers of one hand, who could sometimes barely see. Yet it is one of those extraordinary utterances that prove the truth of Keats's contention that the world is a "vale of Soul-making."[66] As a young man, Williams wrote, "life is valuable—when completed by the imagination. And then only" (*SA,* 107). The "Coda," thirty years later, reveals a life completed by the imagination; despite the ruin of the body, the made soul shines out indestructibly.

As the expression of a philosophy of life, the "Coda" is problematic. Williams's metaphors change, here, from garden, sea, and bomb, to light. "The palm goes / always to the light," he insists,[67] but it is difficult to ascertain the relation the light bears to the whole of human experience. In an important passage, he writes:

So let us love
confident as is the light
in its struggle with darkness
that there is as much to say
and more
for the one side
and that not the darker
which John Donne
for instance
among many men
presents to us.
In the controversy
touching the younger

and the older Tolstoi,
                Villon, St. Anthony, Kung,
    Rimbaud, Buddha
        and Abraham Lincoln
            the palm goes
    always to the light;
            Who most shall advance the light—
                call it what you may!

The general outlines of Williams's belief are clear: against *thanatos,*
against darkness, chaos, and death, "Light, the imagination / and love"
will maintain "all of a piece / their dominance." But in the particular
instance, clarity turns to confusion. It is impossible to tell, for example,
whether John Donne stands for "the darker" side of life, or for the fact
that "there is as much to say / for the one side / and that not the
darker." This ambiguity stems from grammatical confusion, but it is
difficult, too, to decide what Williams *would* say about Donne. He
would not share the pious view of Donne's career as marked by a conversion from sin to godliness, nor would he fault Donne either for his
erotic poetry or, in his religious poetry, for his "murmuring." There is
plenty of darkness in Donne's poetry—despair, a sense of sin, an obsession with death—but there is so much vitality, beauty, intelligence,
joy, and spirit besides that he may well stand for those who suffer intensely and yet do not come down on the side of "the darker." Or he
may not.

A list of wisdom figures follows the lines about Donne. In most cases
these men, like Donne, underwent a radical change or conversion midway through their lives. Williams doubtless perceives an analogy between their histories and his own forced conversion from action to
meditation, sex to celibacy, sense to soul; but with these figures, too,
his meaning is problematic. In the "controversy / touching the
younger / and the older Tolstoi," for instance, who most advanced the
light: the passionate, worldly author of *Anna Karenina,* or the Christian mystic who renounced *Anna Karenina,* worldliness, and passion?
Did Rimbaud advance the light more when he wrote *Une saison en
enfer* and *Illuminations,* or when he abandoned poetry at the age of
nineteen for a life of adventure and gun-running in Africa? The case

would seem clear with the Buddha—surely the founder of a world religion takes the palm over a prince *moyen sensuel*—until one remembers that his enlightenment consisted of the revelation that life is suffering, which can only be overcome by the release of all attachment and the stilling of all desire. An odd companion, he, for Chaucer with his "medieval pageantry," or Villon, who wrote so hot in his prison cell that only the frozen ink in his inkwell reminded him of the cold. Williams's confusion, that is to say, seems to derive from his inability to decide whether one advances the light more by renouncing worldly experience ("Leave me O Love, which reachest but to dust"),[68] or by living intensely, splendidly, fully. Even in "Asphodel," which is partly a poem of repentance, his own example strongly suggests the latter. Still, there is something wonderful about his refusal to discriminate. "It is all / a celebration of the light," he writes; let each individual case be decided as it may. Though the roads are many, though Lincoln is not Chaucer and Confucius is not the Buddha, the light that bathes and sustains each is the same.

So, in their large outlines, are the central human choices. "If a man die," William declares,

> it is because death
> has first
> possessed his imagination.
> But if he refuse death—
> no greater evil
> can befall him
> unless it be the death of love
> meet him
> in full career.
> Then indeed
> for him
> the light has gone out.

In these mighty lines, Williams does not mean to imply a strict causal relationship between imagining death and dying, but to affirm a way it is possible to be. Death can possess the imagination in many ways: One fears death, adores death, becomes obsessed with signs of death,

or simply grows unimaginative and, in that sense, dies. But it is possible—at least at moments—just to live while one is alive. Beautifully,
Williams describes this new dispensation to Flossie:

> In the huge gap
> > between the flash
> and the thunderstroke
> > spring has come in
> > > or a deep snow fallen.
> Call it old age.
> > In that stretch
> > > we have lived to see
> a colt kick up his heels.
> > Do not hasten
> > > laugh and play
> in an eternity
> > the heat will not overtake the light.

An hour, a day, a lifetime: Time itself is a "gap / between the flash / and
the thunderstroke." But when refined, clarified, and intensified by the
imagination, time, which can yawn so vast, reveals itself as the "eternal
moment in which we alone live . . ." (*SA*, 89). From what seemed
nothing, something comes; the world, restored, offers itself anew; and
it does not matter, in this grace-filled time and place, that "colt" cannot
efface "old age," that the world's gift to its lovers may be spring, or it
may be a deep snow. The phrase "deep snow," in fact, only intensifies
the mystery. With the line, "spring has come in," we begin to watch
the world take color, shape, and movement, begin to see a field like
those Williams describes in Book III, "mantled / with white" English
daisies or starred with "the small yellow sweet-scented violet." Then,
magically, Williams sweeps all that away, returns us to the emptiness
of the gap, only this emptiness is charged; with awe we look upon the
silent world and realize that, while we were not watching, it has been
covered up with snow. "Call it old age," Williams writes; then he
abruptly returns to the springtime image of the colt, a world from
which it seems at first the poet and his wife have been excluded. But
the move from spring to snow to age to colt subliminally dislodges our

comfortable expectations about the smooth passage of seasons and hence the smooth continuity of our own individual lives. Anything can happen in this unseasonal season. Life may continue to roll forward from winter to spring, or it may reverse itself, stop, deepen inward, into the hush and mystery of snow. Our lives are utterly contingent; fear is useless. Therefore, Williams urges Flossie to do that all but impossible thing: *be,* like the colt, just exactly where she is. "Do not hasten / laugh and play / in an eternity."

All his life, Williams has been writing "the poem / of his existence . . ." ("The Sparrow," *PB,* 129–32). Each poem, each moment, has been complete in itself, and yet by the time of "Asphodel" they have acquired tremendous cumulative power, too. The first three books of "Asphodel" grow from and commemorate the earlier life and poetry, and the "Coda" grows from and commemorates the first three books of "Asphodel." By the time of the "Coda," then, Williams has created a deep and firm and lasting ground to stand on, one from which, with Flossie, he can

> . . . watch time's flight
>> as we might watch
> summer lightning
>> or fireflies, secure
>>> by grace of the imagination,
> safe in its care.

"Asphodel" is the ground of the made soul, the place of inner standing—but only, paradoxically, as long as it does not stand still, for in Williams's conception of selfhood, the self does not exist apart from its enactment. The poem does stop, of course, on a certain page, at a certain moment. But the snake has its tail in its mouth: Williams reaches the end, only to find there his beginning in what he had "forgot," that "something / central to the sky"; and the poem, which has soared so high, comes full circle to touch down gently on the flower when it was new. "It is all / a celebration of the light," Williams has been saying: a "priest's raiment," the feathers and skins and jewels of a "savage chieftain," or "the pomp and ceremony / of weddings." This makes him think of his own wedding, of the way that, for him and

Flossie, "the light was wakened / and shone." Now, in a great stillness, he remembers that other moment when

> I thought the world
> stood still.
>   At the altar
>   so intent was I
>   before my vows,
>   so moved by your presence,
>   a girl so pale
>   and ready to faint
>   that I pitied
>   and wanted to protect you.

A lifetime has led from and back to this moment. Forgotten and now reclaimed beyond forgetting, it is the moment of wedding, of union, when the self comes into being because it surrenders to and embraces the other, lays itself down with its bride. "As I think of it now," Williams writes,

>   it is as if
>   a sweet-scented flower
>   were poised
>   and for me did open.

The memory releases the splendor. Both the life that led to the poem and the poem that holds the life must come to an end in time, but as the poem ends, a sense of plenitude and sweetness, of beauty beyond measure, begins anew. "Sing me a song to make death tolerable," Williams implores in *Paterson,* "a song / of a man and a woman: the riddle of a man / and a woman" (*P,* 107). "Asphodel" then comes, to be the song that he was seeking. Gravely, now, it closes:

>   Asphodel
>   has no odor
>   save to the imagination
>   but it too

celebrates the light.
It is late
but an odor
as from our wedding
has revived for me
and begun again to penetrate
into all crevices
of my world.

As it draws to silence, it reaches beyond language into the realm where love and memory flow endless and free in the "River of Heaven," and the deathless imagination flowers without ceasing in the light.

Epilogue

We float back to earth and hear the hooves of the great beast stamping.
Death with the deformed toenail comes to search the poet out. Dreams
possess him, and the dance of his thoughts. Once again, passion quickens; once again, Williams becomes aware of

> the tyranny of the image
>   and how
>   men
> in their designs
>   have learned
>   to shatter it
> whatever it may be,
>   that the trouble
>   in their minds
> shall be quieted,
>   put to bed
>   again.
> ("Tribute to the Painters," *PB,* 137)

The result of these designs is *Paterson, V.*

Paterson, V reopens what the Coda of "Asphodel" closes. The radiant centrality of marriage and of the married self to which "Asphodel" comes in the end gives way to a sense of the self as isolate, single— "I, Paterson, the King-self," the Unicorn or "one-horned beast"—and to an urgent affirmation of pursuit, for "the dream / is in pursuit" (*P*, 234, 208, 222). In *Paterson, V*, marriage and adultery are no longer in opposition; instead, they merge with fornication to become virtually identical manifestations of the one ravening hunger to discover the self in its experience, to assert the self by means of its power to penetrate to the ground of its desire: "Paterson, keep your pecker up . . ." (*P*, 235). "Asphodel" moves and flows like "a wave o' th' sea";[1] *Paterson, V*, in contrast, seeks its rhythms in the unappeasable hungers of the satyr.

Near the end of *Paterson, IV*, Williams expresses a rare longing to attain the absolute and surpass the conditions of autobiography:

> Oh that the rocks of the Areopagus had
> kept their sounds, the voices of the law!
> Or that the great theatre of Dionysius
> could be aroused by some modern magic
>   to release
> what is bound in it, stones!
> that music might be wakened from them to
> melt our ears   .
>
>   (*P*, 201)

But existence, for Williams, offers neither Apollonian clarity and order, the self-defining certainties of law, nor lasting Dionysian self-abandon. What remains is the middle ground of measure, the driven, mocking, tragic, playful, celebratory dance. As Williams concludes in *Paterson, V*,

> The measure intervenes, to measure is all we know
>
>   . . . . .
> We know nothing and can know nothing   .
>   but

the dance, to dance to a measure
contrapuntally,
             Satyrically, the tragic foot.
                                    (*P*, 239)

And so, after "Asphodel," Williams wrote *Paterson, V* and the poems in *Pictures from Brueghel*. He left behind notes for *Paterson, VI* when, on March 4, 1963, he died.

That the process of self-discovery is never ending was, for Williams, both a source of despair and a source of affirmation. "Rich as are the gifts of the imagination bitterness of world's loss is not replaced thereby" (*K*, 18). The world is never found, once and for all; one's relation to it is fluid. Nor is the self found, once and for all; it manifests itself in the fluid relation. But "world's loss," and all that it means, to which William's work bears witness, becomes in the end also something else, to which Williams's work bears tribute:

No defeat is made up entirely of defeat—since
the world it opens is always a place
             formerly
                          unsuspected. A
world lost,
             a world unsuspected,
                          beckons to new places . . . .
                                    (*P*, 78; *PB*, 73)

These lines, with their hard-earned serenity and their promise of plenitude rather than conclusions, seem addressed by Williams not only to himself but also to all who would labor both for communion with the world and for a sense of their inner standing—to all who, like Williams, would write their autobiographies.

Notes

Introduction

1. Sherman Paul, *The Music of Survival: A Biography of a Poem by William Carlos Williams* (Urbana, Chicago, London: University of Illinois Press, 1968).

2. Herbert Leibowitz, "'You Can't Beat Innocence': *The Autobiography of William Carlos Williams,*" *American Poetry Review,* 10, no. 2 (March/April 1981), 35–48.

3. *SL,* p. 295; cited in Paul, *The Music of Survival,* p. 41.

4. I am thinking of the fate of Harry Haller, who discovers in *Steppenwolf* that the self is not double but infinite. Hermann Hesse, *Steppenwolf,* trans. Basil Creighton, trans. updated Joseph Mileck (New York: Holt, Rinehart and Winston, 1963).

5. Elizabeth W. Bruss, *Autobiographical Acts: The Changing Situation of a Literary Genre* (Baltimore and London: The Johns Hopkins University Press, 1976).

6. Roy Pascal, *Design and Truth in Autobiography* (London: Routledge and Kegan Paul, 1960), p. 182.

7. Benjamin Franklin, *Autobiography and Other Writings,* ed. Russell B. Nye (Cambridge, Massachusetts: The Riverside Press, 1958), p. 1.

8. Pascal, *Design and Truth in Autobiography,* p. 9.

9. Ibid., p. 10.

10. See William C. Spengemann and L. R. Lundquist, "Autobiography and the American Myth," *American Quarterly,* 17, no. 3 (Fall 1965), 501–19.

11. Jean-Jacques Rousseau, *The Confessions of Jean-Jacques Rousseau,* trans. J. M. Cohen (Harmondsworth, Middlesex: Penguin Books, 1954).

12. Ibid., p. 17.

13. Ibid., p. 169.

14. Ibid., p. 17.

15. Ibid., p. 606.

16. "Telle est sans doute l'intention la plus secrète de toute entreprise de Souvenirs, de Mémoires ou de Confessions. L'homme qui se raconte se recherche lui-même à travers son histoire. . . . La confession, l'effort de remémoration est en même temps recherche d'un trésor caché, d'un dernier mot libérateur rachetant en dernière instance une destinée qui doutait de sa propre valeur" [the translation is mine]. Georges Gusdorf, "Conditions et limites de l'autobiographie," in *Formen der Selbstdarstellung* . . . : *Festgabe für Fritz Neubert,* ed. Gunter Reichenkron (Berlin: Duncker and Humblot, 1956), p. 115. James Olney has translated this essay as "Conditions and Limits of Autobiography," in *Autobiography: Essays Theoretical and Critical,* ed. James Olney (Princeton, New Jersey: Princeton University Press, 1980), pp. 28–48. Gusdorf points out the divergence between the avowed project of an autobiographer and his profound intentions—between the public and the private compulsions. He does not, however, quite clarify the point that the avowed project can vary from autobiographer to autobiographer, and does not consider the possibility that one writer could write more than one autobiography, each attempting a different project. But in general Gusdorf is correct: There are the avowed projects, and then there are the secret intentions. The conflicts between the two—and at times their mutual incompatability—are the points at which the complexities and the fascination arise.

17. Pascal, *Design and Truth in Autobiography,* p. 10. The text of Augustine's *Confessions* I have used is *The Confessions of Saint Augustine,* trans. Rex Warner (New York and Toronto: New American Library, 1963). See also William C. Spengemann, *The Forms of Autobiography: Episodes in the History of a Literary Genre* (New Haven and London: Yale University Press, 1980), for a much fuller discussion of the *Confessions* than I can give here.

18. "God is a circle the circumference of which is nowhere and the center of which is everywhere."

19. I use both "creation" and "discovery" deliberately. Self-discovery, in art, is the process of finding a self which preexisted and which is made manifest by means of artistic creativity; self-creation, in art, is the process of making a self where there was none before. The Romantics looked upon art as a process of self-discovery; certain postmodern writers have looked upon art as a process of self-creation. I believe it is true to say of Williams that he looked upon art as both, simultaneously. In Chapter V, below, I discuss this seeming paradox more fully.

20. Louis Simpson, *Three on the Tower* (New York: William Morrow, 1975), p. 221.

21. Roland Barthes, *Mythologies,* trans. Annette Lavers (New York: Hill and Wang, 1972), pp. 74–75.

22. Pascal, *Design and Truth in Autobiography,* p. 148.

23. Barrett J. Mandel, "Full of Life Now," in *Autobiography: Essays Theoretical and Critical,* p. 51.

24. Ibid., p. 50.

> *Da stieg ein Baum. O reine Übersteigung!*
> *O Orpheus singt! O hoher Baum in Ohr!*

Rainer Maria Rilke, *Duino Elegies and The Sonnets to Orpheus,* trans. A. J. Poulin, Jr. (Boston: Houghton Mifflin, 1977), p. 85.

26. Mandel cites the influence of William Earle, *The Autobiographical Consciousness: A Philosophical Inquiry into Existence* (Chicago, 1972); Earle in turn is influenced by the existentialists and phenomenologists Heidegger, Marcel, Husserl, and Merleau-Ponty. Mandel, p. 50.

27. Ibid., p. 65.

28. Michael Sprinker, "Fictions of the Self: The End of Autobiography," in *Autobiography: Essays Theoretical and Critical,* p. 22.

29. James Olney, "Autobiography and The Cultural Moment," in *Autobiography: Essays Theoretical and Critical,* p. 22.

30. Elizabeth W. Bruss, "Eye for I: Making and Unmaking Autobiography in Film," in *Autobiography: Essays Theoretical and Critical,* p. 298.

31. James Olney, for instance, implies that everything is autobiography when he writes,

> The most fruitful approach to the subject of autobiography . . . is to consider it neither as a formal nor as an historical matter . . . but rather to see it in relation to the vital impulse to order that has always caused man to create and that, in the end, determines both the nature and the form of what he creates. In this view, there is no evolving autobiographical form to trace from a beginning through history to its present state because man has always cast his autobiography and has done it in that form to which his private spirit impelled him, often, however, calling the product not an autobiography but a life-work. If this is so, then the final work, whether it be history or poetry, psychology or theology, political economy or natural science, whether it take the form of personal essay or controversial tract, of lyric poem or scientific treatise, will express and reflect its maker.

(James Olney, *Metaphors of Self: The Meaning of Autobiography* [Princeton, New Jersey: Princeton University Press, 1972], p. 3.) I do not think Olney is wrong, though I disagree with his abandonment of formal and historical questions and a sense of formal and historical developments. Furthermore, it strikes me that, while Olney opens all of literature to autobiography, he confines autobiography still to literature. Surely painting, building barns, and bearing babies are as fully means of casting one's autobiography as are writing tracts and treatises. It is only a little step from seeing all of literature as autobiography to seeing all of life as autobiography—and then, is it not prideful to stop with the human? Are not raccoons and birds, the sand and stars themselves, "*Crying What I do is me: for that I came*"?

32. Friedrich Nietzsche, *Beyond Good and Evil,* section 6; quoted in Ronald Hayman, *Nietzsche: A Critical Life* (Harmondsworth, Middlesex, 1980), n.p.

33. Jorge Luis Borges, *Dreamtigers,* trans. Mildred Boyer and Harold Moreland (Austin, Texas, 1964), p. 93. William C. Spengemann quotes this passage in *The Forms of Autobiography,* p. 167.

Chapter 1

1. See Robert F. Sayre, *The Examined Self: Benjamin Franklin, Henry Adams, Henry James* (Princeton, New Jersey: Princeton University Press, 1964); and William C. Spengemann, *The Forms of Autobiography: Episodes in the History of a Literary Genre* (New Haven and London: Yale University Press, 1980), for excellent discussions of Franklin's *Autobiography.* See David Levin, "*The Autobiography of Benjamin Franklin:* The Puritan Experimenter in Life and Art," in *In Defense of Historical Literature* (New York: Hill and Wang, 1967), for a defense of Franklin against charges such as those Williams makes, or D. H. Lawrence makes in *Studies in Classic American Literature.*

2. Benjamin Franklin, *Autobiography and Other Writings,* ed. Russel B. Nye (Cambridge, Massachusetts: The Riverside Press, 1958), p. 56.

3. Sherman Paul, *The Music of Survival: A Biography of a Poem by William Carlos Williams* (Urbana: University of Illinois Press, 1968), p. 49. Paul also points out the resemblance between Williams's persona in his *Autobiography* and Franklin's persona in his.

4. The Stecher trilogy—*White Mule, In the Money,* and *The Build-up*—is, like *The Autobiography,* conventionally mimetic, and since Williams appears as a character in the last of the novels, the trilogy is at least partly autobiography. Primarily, however, the novels concern Flossie's family and above all Flossie herself, who is born in the first chapter of *White Mule* and is about to marry Charlie (Williams himself) at the end of *The Build-up.* Williams is very little concerned with his own history and image, and very much concerned both with the history of Flossie's family, particularly their struggle to establish themselves as recent immigrants in the New World, and with his imaginative creation and apprehension of his wife. A man "must create a woman of some sort out of his imagination to prove himself," Williams writes in his play *A Dream of Love.* "Just as a woman must produce out of her female belly to complete herself—a son—so a man must produce a woman, in full beauty out of the shell of his imagination and possess her, to complete himself also . . ." (p. 200). Flossie, his actual wife, becomes by this means also his *anima,* his daughter, his Venus; by writing her story, Williams can return to the beloved fertile ground and know it for the first time.

5. William Butler Yeats, "A Crazed Girl," in *The Collected Poems of W. B. Yeats* (New York: Macmillan, 1956), p. 301.

Chapter 2

1. In "You Can't Beat Innocence," Herbert Leibowitz discusses the centrality of "Innocence" in Williams's *Autobiography* as "a convenient strategem for Williams: an ingrained psychological defense against his own ambitions, captious moods, and the possibility of failure." Leibowitz correctly perceives that for Williams innocence is both "the royal road to approval and reward" and "a second skin that shields a person from attack" (*American Poetry Review*, 10, no. 2 [March/April 1981], 36). However, Leibowitz underestimates the degree to which Williams's innocence is genuine, and one source of his astonishing exuberance, freshness, and creativity.

2. Williams and Flossie were in Italy for most of March 1924; thence they traveled to Vienna, where they stayed through April. "Rome" is by far the rawest and most immediate of the European writings. Written partly in Rome, partly in Vienna, and partly back home in Rutherford, it attempts, as Steven Ross Loevy says, to enact "that vibrant place in the mind where self and circumstance breed intense living in writing" (Introduction to "Rome," p. 7).

Williams wrote *A Voyage to Pagany* during his separation from Flossie in 1927–28, in which he stayed in Rutherford and she spent the school year with their sons in Europe; this was a dark time in their marriage. Loevy argues that Williams considered working the "Rome" improvisations into the later novel, as an example of Dev Evans's writing (p. 8). The chapter "Night" and the following thoughts from "Carcassonne" bear eloquent witness to the darkness so firmly suppressed in the *Autobiography*:

> Just go. Why? He couldn't let himself do that. Why not just kill yourself. It's more sensible. . . . But if he should go loose, he would die, of this he was convinced, since to go loose to him was to go totally ungoverned, drunken, syphilitic, starved, jailed, murderous: Finis. . . . This had been his excuse. Not an excuse. It was the wall over which he could not climb, short of annihilation. . . . Yet, that was what he wanted to be—really; abandoned (*VP*, 49).

3. Marcel Proust, *The Past Recaptured*, in *Remembrance of Things Past*, trans. Andreas Mayor (New York: Vintage Books, 1971), p. 126. When one keeps in mind Williams's own illness, the passage becomes especially poignant:

> . . . [T]he Baron at this moment . . . was flinging down his words with greater force, as the tide, on days of bad weather, flings down its little contorted waves. And the traces of his recent attack caused one to hear at the back of his words a noise like that of pebbles dragged by the sea. Continuing to speak to me about the past, no doubt to prove to me that he had not lost his memory, he evoked it now . . . by reciting an endless list of all

the people belonging to his family or his world who were no longer alive, less, it seemed, with any emotion of grief that they were dead than with satisfaction at having survived them. He appeared, indeed, as he recalled their extinction, to enjoy a clearer perception of his own return towards health and it was with an almost triumphal sternness that he repeated, in a monotonous tone, stammering slightly and with a dull sepulchral resonance: "Hannibal de Bréauté, dead! Antoine de Mouchy, dead! Charles Swann, dead! Adalbert de Montmorency, dead! Boson de Talleyrand, dead! Sosthène de Doudeauville, dead!"

4. "The Wanderer," first published in 1914 and published in *Al Que Quiere!* in 1917, first uses the symbol of the river and asks the poet's central question, "How shall I be a mirror to this modernity?" As J. Hillis Miller comments, "In *Paterson* the plunge into the Passaic which the poet had made in 'The Wanderer' is explored in its deepest implications . . ." (*Poets of Reality* [Cambridge, Massachusetts: Harvard University Press, 1965], pp. 303–4). In 1926 Williams's short poem "Paterson" won the Dial Award, and in 1928 Williams began to plan the epic version (see Louis Simpson, *Three on the Tower* [New York: William Morrow, 1975], p. 291). Books I through IV of *Paterson* were published in 1946, 1948, 1949, and 1951; Book V was published in 1958.

5. See Paul L. Mariani, *William Carlos Williams: The Poet and His Critics* (Chicago: American Library Association, 1975), for a full account of critical reactions to *Paterson*.

6. As an anonymous reader of this book has pointed out, Williams also brought together *Collected Earlier Poems* and *Collected Later Poems* at this time. Williams writes, "There are several books still to be written: a biography of my mother, the continuation of the *White Mule* series; the prose, essays, prefaces and miscellaneous comment should be collected, and so forth. That will all come" (*A,* 348). Here, he does not mention plans to write any more poems. In a letter to Louis Martz dated May 27, 1951, he does write,

> I must now . . . make myself clear. I must gather together the stray ends of what I have been thinking and make my full statement as to their meaning or quit. . . .
> The first effect is in the writing itself. I begin to see what I have been after. . . . Verse form, the actual shape of the line itself, must be as it is the first visible thing. I'm finally getting to understand what I want to do. (*SL,* 298–99)

It is hard to tell, therefore, whether Williams intended to summarize his meaning in poetry or in prose. Whichever, he seems not to have intended the radical new beginning that issued, in fact, from the *Autobiography*.

7. Other examples include "The High Bridge above the Tagus River at Toledo," "The Desert Music," "To a Dog Injured in the Street," and parts of "Asphodel, That Greeny Flower." In each case, what seem to be rather inconsequential anecdotes when reported in the *Autobiography* become keys to the recesses of memory, metaphors for poetry, images by means of which the self is apprehended

across the abysm of time. As Williams writes of the sheep and dogs that crowded him in 1910 on the bridge above the Tagus at Toledo,

> In old age they walk in the old man's dreams and still
>> walk in his dreams, peacefully continuing in his verse
>> forever.

(PB, 53)

8. My phrasing is intentional. Writing the *Autobiography,* especially its final chapters, Williams identified not only with Franklin but also with Whitman, who, in fame, was the Good Gray Poet. In the *Autobiography,* Williams explains the end of *Paterson, IV* as follows: "[T]he man rises from the sea where the river appears to have lost its identity and accompanied by his faithful bitch, obviously a Chesapeake Bay retriever, turns inland toward Camden where Walt Whitman, much traduced, lived the later years of his life and died" (*A,* 392). The "man" is Williams's persona; the parallel with Whitman occurs only in the *Autobiography.*

9. See especially "Jacataqua," in *IAG,* pp. 174–87. A beautiful passage in *Paterson, Book I* also employs these metaphors, with the exception that "the giants" replace "the gods":

> we sit and talk
> I wish to be with you abed, we two
> as if the bed were the bed of a stream
> —I have much to say to you
>
> We sit and talk,
> quietly, with long lapses of silence
> and I am aware of the stream
> that has no language, coursing
> beneath the quiet heaven of
> your eyes
>
> . . .
> We sit and talk and the
> silence speaks of the giants
> who have died in the past and have
> returned to those scenes unsatisfied
> and who is not unsatisfied, the
> silent, Singac the rock-shoulder
> emerging from the rocks—and the giants
> live again in your silence and
> unacknowledged desire—

(P, 24–25)

10. I wish to be quite clear: It is not sex that offends me here, but a failure of imagination. If it were true (which it is not) that "that has nothing to do with me," there would not be much justification for going to bed with women and tormenting one's wife. See chapter 3 on *A Dream of Love* for a discussion of the theme of adultery.

11. Sherman Paul, *The Music of Survival* (Urbana, Chicago, London: University of Illinois Press, 1968), pp. 42 and 43; and Williams's letters to Wallace Stevens, April 25, 1951, and to Marianne Moore, June 23, 1951 (*SL,* 295–96 and 304–5). Also important in this context are the death of Williams's mother in 1949 and the Library of Congress affair, when Congress made impossible his appointment to a Chair of Poetry at the Library of Congress. See Sherman Paul, pp. 42–43; Reed Whittemore, *William Carlos Williams: Poet from Jersey* (Boston: Houghton Mifflin, 1975), pp. 306–14; and Paul Mariani, *William Carlos Williams: A New World Naked* (New York: McGraw-Hill, 1981), chapters 12 and 13, passim.

12. Draft of the *Autobiography, YALC.* The fact that there are so few changes among the manuscript and typescript drafts of the *Autobiography* makes Williams's excision of this passage all the more striking.

13. Paul, *The Music of Survival,* p. 67.

14. Peter Matthiessen writes, "The deep, resonant *Om* is all sound and silence throughout time, the roar of eternity and also the great stillness of pure being; when intoned with the prescribed vibrations, it invokes the All that is otherwise inexpressible" (*The Snow Leopard* [New York: Bantam Books, 1979], p. 108). To chant *Om* is a means, and to perceive *Om* is an end, of Buddhist meditation—though to say "an end" is false, since, seeking an end, one will never find it.

Sherman Paul describes the music as that of a "'still, sad music of humanity' such as Wordsworth said he heard, 'Not harsh nor grating, though of ample power / To chasten and subdue . . . '" (p. 95). Perhaps. But though Williams was no Buddhist, the "deep cello tone" seems to me to be, like "Om," beyond sentiment entirely.

Chapter 3

1. Jean-Jacques Rousseau, *The Confessions of Jean-Jacques Rousseau,* trans. J. M. Cohen (Harmondsworth, Middlesex: Penguin Books, 1954), p. 17.

2. Several of the meanings of "confession" are applicable here, and indeed to all autobiographies entitled *Confessions.* A confession is "an admission of guilt, as by a person charged with a crime"; "the confessing of sins to a priest in order to receive absolution"; "a form used in public worship, expressing a general acknowledgement of sin"; "declaration of faith; creed"; "a group of people adhering to a certain creed; church; sect; denomination"; and "the tomb or shrine of a martyr or confessor" (*Webster's New World Dictionary*). In general parlance, "confession" has come to indicate guilt but not the substratum of faith or belonging without which there would be no guilt.

3. "The Poet," in Ralph Waldo Emerson, *Essays & Lectures,* ed. Joel Porte (New York: The Library of America, 1983), pp. 448, 454.

4. *A Dream of Love* was published in 1948, the same year as *Paterson, Book II. Book I* of *Paterson* was published in 1946; *Book III* in 1949.

5. I use the dominant metaphors of Saint Augustine's *City of God* intentionally; they resonate throughout the poem. Like Augustine, Williams divides "those who prefer gods of their own creation" and therefore dwell in the city of man from "those who love deity" and whose desire is directed toward the City. But Williams works outside a religious tradition, as my subsequent remarks make clear.

The phrases quoted are from F. C. Gardiner, *The Pilgrimage of Desire: A Study of Theme and Genre in Medieval Literature* (Leiden: E. J. Brill, 1971), p. 13.

6. This image also foreshadows the image of "Beautiful Thing" in *Paterson, Book III:*

> But you!
> —in your white lace dress
>   "the dying swan"
> and high-heeled slippers—tall
> as you already were—
>   till your head
> through fruitful exaggeration
> was reaching the sky and the
> prickles of its ecstasy
>   Beautiful Thing!
>
> (*P,* 126–27)

Both images recall Williams's poems about the "Beautiful Thing" which is love, the poem, and New York City, first published in *Spring and All:*

> The Easter stars are shining
> above lights that are flashing—
> coronal of the black—
>   Nobody
>
> to say it—
>   Nobody to say: pinholes
>
> Thither I would carry her
> among the lights—
> Burst it asunder
> break through to the fifty words
> necessary—.
>
> (*SA,* 99)

This is not to say, of course, that love is New York City. The visual splendor of a city at night, a "cornucopia / of glass," is what is being described—as well, perhaps, as the poignancy of an ordinary evening in Rutherford.

7. One thinks of the epiphanic moment in *The Prelude* when, having ascended Snowden, Wordsworth looks up and sees the moon:

> . . . and lo! as I looked up,
> The Moon hung naked in a firmament
> Of azure without cloud, and at my feet
> Rested a silent sea of hoary mist.

(William Wordsworth, *The Prelude* [*Or, Growth of a Poet's Mind*], XIV, 39–42, in *The Prelude: A Parallel Text,* ed. J. C. Maxwell [New Haven: Yale University Press, 1981], p. 513.)

8. Gardiner, *The Pilgrimage of Desire,* p. 19.

9. Ibid., p. 24.

10. The fire is a good deal more powerful than the fire on which Gulliver urinates while among the Lilliputians, but the images are strikingly similar. Williams's conflict is whether to "spit on" or enter into passion, the making of poems, and the consequent despair.

11. J. Hillis Miller's *Poets of Reality* (Cambridge, Massachusetts: Harvard University Press, 1965) has an excellent discussion of Williams's sense of the erotic: see pp. 321–37.

12. Williams's sense of the duality and complementarity of all existence is strikingly similar to the Taoist concept of *yin* and *yang.* Alan Watts writes, "they are associated with the masculine and the feminine, the firm and the yielding, the strong and the weak, the light and the dark, the rising and the falling, heaven and earth." This "principle of polarity" is "not to be confused with the ideas of opposition or conflict," or with the ideas of purification and progress, that pervade Western culture. (*Tao: The Watercourse Way* [New York: Pantheon Books, 1975], pp. 21, 19.) There is another striking similarity as well. What Taoists mean by a life and art that "goes with the grain" is very much like what Williams means by a life and art "in the American grain": a life and art lived and practiced not in domination but in participation.

13. See "The Basis of Faith in Art," in *SE,* particularly pp. 187–95. There are three valid arguments against Williams's theories about adultery, it seems to me. Traditional Christianity would argue that it is a sin, a breaking of a covenant; Zen Buddhism would argue that all striving after "Beautiful Thing" is pointless, is, in fact, counterproductive, for enlightenment simply *is* and cannot be *found;* and feminism would argue that to see women as symbols, either of "wife" or of "Beautiful Thing," obliterates them as persons. I find all three true, but my aim here is to try to understand Williams. Furthermore, I think that Williams himself became aware of precisely these three problems, and to a great extent grew beyond them. "Asphodel, That Greeny Flower" is a magnificent celebration of a covenant, a way of being where one is, and a powerful acknowledgment of Flossie as a person, not just as a wife; and the short stories, particularly "The Farmers' Daughters," show the extent to which Williams came to see the personhood of women.

14. Emerson, "The Poet," in *Essays & Lectures,* p. 450.

15. Doc's reply is, "Give me time." He, of course, has no time, since he dies the next afternoon. But the phrase is echoed in "Asphodel," where at last the plea is granted:

> Only give me time,
>   time to recall them
>   before I shall speak out.

> Give me time,
>
>   time . . .
>
>   (*PB*, 154)

A note in the Yale Collection reveals the justice of Myra's remark and Williams's sense of the tragedy in *A Dream of Love*. Planning the play, Williams writes,

> . . . for the first time in his life he sees the implications and the fact of monogamy (the whole man and the man whole).
>
> He SEES—and the light it casts through and through his life is brilliant—he stands in amazement before it . . . before her, her life given; desperately assailed by the tragedy of her life.

(Linda Welshimer Wagner quotes this passage as well in *The Prose of William Carlos Williams* [Middletown, Connecticut: Wesleyan University Press, 1970], p. 147.) To express this sense of monogamy is one of the things for which Williams needed "time"; it is present throughout "Asphodel," though not overtly in *A Dream of Love*.

16. It does no good, for Williams, to be extraordinary and right. Like Wordsworth, Emerson, and Whitman, he cares not only about his own poethood but also about the potentiality for all men to become "poets."

17. "All the world" is no exaggeration; Doc's death receives an active press, and the reporters soon come calling. As the Milkman remarks, with delightful illogic, "To take a woman to a hotel that wasn't his wife? Sure, it could be any man at all—those things happen every day. I will admit you don't have to drop dead in bed with her. That was bad—in fact, that ended the doc" (*DL*, 156).

18. "The proof of a poet is that his country absorbs him as affectionately as he has absorbed it," Whitman writes in the 1855 *Preface* to *Leaves of Grass*. The sentiment is excised from later versions of the preface; Whitman quickly learned that to define poethood by the country's affection was to hoist oneself on one's own petard. (*Complete Poetry and Selected Prose*, ed. James E. Miller, Jr. [Cambridge, Massachusetts: The Riverside Press, 1959], p. 427.)

19. Wagner, *The Prose of William Carlos Williams*, p. 146. Steven Ross Loevy concurs with Wagner:

> At the moment Doc and Dotty make contact, the lights go out and in the darkness we witness a mock battle scene with gun fire, flashes of light, fife and drum, and a final explosion. Our side wins the battle. This sexual consummation has the magnitude of the conclusion of a war. The violence destroys the old order and leads to victory on the home front in the name of love, marriage, forgiveness, the American language, and the imagination. This final gesture of Myra's dream, the last moment before waking, acknowledges that death attends such accomplishments.

(*William Carlos Williams's A DREAM OF LOVE* [Ann Arbor, Michigan: UMI Research Press, 1983], p. 73.) David A. Fedo does not discuss this moment of consummation but comments that Myra's final arrival "at the peace that comes after great pain" seems to him insufficiently motivated; for him, the end of *A Dream of Love* is a dramatic failure. (*William Carlos Williams: A Poet in the American Theatre* [Ann Arbor, Michigan: UMI Research Press, 1983], p. 123.)

Chapter 4

1. Interestingly, Bates was just about right, though perhaps "fifteen years" would have been more accurate.

2. This information was given me by Dr. Donald Gallup, formerly Curator of the Collection of American Literature at the Beinecke Library, Yale. All subsequent quotation from the poem is from the manuscript version in the Yale Collection.

3. See Frank Kermode, *Romantic Image* (New York: Vintage Books, 1957), chapters 1 and 2, for a discussion of this theme. Kermode's primary subject is Yeats.

4. Williams knew *Hamlet;* his father read Shakespeare aloud in the home, and as a student at the University of Pennsylvania, Williams joined the Mask and Wig Club and played Polonius in *Mr. Hamlet of Denmark* (*A*, 15, 52).

5. Reed Whittemore, *William Carlos Williams: Poet from Jersey* (Boston: Houghton Mifflin, 1975), p. 68.

6. Letter to Edgar Williams; quoted in ibid., p. 52.

7. The metaphor of "the woods of your / own nature" (*PB*, 33) seems rooted in Williams's experiences in Kipp's woods, where Williams wandered as a boy. In *The Autobiography,* he writes:

> What I learned was the way the moss climbed about a tree's roots, what growing dogwood and iron wood looked like; the way rotten leaves will mat down in a hole—and their smell when turned over—every patch among those trees had its character, moist or dry. . . .
>
> It is a pleasure for me now to think of these things, but especially of the flowers I got to know in those precincts. It was a half-ashamed pleasure, I think. . . . There is a long history in each of us that comes as not only a reawakening but a re-possession when confronted by this world. To look up and see on a tree blooms, yellow and green, as large and heavy as the tulip, was something astonishing to me. The tassels of the chestnut— young and old trees, beggar's lice, spiders, shining insects—all these things were as much a part of my expanding existence as breathing. (*A*, 20–21)

8. As a boy, Williams was fascinated by the "three volumes of the famous illustrated translation of Dante's *Divine Comedy,*" but the fascination lay primarily in trying to discover the "anatomical secrets" of "Gustave Doré's pictures of those beautiful but damned ladies . . ." (*A*, 15).

9. *YALC;* quoted also in Whittemore, *William Carlos Williams,* p. 23.

10. See Whittemore, pp. 14–15, and Paul Mariani, *William Carlos Williams: A New World Naked* (New York: McGraw-Hill, 1981), pp. 14–16.

11. James Joyce, *Dubliners* (New York: The Viking Press, 1968), p. 31.

12. The failure of language in "Philip and Oradie" is not unique to that poem; nearly all of Williams's early verse strikes a similar pose. Particularly memorable examples include the "Keatsian" sonnet for H.D., "The Uses of Poetry," printed in Williams's *Poems* of 1909, and the rather haunting "An After Song," printed in *The Tempers* in 1913. "I've fond anticipation of a day," the first begins,

> O'erfilled with pure diversion presently,
> For I must read a lady poesy
> The while we glide by many a leafy bay. . . .

The second attempts to sustain a heroic note imitative of Ezra Pound:

> So art thou broken in upon me, Apollo,
> Through a splendor of purple garments—
> Held by the yellow-haired Clymene
> To clothe the white of thy shoulders—
> Blue from the day's leaping of horses.

The poem's last line, however, points to its problem: "This is strange to me, here in the modern twilight" (*CP*, 21, 7). See James Breslin, *William Carlos Williams: An American Artist* (New York: Oxford University Press, 1970), pp. 10–17, for a valuable discussion of Williams's first two books, *Poems* and *The Tempers;* Rod Townley discusses these books in much greater detail in *The Early Poetry of William Carlos Williams* (Ithaca and London: Cornell University Press, 1975), pp. 39–71.

13. William Wordsworth, "Ode: Intimations of Immortality from Recollections of Early Childhood," in *The Poems,* ed. John O. Hayden (New Haven: Yale University Press, 1981), 1: 525.

14. Ibid.

15. John Keats, "Hyperion: A Fragment," III, 113, in *The Poems of John Keats,* ed. Jack Stillinger (Cambridge, Massachusetts: Harvard University Press, 1978), p. 355.

16. Many influences combined, of course, to effect Williams's transformation from the poet of "Philip and Oradie" to the poet of "The Wanderer." Among them were Pound's tutelage and criticism, Williams's marriage to Flossie in 1912, the Paterson silk strike in 1913, the Armory show also in 1913, and the general climate of artistic ferment and revolution which Williams found so exciting. All such transformations are overdetermined. But if Philip had not died, if "Philip and Oradie" had not failed, the Williams who could benefit from these influences would not have existed.

James Breslin, *William Carlos Williams: An American Artist;* Rod Townley, *The Early Poetry of William Carlos Williams;* Paul Mariani, *William Carlos Williams: A New World Naked;* J. Hillis Miller, *Poets of Reality;* and Bram Dijkstra, *The Hieroglyphics of a New Speech: Cubism, Stieglitz, and the Early Poetry of William*

Carlos Williams (Princeton, New Jersey: Princeton University Press, 1969) are among the critics who discuss Williams's transformation to become the poet of "The Wanderer."

17. Keats, "Endymion: A Poetic Romance," I, 3, in *The Poems of John Keats,* p. 103.

Chapter 5

1. For Williams's account of his early medical practice in New York City, which came abruptly to an end when he refused to participate in corruption at Nursery and Child's Hospital, see *A,* 71–105.

2. "Stealing" was, for Williams, a Promethean activity, as well as a means of rebellion against the constraints of middle-class domesticity. The passage from which I quote occurs in *The Great American Novel:*

> He smiled and she, from long practice, began to read to him, progressing rapidly until she said: You can't fool me.
>
> He became very angry but understood at once that she had penetrated his very mystery, that she saw he was stealing in order to write words. She smiled again knowingly. He became furious. (*GAN,* 161)

The characters are Williams and Flossie. Reed Whittemore emphasizes "stealing" (the title of one of his chapters) in *William Carlos Williams: Poet from Jersey.*

3. Of the "renegades, dirty-minded and -fisted," who were his classmates at school, Williams writes:

> There again, a word: their perfections. They were perfect, they seem to have been born perfect, to need nothing else. . . .
>
> It isn't because they fascinated me by their evildoings that they were "bad" boys or girls. Not at all. It was because they were there full of perfection of the longest leap, the most unmitigated daring, the longest chances. (*A,* 287–88)

4. The phrase "Beautiful Thing" first occurs in Williams's essay on Columbus in *In the American Grain.* Williams quotes from Columbus's diaries:

> On shore I sent the people for water, some with arms, and others with casks; and as it was some little distance, I waited two hours for them.
>
> During that time I walked among the trees which was the most beautiful thing which I had ever seen. (*IAG,* 26)

In the epiphanic moment, reality reveals itself to be coequal in beauty with the imagination, and therefore adequate fulfillment for the imagination. See also *Paterson, III,* in which "Beautiful Thing" becomes central.

"Poverty" is as rich a condition for Williams as it is for Wallace Stevens, who writes in "L'Esthetique du Mal":

> The greatest poverty is not to live
> In a physical world, to feel that one's desire
> Is too difficult to tell from despair.

. . .

And out of what one sees and hears and out
Of what one feels, who could have thought to make
So many selves, so many sensuous worlds,
As if the air, the mid-day air, was swarming
With the metaphysical changes that occur,
Merely in living as and where we live.

For Williams and Stevens both, "poverty" is the plenitude of our condition. For neither, however, is it a simple matter to learn to live "as and where we live." (*The Palm at the End of the Mind,* ed. Holly Stevens [New York: Vintage Books, 1972], p. 262.)

5. *The Poetry of Robert Frost* (New York, Chicago, San Francisco: Holt, Rinehart and Winston, 1969), p. 338. In general, however, Frost seems a lot less sanguine about getting help from the universe than Williams.

6.   Are facts not flowers
                                    and flowers facts
        or poems flowers
            or all works of the imagination
                interchangeable?
("Asphodel, That Greeny Flower," *PB,* 178)

7. *Walden,* in *Walden and Other Writings of Henry David Thoreau,* ed. Brooks Atkinson (New York: Modern Library, 1937, 1950), p. 291. The phrase occurs in Thoreau's story of the man of Kouroo.

Whittling his staff, striving for perfection, the artist of Kouroo attains a state of freedom from the *kalpas* of death and birth, a sempiternal selfhood in art. In so doing, he becomes a central figure to Modernist autobiography: his staff is Eliot's music in *Four Quartets,* Proust's cathedral-of-a-book in *A la recherche du temps perdu,* Williams's tapestry in *Paterson, V,* Joyce's endless dream in *Finnegans Wake.*

Modernist autobiography developed, of course, out of Romantic autobiography, in which the tension recurs between the idea that selfhood can be realized in the life by means of writing one's autobiography, and the idea that selfhood can be attained and can endure only within the autobiography itself. For a discussion of this tension and this development in the nineteenth century, see William Spengemann, *The Forms of Autobiography: Episodes in the History of a Literary Genre* (New Haven and London: Yale University Press, 1980). See also Geoffrey Hartman, "Poem and Ideology," in *The Fate of Reading* (Chicago and London: University of Chicago Press, 1975), pp. 124–47, for related remarks with regard to Keats's "To Autumn."

8. Here, Williams resembles Gerard Manley Hopkins:
        As kingfishers catch fire, dragonflies draw flame;
        As tumbled over rim in roundy wells
        Stones ring; like each tucked string tells, each
            hung bell's

> Bow swung finds tongue to fling out broad its
>   name;
> Each mortal thing does one thing and the same;
> Deals out that being indoors each one dwells;
> Selves—goes itself; *myself* it speaks and spells,
> Crying *What I do is me:* for that I came.

(*Poems and Prose of Gerard Manley Hopkins,* ed. W. H. Gardner [Harmondsworth, Middlesex: Penguin Books, 1963], p. 51.) He resembles Joyce as well: Stephen Dedalus tells Lynch,

> When you have apprehended that basket as one thing and have then ana-
> lysed it according to its form and apprehended it as a thing you make the
> only synthesis which is logically and esthetically permissible. You see that
> it is that thing which it is and no other thing. The radiance of which [Aqui-
> nas] speaks [as *claritas*] is the scholastic *quidditas,* the *whatness* of a thing.
> This supreme quality is felt by the artist when the esthetic image is first
> conceived in his imagination.

(*A Portrait of the Artist as a Young Man* [New York: The Viking Press, 1972], p. 213.) Like Joyce, but unlike either Hopkins or Eliot, Williams does not infer a divine purpose, a Christ or universal truth, from the *quidditas* of phenomena.

9. "Damnation" as the source of art receives its fullest treatment in *Kora in Hell* and the chapter entitled "Night" in *A Voyage to Pagany;* see also "These" (*CP,* 458–59).

10. Thoreau, *Walden,* in *Walden and Other Writings,* pp. 290–91.

11. "To an Old Jaundiced Woman," *SA,* 129–30, *CP,* 215, and *CEP,* 268: "To a Poor Old Woman," *CP,* 383 and *CEP,* 99; "A Negro Woman," *PB,* 123; "The Lonely Street," *CP,* 174 and *CEP,* 227.

In the idea that the people *are* the poems, Williams is most like Whitman. Compare also Emerson's "The Poet":

> I look in vain for the poet whom I describe. . . . We have yet had no
> genius in America, with tyrannous eye, which knew the value of our in-
> comparable materials, and saw, in the barbarism and materialism of the
> times, another carnival of the same gods whose picture he so much admires
> in Homer. . . . Our log-rolling, our stumps and their politics, our fisheries,
> our Negroes and Indians, our boats and our repudiations, the wrath of
> rogues and the pusillanimity of honest men, the northern trade, the south-
> ern planting, the western clearing, Oregon and Texas, are yet unsung. Yet
> America is a poem in our eyes. . . .

(Ralph Waldo Emerson, *Essays & Lectures,* ed. Joel Porte [New York: The Library of America, 1983], pp. 464–65.) This passage seems, of course, directly to address both Whitman and Williams. "It's all of the gods, there's nothing else worth writing of. They are the same men they always were—but fallen" (*K,* 61).

12. See, for instance, Joseph N. Riddel, *The Inverted Bell: Modernism and the Counterpoetics of William Carlos Williams* (Baton Rouge: Louisiana State Univer-

sity Press, 1974); J. Hillis Miller's review of Riddel, "Deconstructing the Decon-
structers," *Diacritics* (Summer 1975), 24–31; and Riddel's reply to Miller, *Diacritics* (Fall 1975), 56–65.

13. "The Farmers' Daughters" and "The Girl with a Pimply Face," in *FD,*
354–72 and 117–30.

14.   . . . we understood
> Her by her sight, her pure and eloquent blood
> Spoke in her cheekes, and so distinckly wrought,
> That one might almost say, her bodie thought.

(John Donne, "The Second Anniversary: Of the Progres of the Soule," in *The
Complete Poetry of John Donne,* ed. John T. Shawcross [Garden City, New York:
Doubleday, 1967], p. 298.)

This passage describing Elizabeth Drury is, of course, a famous description of
the unified sensibility the absence of which, in twentieth-century poetry, T. S.
Eliot laments, and the presence of which Williams demonstrates. (See T. S. Eliot,
"The Metaphysical Poets," in *Selected Essays of T. S. Eliot* [New York: Harcourt,
Brace and World, 1964], pp. 241–50.)

15. The passage from which I quote occurs in *Paterson, II:*
> Why should I move from this place
> where I was born? knowing
> how futile would be the search
> for you in the multiplicity
> of your debacle. The world spreads
> for me like a flower opening—and
> will close for me as might a rose—
> wither and fall to the ground
> and rot and be drawn up
> into a flower again. But you
> never wither—but blossom
> all about me. In that I forget
> myself perpetually—in your
> composition and decomposition
> I find my
>   despair!
>   (*P,* 75)

In its final version, the passage is addressed to "Beautiful Thing," but Sister M.
Bernetta Quinn writes that, in Williams's manuscript, "you" referred to God (*The
Metamorphic Tradition in Modern Poetry* [New Brunswick, New Jersey: Rutgers
University Press, 1955], p. 109).

16. *YALC.* Here again, Stevens's thought seems to intersect with Williams's:
> One sits and beats an old tin can, lard pail.
> One beats and beats for that which one believes.
> That's what one wants to get near. Could it after
>   all

> Be merely oneself, as superior as the ear
> To a crow's voice? Did the nightingale torture the
> > ear,
> Pack the heart and scratch the mind? And does the
> > ear
> Solace itself in peevish birds?

("The Man on the Dump," *The Palm at the End of the Mind,* p. 164.) "The Man on the Dump" as a whole provides an interesting comparison with "Pastoral," discussed earlier in this chapter.

17. See J. Hillis Miller's discussion of "Young Sycamore" in his Introduction to *William Carlos Williams: A Collection of Critical Essays* (Englewood Cliffs, New Jersey: Prentice-Hall, 1966), pp. 3–13. Two essays which have influenced my readings in this chapter are Donald M. Kartiganer, "Process and Product: A Study of Modern Literary Form," *Massachusetts Review* 12.2 (Spring 1971), 297–328; and Charles Altieri, "From Symbolist Thought to Immanence: The Ground of Postmodern American Poetics," *boundary 2,* no. 1 (1973), 605–41.

18. Bram Dijkstra, *The Hieroglyphics of a New Speech: Cubism, Stieglitz, and the Early Poetry of William Carlos Williams* (Princeton, New Jersey: Princeton University Press, 1968), p. 172.

19. *YALC.* In *The Great American Novel,* Williams writes:

> At that table [at Mrs. Chain's boarding house] I met one of my dearest friends. Will you have some bread? Yes. That look. It was enough. Youth is so rich. It needs no stage setting. Out went my heart to that face. There was something soft there, a reticence, a welcome, a loneliness that called to me. And he, he must have seen it in me too. We looked, two young men, and at once the tie was cemented. It was gaged accurately at once and sealed for all time. (*GAN,* 207)

Chapter 6

1. William Shakespeare, *Pericles,* V, i, ed. Ernest Schanzer (New York and Toronto: New American Library, 1965), p. 134.

2. Paul Mariani, *William Carlos Williams: A New World Naked* (New York: McGraw-Hill, 1981), pp. 648–49.

3. Ibid., p. 651ff.

4. *Myra:* What would you do without all your women, darling?
    Doc: I'd find one up a tree somewhere.
    Myra: You sure would. And drag her down by the hair—if she didn't drop on you first from a low branch. I don't care—so long as I have my garden. (*DL,* 117)

5. Mariani, *A New World Naked,* pp. 661–62.

6. Quoted in Linda Welshimer Wagner, *The Prose of William Carlos Williams* (Middletown, Connecticut: Wesleyan University Press, 1970), p. 147.

7. Mariani, *A New World Naked,* p. 661.

8. "The local is the only thing that is universal. . . . The classic is the local fully realized, words marked by a place" ("Kenneth Burke," in *Imaginations,* p. 356). The idea runs throughout Williams's writings; cf. also "The local is the universal" ("Introduction," in *SE,* p. 233).

9. Henry David Thoreau, *Walden,* in *Walden and Other Writings,* ed. Brooks Atkinson (New York: Modern Library, 1937, 1950), p. 85.

10. William Blake, Marginalia to Richard Watson's *Apology for the Bible,* in *The Complete Poetry and Prose,* ed. David V. Erdman (Garden City, New York: Anchor Books, 1982), p. 617.

11. Sigmund Freud, *Civilization and Its Discontents,* trans. and ed. James Strachey (New York: W. W. Norton, 1962), p. 92.

12. James Strachey, fn. to Freud, *Civilization and Its Discontents,* p. 92.

13. In *Beyond the Pleasure Principle,* Freud discusses the repetition of unpleasant stimuli as an effort to master them and bring them under the dominance of the pleasure principle. He remarks, ". . . the artistic play and artistic imitation carried out by adults . . . do not spare the spectators . . . the most painful experiences and yet can be felt by them as highly enjoyable. This is convincing proof that, even under the dominance of the pleasure principle, there are ways and means enough of making what is in itself unpleasurable into a subject to be recollected and worked over in the mind." Trans. James Strachey (New York: Bantam Books, 1959), p. 37.

14. Galway Kinnell, interview with Margaret Edwards in *Walking Down the Stairs: Selections from Interviews* (Ann Arbor: University of Michigan Press, 1978), p. 112.

15. *Paterson II* is a milestone for me. One of the most successful things in it is a passage in section three of the poem which brought about—without realizing it at the time of writing—my final conception of what my own poetry should be; a passage which, sometime later, brought all my thinking about free verse to a head. . . .

My dissatisfaction with free verse came to a head in that I always wanted a verse that was ordered, so it came to me that the concept of the foot itself would have to be altered in our new relativistic world. . . . I had a feeling that there was somewhere an exact way to define it; the task was to find the word to describe it, to give it an epitaph, and I finally hit upon it. The foot not being fixed is only to be described as variable. If the foot itself is variable it allows order in so-called free verse. Thus the verse becomes not free at all but just simply variable, as all things in life properly are. From the time I hit on this I knew what I was going to have to do. (*IWW,* 80, 82)

See Stephen Cushman, *William Carlos Williams and the Meanings of Measure* (New Haven and London: Yale University Press, 1985), pp. 84–92 and passim, for a full discussion of Williams's variable foot and triadic line.

16. T. S. Eliot, "Little Gidding," *Four Quartets,* in *Collected Poems: 1909–1962* (New York: Harcourt, Brace and World, 1963), p. 205.

17. *YALC.* The scrap of paper also contains the working title for "Book V" (the planned extension of *Paterson* that became "Asphodel"), "The River of Heaven."

18. James Breslin is among the earliest of Williams's critics to write of the importance of descent in Williams's poetry. See *William Carlos Williams: An American Artist,* pp. 53–65 passim; also 187–202 passim.

19. Louis L. Martz, *The Poetry of Meditation: A Study in English Religious Literature of the Seventeenth Century* (New Haven and London: Yale University Press, 1954), p. 36ff.

20. *Doc:* I died when I walked upon the grass. I died in everything. I died when I was born. . . . From which you once rescued me—hence my devotion. (*DL,* 201)

21. *YALC.* See Paul Mariani, "The Eighth Day of Creation: Rethinking *Paterson,*" in *A Usable Past* (Amherst: University of Massachusetts Press, 1984), p. 59ff., for a full discussion of Williams's use of this phrase. See also Mariani, *A New World Naked,* pp. 701–2.

22. Cf. the opening line of the *Aeneid: "Arma virumque cano"* ("Arms and the man I sing").

23. Homer, *The Odyssey,* trans. Robert Fitzgerald (Garden City, New York: Doubleday, 1961), pp. 201–3. This is the only mention in Homer of asphodel.

24. Cushman, *William Carlos Williams and the Meanings of Measure,* and Henry M. Sayre, *The Visual Text of William Carlos Williams* (Urbana and Chicago: University of Illinois Press, 1983), both offer excellent discussions of the visual nature of the triadic line and variable foot.

25. J. Hillis Miller, *Poets of Reality: Six Twentieth-Century Writers* (Cambridge, Massachusetts: Harvard University Press, 1965), p. 355.

26. T. S. Eliot, "Dry Salvages," *Four Quartets,* p. 198.

27. Breslin, *William Carlos Williams: An American Poet,* p. 188, and Cushman, *William Carlos Williams and the Meanings of Measure,* emphasize the element of descent in the triadic line.

28. Mariani, *A New World Naked,* pp. 598–600. Williams is aligning himself especially with Whitman—his persona "turns inland toward Camden where Walt Whitman, much traduced, lived the latter years of his life and died"—and declaring his intention to continue Whitman's struggle against the "dominance of the iambic pentameter in English prosody" by discovering "a new construction upon the syllables" (*A,* 392). Benjamin Sankey, *A Companion to William Carlos Williams's PATERSON* (Berkeley: University of California Press, 1971), p. 193ff., also emphasizes the identification with Whitman—an identification which is not

overtly made in the published version of *Paterson,* but which both manuscript evidence and the reference in the *Autobiography* establish.

29. Joseph N. Riddel, *The Inverted Bell: Modernism and the Counterpoetics of William Carlos Williams* (Baton Rouge: Louisiana State University Press, 1974), p. 95.

30. Mariani, *A New World Naked,* p. 645.

31. Mariani discusses this poem at some length in "The Hard Core of Beauty," in *A Usable Past,* pp. 79–84.

32. Cf. Wordsworth's remark on "this degrading thirst after outrageous stimulation"—a thirst which he attributes to the monotony of modern urban life. (Preface to *Lyrical Ballads,* in *The Poems,* ed. John O. Hayden [New Haven: Yale University Press, 1981], I, 873.)

33. In some accounts of the birth of Venus, she is "portrayed as having been produced by the seafoam caused by the severed genitals of Ouranos, who had been castrated by his son, Cronos." (Charlene Spretnak, *Lost Goddesses of Early Greece: A Collection of Pre-Hellenic Myths* [Boston: Beacon Press, 1978], p. 61.) The link between love, nature, and violence is there from the beginning.

34. Wallace Stevens, "Sunday Morning," in *The Palm at the End of the Mind,* ed. Holly Stevens (New York: Vintage Books, 1972), pp. 5–8.

35. Freud, *Civilization and Its Discontents,* p. 12. He is quoting from Grabbe's *Hannibal: "Ja, aus der Welt werden wir nicht fallen. Wir sind einmal darin."*

36. Joseph Conrad, *Lord Jim* (Harmondsworth, Middlesex: Penguin Books, 1957), p. 163.

37. An anecdote in the *Autobiography* reveals the same ambivalence about marriage, expressed through an ambivalence about gardening:

> I had begun to dig a three-foot trench following the foundation along the front of the house. I planned to fill it with leaves and throw back the dirt against the time I'd be ready to plant rhododendrons there. As I sweated at the job a young woman of my acquaintance, passing up the street, paused and said to me, "Happy?"
>
> It stopped me cold.
>
> "Sure, why not?" I said. She laughed and went on.
>
> "What's biting her, I wonder," I said to myself. "But am I," I wondered, "happy? Who can tell?" (pp. 132–33)

38. Alexander Welsh, *The City of Dickens* (Oxford: The Clarendon Press, 1971), has a wonderful discussion of the ways in which marriage, by its fixity, can become a living death. He shows how the promised happy endings in Dickens's novels often have sinister undertones for this reason.

39. Mariani, "Reassembling the Dust," in *A Usable Past,* p. 35.

40. The configuration is particularly dominant in *Paterson, V.* For example, Williams writes,

> —every married man carries in his head
> the beloved and sacred image

                                        of a virgin
                    whom he has whored.
                                                    (*P*, 234)
In *YALC* occur these cancelled lines from *Paterson, V:*
                    (the whole flower episode
                        is an image of 'my wife')—as an image,
                    a beloved image, a secret image
                        of an inviolate virgin
                    —whom I whored   .   .   (as all men do) to their wives.
Joseph Riddel quotes this and comments: "It is clear throughout *Paterson* that the
woman is the poem the poet makes, and the idea of the perfect or 'whole' poem he
violates in his making" (*The Inverted Bell*, p. 288). Riddel's own language,
though, is revealingly confusing: Does he mean just that the poet can conceive of
his poem as a woman, born, as Williams says, "in full beauty out of the shell of his
imagination" (*DL*, 200), or does he mean that any given woman is a "poem the
poet makes"? Paul Mariani is thinking along the same lines as Riddel when, in
"The Eighth Day of Creation," he writes of the "virgin/whore" as "the hag language whored and whored again but transformed by the poet-lover's desire into
something virginal and new," and adds, "[The] poem, like the tapestries [of *Paterson, V*] themselves, can be possessed a thousand thousand times and yet remain
as fresh and virginal as on the day they were conceived, like Venus, from the head
of their creator" (*A Usable Past*, p. 69). The trouble with this equating of woman
with poem, life with art, is summed up by the fact that, contrary to Mariani, Venus
was *not* conceived and born from any man's head. To write a poem is not to "make"
a woman; to use language is not to "whore" a woman. And the idea that having
sexual intercourse is best described as "whoring" is pretty silly anyway.

    41. The reference is somewhat equivocal, as if Williams is embarrassed at ad-
mitting to a highly androgynous nature, but though Williams questions the
poem's other speaker, he does not dissociate himself from him:

                    First he said:
                    It is the woman in us
                    That makes us write—
                    Let us acknowledge it—
                    Men would be silent.
                    We are not men
                    Therefore we can speak
                    And be conscious
                    (of the two sides)
                    Unbent by the sensual
                    As befits accuracy.

                    I then said:
                    Dare you make this
                    Your propaganda?

And he answered:
Am I not I—here?
("Traditional," *CP,* 40; *CEP,* 34)
Cf. *SL,* p. 311, to Kay Boyle: The poet "must be in essence a woman as well as a man."

42. Mariani, "The Hard Core of Beauty," in *A Usable Past,* p. 86. Cf. Mariani, *A New World Naked,* pp. 536, 581–82, 672.

43. In "The Young Housewife," Williams shows himself to be at least subliminally aware of just this fact. Here he is Pluto, metaphorically crushing the fallen leaf, as he drives past the avatar of Persephone, bowing and smiling (*CP,* 57; *CEP,* 136).

44. W. B. Yeats, "The Circus-Animals' Desertion," in *The Collected Poems of W. B. Yeats* (New York: The Macmillan Company, 1956), p. 336.

45.   What thou lovest well remains,
                              the rest is dross
What thou lov'st well shall not be reft from thee
What thou lov'st well is thy true heritage
Whose world, or mine or theirs
                              or is it of none?
First came the seen, then thus the palpable
        Elysium, though it were in the halls of hell,
What thou lovest well is thy true heritage.
(Ezra Pound, Canto LXXXI, in *The Cantos of Ezra Pound* [New York: New Directions, 1977], pp. 520–21.) I can think of no more eloquent gloss on "Asphodel, That Greeny Flower" than these lines.

46. Freud, *Beyond the Pleasure Principle,* pp. 71–72, 78–79, and passim.

47. Carl Jung, "Aion," in *Psyche and Symbol: A Selection from the Writings of C. G. Jung,* ed. Violet S. de Laszlo (New York: Doubleday, 1958), p. 60.

48. Quoted by Jonathan Cott in "Forever Jung: A Conversation with Analyst Marie-Louise von Franz," in *Rolling Stone,* 21 November 1985, p. 84.

49. Susan Griffin, *Pornography and Silence: Culture's Revenge Against Nature* (New York: Harper and Row, 1981).

50. Such attempts to get us to confront the effects of nuclear disaster as the television special "The Day After" work upon precisely this mixture of courage and ghoulishness.

51.   Labour well the Minute Particulars, attend to the
                              Little-ones:
And those who are in misery cannot remain so long
If we but do our duty: labour well the teeming Earth.
                              . . .
He who would do good to another, must do it in Minute
                              Particulars
General Good is the plea of the scoundrel hypocrite &
                              flatterer:

> For Art & Science cannot exist but in minutely organized
>   Particulars
> And not in general Demonstrations of the Rational Power.
> The Infinite alone resides in Definite & Determinate
>   Identity. . . .

(William Blake, *Jerusalem,* in *The Complete Poetry and Prose,* p. 205.)

52.
> Two things of opposite natures seem to depend
> On one another, as a man depends
> On a woman, day on night, the imagined
>
> On the real. This is the origin of change.
> Winter and spring, cold copulars, embrace
> And forth the particulars of rapture come.

(Wallace Stevens, "Notes Toward a Supreme Fiction," in *The Palm at the End of the Mind,* p. 218.)

53. Here, too, an analogy can be made between pornography and the bomb in that each relies for its power upon a high degree of abstraction. Williams's life bears witness that, when one looks attentively, the "Little-ones" simply prove to be more interesting than either.

54. D. H. Lawrence, "Introduction to These Paintings," in *Phoenix: The Posthumous Papers (1936),* ed. Edward McDonald (New York: The Viking Press, 1968), p. 570.

55. Lawrence, "Introduction to These Paintings," p. 578.

56. Lawrence, "Introduction to These Paintings," p. 569.

57. Williams's language in these lines suggests not only the Cubist but also the American tinker. He doubtless intends a contrast with "the abstractions of Hindu painting," but since Hindu painting is not very abstract, the contrast is difficult to see. I daresay the true contrast is between Hindu thought and Williams's.

58. Edmundo O'Gorman, *The Invention of America* (Bloomington: Indiana University Press, 1961), gives a detailed and fascinating account of the unintended changes Columbus's voyages and the consequent "invention" of America wrought in the medieval world picture. See also Mariani, *A New World Naked,* p. 675.

59. Though the movement of "Asphodel" from hell in Book I to heaven in the "Coda" sometimes causes it to be compared with Dante's *Divine Comedy,* the profound difference between them is that, for Williams, "hell" and "heaven" are simply two ways of experiencing earth and human existence. As Sayre comments, Williams's poem celebrates his "love for Flossie, not for some Beatrice," and is "in the 'earthly' tradition" (*The Visual Text of William Carlos Williams,* p. 120). In "Against the Weather," in fact, Williams seeks to bring Dante back to earth:

> The dogmatist in Dante chose a triple multiple for his poem, the craftsman skillfully followed orders—but the artist?
>
> Note that beginning with the first line of the *terza rima* at any given onset, every four lines following contain a dissonance. . . . Throughout the

Commedia this fourth unrhymed factor, unobserved, is the entrance of Pan
to the Trinity which restores it to the candid embrace of love. (*SE,* 207)
Williams's remarks on Dante, and his dedication of "Asphodel" to Flossie, contrast
importantly with his despair at writing about "a wife" in the much earlier *Great
American Novel,* published in 1923:

> I perceive that it may be permissible for a poet to write about a poetic
> sweetheart but never about a wife—should have said possible. It is not
> possible. All men do the same. Dante be damned. Knew nothing at all.
> Lied to himself all his life. Profited by his luck and never said thanks. God
> pulled the lady up by the roots. Never even said thank you. Quite wrong.
> Look what he produced. Page after page. (p. 166)

60. Mariani, *A New World Naked,* p. 675.

61. The poet will ... be the *expression* of nature itself, or his part will be to
seek it, if men have lost sight of it. Hence arise two kinds of poetry, which
embrace and exhaust the entire field of poetry. ...

... [T]he poet *is* nature, or he *seeks* nature. In the former case, he is a
simple [or naive] poet, in the second case, a sentimental poet.

(Friedrich von Schiller, "On Simple [or Naive] and Sentimental Poetry," anon.
English translation, *Essays Aesthetical and Philosophical,* in *Criticism: The Major
Texts,* ed. Walter Jackson Bate [New York: Harcourt, Brace and World, 1952],
pp. 410–11.)

62. ... [W]hen man enters the state of civilisation, and art has fashioned him,
this *sensuous* harmony which was in him disappears, and henceforth he can
only manifest himself as a *moral unity,* that is, as aspiring to unity. The
harmony that existed as a *fact* in the former state, the harmony of feeling
and thought, only exists now in an *ideal* state.

(Schiller, "On Simple and Sentimental Poetry," p. 411.)

63. Mariani, *A New World Naked,* pp. 675–77.

64. "I see in you / all women / as I saw in that man / all men, myself" (*YALC*).

65. William Blake, Letter to George Cumberland, 12 April 1827, in *The Complete Poetry and Prose,* p. 783.

66. John Keats, Letter to George and Georgiana Keats, 14 February–3 May
1819, in *The Complete Works of John Keats,* ed. H. Buxton Forman (New York:
AMS Press, 1970), V, 53.

67. My own work on "Asphodel" was complete before the publication of Marilyn Kallet's *Honest Simplicity in William Carlos Williams' "Asphodel, That Greeny
Flower"* (Baton Rouge and London: Louisiana State University Press, 1985).
This book contains a thoughtful interpretation of the mythic and ritual substrata
of the poem, particularly in the Eleusinian mysteries, and a valuable chapter on
the worksheets for "Asphodel" in the Yale Collection. Accuracy does not extend,
however, to Kallet's description of the "poets, explorers, and great men of culture"
moving "through the lines of 'Asphodel' with their 'palms going / always to the
light'" (pp. 115–16). Williams refers to the palm of victory, not the palms of the
hands, and his sense is not that these great men advance serenely toward the light,

but that, in the struggle between light and darkness evident for instance in the lifeworks of these men, victory goes to the light:

the palm goes
always to the light:
Who most shall advance the light—
call it what you may!

(*PB*, 180–81)

68. Sir Philip Sydney, *The Poems of Sir Philip Sidney,* ed. William A. Ringler, Jr. (Oxford: Clarendon Press, 1962), p. 161.

Epilogue

1. The phrase comes from *The Winter's Tale.* Florizel speaks to Perdita:

When you do dance, I wish you
A wave o' th' sea, that you might ever do
Nothing but that—move still, still so,
And own no other function.

(IV, iv, 140–43)

With its flowers and quickening *eros,* the scene powerfully resembles the initial marriage site of "Asphodel, That Greeny Flower."

Index

"absence" and "presence," 97–99
Arensberg, Walter, 34
asphodel, 128, 132–33
Augustine, Saint, 4, 7, 21, 119, 192–93n.
  5
autobiography
  conventional definitions of, 9, 14
  private, 4–10, 13, 22
  public, 3–4, 7–8, 22–23

Barthes, Roland, 9, 12
Bates, Arlo (English professor), 64
Baxter, Viola (friend of WCW), 65
Beach, Sylvia, 35
"Beautiful Thing," 47, 50–54, 95, 97, 100,
  162
  and "Pastoral," 89–90
  first mention of, by Williams, 198n. 4
  in *Paterson,* 51, 53, 141, 193n. 6
Blake, William, 172
  and "minute particulars," 156, 207–8n.
  51
  and prophecy, 120

Boecklin, Arnold
  "Insel des Todes," 64
bomb, nuclear, 120, 139, 142, 147, 153–
  58, 160
Boone, Daniel, 18, 22, 23
Borges, Jorge Luis, 13
Brancusi, Constantin, 34
Bruns, Gerald, xi
Bruss, Elizabeth
  "autobiographical acts," 2–3
Burns, Robert, 62

Cézanne, Paul, 119, 158–61
Chain, Mrs. (boarding-house keeper), 110,
  202n. 19
Chaucer, Geoffrey, 175
Clemens, Samuel Langhorne ("Mark
  Twain"), 35
Cold War, 122
Columbus, Christopher, 119, 160–61,
  198n. 4, 208n. 58
confession, 192n. 2

Conrad, Joseph
  Lord Jim, 144–45
consciousness and "the true self," 10
Crane, Hart, 36
Cubists, 160, 208n. 57
Curie, Marie, 18–19

dance, 44
  of Kali, 156
  of Shiva, 13
  the self as a, ix–x, 13
Dante, 196n. 8, 208–9n. 59
Darwin, Charles, 119, 160
deconstruction, 12
Demeter and Persephone, 148–49, 169,
    171
Demuth, Charles, 9, 14, 36
  and his first meeting with WCW, 110
  and "The Crimson Cyclamen," 108–14
  and the painting "Tuberoses," 109
  death of, 113
Derrida, Jacques, 12
Dickens, Charles, 205n. 38
Donne, John, 102, 174, 201n. 14
Doolittle, Hilda ("H.D."), 32, 71–72
Duchamp, Marcel, 34–35
Dunbar, Paul Laurence, 74

Eliot, T. S., 21
  and "feud" with Williams, 34, 36
  and Prufrock, 94
  Four Quartets, 127, 138
Emerson, Ralph Waldo
  "The Poet," 46, 55, 57, 200n. 11
eros and *thanatos,* 39–42, 46
  Freud on, 121–22
  in "Asphodel, That Greeny Flower,"
    153–55
  in "The Birth of Venus," 142–43

flowers, as symbol, 139, 145–47
Ford, Ford Madox, 35
Foucault, Michel, 12
Franklin, Benjamin
  and "denial," 17–18
  Autobiography, 3, 14, 19–22, 32, 45,
    103
  See also autobiography, public

Freud, Sigmund, 148
  Beyond the Pleasure Principle, 154
  Civilization and Its Discontents, 121–22,
    144
Freytag Loringhoven, Baroness Else von,
    25, 36
Frost, Robert
  "The Most of It," 90

garden, as symbol. *See* flowers
Gardiner, F. C., 50
Grabbe, Christian Dietrich, 144, 205n. 35
Griffin, Susan
  Pornography and Silence, 155
Gris, Juan, 160
"ground of one's desire, the," 22–23
Gusdorf, Georges, 6, 186n. 16

Hamilton, Alexander, 18
Hartley, Marsden, 36, 166–67
Herman, Charlotte, 72–74, 81
  See also *princesse lointaine*
Hitler, Adolf, 122, 160
Hoheb, Carlos (uncle of WCW), 70, 74
Homer, 119, 140, 160
  Iliad, 149–50
  Odyssey, 133–34
Hopkins, Gerard Manley, 199–200n. 8
Husband, John (guest of WCW), 37

Ignatius of Loyola, Saint, 120–21
imagination, 96–99, 154–55

Joyce, James, 34–36
  "Araby," 82
  Portrait of the Artist as a Young Man, A,
    200n. 8
Jung, C. G.
  "Aion," 155

Kali, dance of, 156
Kallet, Marilyn, 209–10n. 67
Keats, John, 9
  and his influence on WCW, 63–64, 71,
    73, 76, 82, 88, 97, 197n. 12
  and the "vale of Soul-making," 173
  Endymion, 86
  "Ode to a Nightingale," 104
  on the egotistical sublime, x, 84–85

Kinnell, Galway, 123–24
Kore. *See* Demeter and Persephone

Lacan, Jacques, 12
Larbaud, Valery, 34
Lawrence, D. H., 160
  "Introduction to These Paintings," 159
Leibowitz, Herbert, 1, 189n. 1
Library of Congress affair, 116
light, as symbol, 173–79

Mandel, Barrett J., 10–12
Mann, Thomas
  Doctor Faustus, 25
Mariani, Paul, 147, 204–5n. 28, 206n. 40
marriage, 48, 52–53
  in "Asphodel, That Greeny Flower," 118,
    131, 145–48, 162, 170, 176–79,
    210n. 1
Martz, Louis, 130–31
Matthiessen, Peter, 192n. 14
McAlmon, Robert, 33, 35–36
meditation, Ignatian, 120–21, 134
Melville, Herman, 119, 167
Miki, Roy, xi
Miller, J. Hillis, 138, 190n. 4
Modernism, 24, 70, 199n. 7
Moore, Marianne, 80

Nietzsche, Friedrich, 13

O'Gorman, Edmundo, 280n. 58
Olney, James, 12, 187n. 31
Olson, Charles, 21–23
Orpheus and Eurydice, 164–65, 169

Pan, 167–68
Pascal, Roy, 3, 7, 9–10
  See also *Selbstbestinnung*
Passaic Falls, 18, 37–38
Passaic River, x, 8, 15, 85
Paul, Sherman, 22, 42, 192n. 14
Perón, Juan, 119–20, 160
Persephone. *See* Demeter and Persephone
postmodernism, 186n. 19
Pound, Ezra, 27, 32, 36, 70–71
princesse lointaine, 72–74, 81–82, 102

Proust, Marcel
  and Baron de Charlus, 36, 189–90n. 3
  Remembrance of Things Past, 10–11

Quinn, Sister M. Bernetta, 201n. 15

Riddel, Joseph, 142, 206n. 40
Rilke, Rainer Maria
  The Sonnets to Orpheus, 11
Rimbaud, Arthur, 11, 174
Romanticism, 5, 25, 65, 73–74, 82, 90, 96,
    97, 158, 186n. 19, 199n. 7
  influence of, on Williams, 66–67
Rosenberg, Julius and Ethel, 119–20, 161
Rousseau, Jean-Jacques
  and transparence, 5
  Confessions, 5–7, 9–10, 14, 45–46, 55,
    103
  See also autobiography, private; Romanti-
    cism
Rutherford, New Jersey, 25–27, 72–73,
    78, 88

Schiller, Friedrich von, 209n. 61
sea, as symbol, 139–47, 153
Second World War, 142
Selbstbestinnung ("a search for one's inner
    standing"), 3, 7, 9–10, 119
self
  and "innocence," 14
  and self-surrender, 80–81, 84, 90
  and solipsism, 84
  as a dance, ix–x
  as a "deep self," 11–12
  as an illusion, 12–13
  as "Root, Branch, & Flower," 2–3, 27,
    103–4
  "making something of," 87–91
Shakespeare, William, 67, 74, 116
  Hamlet, 65, 196n. 4
  Richard II, 98, 103
  Sonnets, 107
  The Winter's Tale, 210n. 1
Sheeler, Charles and Musya, 21
Shiva, dance of, 13
Simpson, Louis, 8, 13
Stein, Gertrude, 23, 36
Stevens, Wallace

"Esthétique du Mal," 198–99n. 4
"Man on the Dump, The," 201–2n. 16
"Notes Toward a Supreme Fiction,"
    156–57, 208n. 52
"Sunday Morning," 143
Stieglitz, Alfred, 36
symbolism. *See* "Beautiful Thing"; bomb;
    flowers; light; sea

Thoreau, Henry David, 91, 119, 199n. 7
Tolstoy, Leo
    Anna Karenina, 174
triadic line, 136–38

University of Pennsylvania, 63, 70–72

variable foot, 136–38
Venus and the venereal, 31–32, 33, 39, 47,
    188n. 4, 205n. 33
    in "The Birth of Venus," 142–43
Villon, François, 174–75

Watts, Alan, 194n. 12
Wellcome, Emily Dickinson (grandmother
    of WCW), 74, 86
Welsh, Alexander, 205n. 38
Whitman, Walt, 104, 140, 191n. 8, 200n.
    11, 204–5n. 28
Williams, Edgar (brother of WCW), 64,
    70–72, 128
Williams, Florence Herman ("Flossie"), xi,
    15, 26, 81, 128
    and "Asphodel, That Greeny Flower,"
        116, 131–32, 135, 147–53, 162–
        73, 176–79
    and trip to Europe, 33–34, 160, 189n.
        2
    and Williams's infidelities, 116–18
    as "the rock on which I have built,"
        27
    courtship of, 73–74
Williams, Paul (grandson of WCW), 37
Williams, Raquel Hélène Hoheb (mother of
    WCW), 24, 70, 74, 128
    and "Philip and Oradie," 78–80
    death of, 80
    life and character of, 78–80

Williams, William Carlos
    and adultery, 50–53, 116–18, 147–53,
        191n. 10, 194n. 13
    and divorce, 52
    and marriage, 48, 52–53, 117–18
    and sex, 31–32, 33, 39–40, 71, 191n.
        10
    in *A Dream of Love,* 45–62
    in "Love Song," 93–95
    in "Queen-Ann's Lace," 102–3
    and striving for perfection, 70–71
    and the profession of writing, 64
    as a medical student, 70–72
    as a physician, 23, 26–28, 32–33
    courtship of, 72–74
    death of, 183
    illnesses of, 40–41, 116
    "innocence" of, 14, 31–44
    marriage of. *See* Williams, Florence Her-
        man ("Flossie")
    "nameless religious experience" of, 80–81
    oppositions in the life of, 24–26
    trips to Europe of, 27, 33–35, 128, 160
    WORKS:
    "Adam," 74–75
    Adam & Eve & The City, 108
    "Address," 62, 127
    Al Que Quiere!, 76, 84, 87, 91
    "Asphodel, That Greeny Flower," xi, 15,
        86, 95, 115–79, 190n. 7, 194n. 13
        "abiding love" in, 134
        Book I of, 149–53, 163
        Book II of, 153–62
        Book III of, 162–72, 176
        "Coda" of, 135, 172–79
        composition of, 116
        death and love in, 115, 121–22,
            153–55
        major symbols in, 139
        organic metaphor in, 104
        regenerated marriage in, 118
    *Autobiography of William Carlos Wil-
        liams, The,* 1–2, 8, 14, 17–44, 50–
        51, 89, 188n. 4, 205n. 37
        and Benjamin Franklin, 19–20
        and Charles Demuth, 113
        and "innocence," 31–44, 189n. 1
        and Marsden Hartley, 166